Christian Anthropology

To
Edwin B. Broderick
Bishop of Albany

CHRISTIAN ANTHROPOLOGY
A Meaning for Human Life

John F. O'Grady

PAULIST PRESS
New York/Paramus, N.J./Toronto

Cover Photo and Sculpture
by Brother Damian Ball

IMPRIMATUR
✠ Edwin B. Broderick, D.D., Ph.D.
Bishop of Albany

The Feast of the Sacred Heart of Jesus
June 6, 1975

Library of Congress
Catalog Card Number: 75-32307

ISBN 0-8091-1907-2

Published by Paulist Press
Editorial Office: 1865 Broadway, N.Y., N.Y. 10023
Business Office: 400 Sette Drive, Paramus, N.J. 07652

Printed and bound in the
United States of America

Contents

Preface

Dreams make life. Questions can bring dreams. Man has always dreamed and questioned. Today is no different than the thousands of dreams and questions that have preceded it. What does it mean to be alive? Is life worth living? What is important in life and where is it found? We are a generation preoccupied with ourselves and the meaning of life, and there are as many responses as there are platforms and podiums for speakers to present their views. The questions abound; the dreams are equally present in the hopes for peace and love and harmony and brotherhood. The time has come to study the dream and ask the question about the meaning of man himself:

> An aloof and alien technological society has already shocked man into a rediscovery of his own humanity with all its hopes and miseries. In every faith and in every believer, there is once again a burgeoning awareness of God—or at least a sense that every man is a priest to his fellow-man.[1]

Many have offered their understanding of man. In most cases this has included some aspect of religion. Rediscovering humanity today seems to involve at least the priesthood of man to man, and possibly man to God.

Christianity has its understanding of man and human life. It must offer this understanding to contemporary man or else it can look forward to becoming another museum piece, an artifact from a bygone generation. To someone in search of meaning, the Christian religion offers a particular understanding that can make sense. If it helps some, perhaps it will be able to help many. This book is concerned with the Christian meaning of man.

To try to put between the covers of a single look the full Christian understanding of man is a task too vast for any author to tackle. What is offered here is a foundation for a Christian anthropology as found in Scripture and understood in Christian tradition. Every effort is made to relate the findings of contemporary sciences to the biblical and Christian image of man, but always the basis is found in the Bible and in Christian tradition; within this framework one can evaluate contemporary findings.

The approach is systematic and historical. If we can appreciate how Christians in the past understood themselves, we can come to a better grasp of knowing ourselves today; if we can organize ideas and images around some central core, we stand a better chance to move from the level of the conceptual to the practical. It is on the latter level that we all must live, and this book will prove of value only if it aids people in living the daily commonplace ups and downs of life.

When any author presents a manuscript to the public, he must be honest enough to evaluate its value and, in particular, have an audience in mind that may benefit from his work. This work is directed to a specific group with the hope that it can prove beneficial to a larger group.

Today in the United States there is a continual upheaval in religious education. Many people are confused and even greatly discouraged with the prospect of overcoming that confusion. If there is to be a quality religious education today, then that education must be based on the best of biblical studies as well as on Christian tradition. It must also respond to contemporary people and their religious needs. The present work on Christian anthropology is directed to that need.

Finally, much of what appears here has been learned from others and from the experience of living. I am particularly indebted to the Reverend Magnus Lohrer, O.S.B., of Rome, Italy, for his insights into Christian anthropology. His powerful influence will be found throughout much of what follows. I am also indebted to the students of the Seminary of Our Lady of Angels, Albany, New York, 1969-1972, and the students of Providence College Summer School, 1970-1973, who heard these words and reacted in a friendly and critical way, much to the benefit of the author. Words of gratitude are also offered to Mrs. John Roman who typed the final manuscript, not only with accuracy but with personal interest, and to the Reverend George Worgul, S.T.D., for his helpful comments. May what proved helpful to some students prove helpful to many readers.

Albany, New York March 19th, 1975

Notes

[1] *Time*, December 26, 1969.

Introduction

The behavioral sciences are continually expanding their insights into the meaning of human life. Psychology, sociology, cultural and social anthropology, as well as the developments of the new biology offer an ever-increasing appreciation of the mystery of life with a speed that often brings great anxiety, as well as a multiplication of questions. What is life? When does human life begin? What are the effects of social pressures on human relationships? How does society function while maintaining the dignity and rights of the individual? What are the implications of the advances in genetics and what is the future of the human race? These and a host of other possibilities and unanswered queries have their effect on theology and on the religious understanding of life. In the midst of this knowledge expansion, however, the task of Christian anthropology remains the same: to seek to continue to grow in the understanding of life in the light of the Word of God.

Christian anthropology seeks to judge, evaluate, and integrate everything pertaining to man and his environment and habits and customs, as well as his search for meaning, within the orientation of Christianity as based on the Bible. The result is a mutual interaction between anthropologists, psychologists, and theologians.

Christian Anthropology as Theology

In some ways, the entire history of Christian theology is a history of Christian anthropology. The earliest controversies over Original Sin and its historical development involve an appreciation of person and life. Something similar could be said of the history of grace. In each instance, however, theology has treated only aspects of the meaning of human life without trying to consider systematically the whole that is man and woman in the sight of God. It is only recently that theologians have attempted a systematic reflective approach to Christian anthropology. But while the system may be new, its roots are in the very meaning of Christianity.

The Bible is filled with themes of anthropology. It is the history of salvation, the history of man's relationship to God and to his fellow-man. Mankind is created in the very image of God; sin has permeated the person, but grace has abounded. People need others to live, while individuals live in continual conflict within and without. Even much of what we believe is the result of twentieth-century psychology can be found in the subtle wisdom of the Bible.

The early history of the Church and theology gives further witness to the place of anthropology. The early Fathers combined their biblical tradition with the Greek philosophical tradition and engaged in the discussion of the immortality of the soul, the relationship between matter and spirit, and the psychic structure of the human person. But like their theological source in Scriptures, the early Fathers did not present a unified picture of Christian life. They were interested in scattered questions and at times too much concerned and affected by their philosophy. The result was a somewhat uneven approach to a Christian anthropology.

The theology of the Middle Ages also proffered its insights into the meaning of life, but cast its theologizing throughout various tracts. The principal reason for this piecemeal approach was the tendency to consider the human person not as a subject but as an object among objects.[1] Thomas Aquinas, for example, in his *Summa* treats creation in general, then angels, followed by irrational creatures and man.[2] The problem with such a progression is that it places theological anthropology on the same level with cosmology and angelology, rather than seeing the creation of man and woman as the pinnacle of creation and thus giving an anthropological overtone to all of the theological corpus.

While there are valid insights into anthropology in the Scholastic approach, it is far from a sufficient presentation of the Christian meaning of human life.

In modern times the evolution and development of anthropology has been limited almost exclusively to philosophy and biology. Descartes, Kant, Hegel, Marx, Darwin, as well as the contemporary existentialists and phenomenologists and process thinkers, have influenced the spirit of anthropology far more than any theology. Moreover, the continual development of evolutionary thought over the past century has radically changed the contemporary image of the person. People no longer see themselves living in a world created by God to be contemplated. Instead, the individual man and woman become the dynamic center of the evolutionary process, capable of doing what he or she chooses without any assistance from any god.[3]

The combination of these two modern movements—the more philosophical movement emphasizing man as body-subject with consciousness and freedom, and the scientific movement culminating in the power of the individual in the universe as the human person evolves into greater consciousness—is the matrix in which we must speak of a Christian anthropology. The theologian must also have his say when it comes to the meaning of human life.

In the continual interplay between theology and other disciplines there is always a tendency to fall into an extreme position. Either the theology can override the science or the science can override the theology. For this reason, some theologians today are concerned with the new approach to the Christian meaning of human life and protest that some contemporary theologians are doing nothing more than repeating the mistakes of the theological liberalism of the nineteenth century with its emphasis on man to the detriment of God.[4] They look upon the false immanentism of the final quarter of the last century and the first quarter of the present century lying buried through the efforts of Karl Barth and his famous commentary on Romans.[5] This, however, is not the case.

Today, as we look back on earlier attempts to introduce a truly Christian anthropology, we recognize that any theology that caters exclusively to man is doomed to failure. Within the Christian tradition, however, God is accepted as one who has manifested himself humanly in Jesus of Nazareth. Even Barth himself recognized a need for tempering his thought in the final period of his life.[6] The revelation of the Christian God did not come to us as a cosmology, nor as a strict theology, but as a theological anthropology in Jesus.

If we seek to speak about God in our theology, then we are intrinsically concerned with man, since for Christianity that is how God has revealed himself to us. Christian theology has as its root of expression an anthropology, for it is Jesus of Nazareth as a man that is the revelation of God.

The Bible is so oriented to human life that even creation is viewed in this relationship. The historical, earthly, and cosmic dimensions of human life are presented in Genesis and found throughout the Old Testament. Wisdom literature in particular offers valuable insights into the relationship between man and his environment. The same theme will be echoed when Jesus as the new man is presented with cosmic dimensions in Colossians or when Paul speaks of the groaning of all creation awaiting the revelation of the sons of God in the eighth chapter of Romans. The conclusion is simple enough; no cosmology, no understanding of the world is complete without the crown of creation: human life. Nor is human life understood apart from its natural environment.

This cosmic dimension of Christian anthropology also emphasizes the need for the theologian to include in his purview the findings of other disciplines. Theology can never be an esoteric science that seeks to disclose hidden aspects of life and the world entirely unknown to the inquisitive mind of men and women. Christian theology is a human effort to understand the revelation that is Jesus of Nazareth, and to do this well it presupposes the use and application of all branches of human science and knowledge. Isolation from study and the pursuit of truth is quite impossible if there is ever to be found a truly integrated Christian anthropology.

Finally, it must be emphasized that the Christian understanding of human life is not a peripheral part of theology. Rather, Christian anthropology influences the whole of the theological endeavor with implications that are at present relatively untouched.

As long as man was considered as an object among objects, the knowing and loving subject who lives and theologizes was overlooked. With the return to an emphasis on the human person with freedom, consciousness, and responsibility, a transcendental dimension permeates theology. To speak of faith as man's response to God presupposes the knowing/loving subject. Grace as God's gift of himself also involves the transcendental structure of man as knowing and loving.

On a more practical level, how can we begin to examine liturgy as the expression of Christian worship until we appreciate the need for all peoples to express themselves symbolically? Even the frequency of liturgical celebrations depends on the historical nature of the human person as well as on the historical nature of Christianity calling the individual into a future.[7]

In the field of Christian morality, Roman Catholic and Protestant theologians have developed a new approach to the moral life.[8] For Roman Catholics, the meaning of natural law is changed; the possibility of sin and the fundamental option are all based on a reinterpretation of the individual person. Historical consciousness, the dynamic-becoming-nature of man, the influence of freedom—all these have changed moral interpretations and all are founded on a more complete image of human life.

The very heated debate today on authority and power and its place in society and religion also depends on a more fundamental anthropology.[9] The age of freedom and personal responsibility, as well as the age that has witnessed the abuse of power and authority at the highest levels, heralds changes in the sphere of all institutions and the efforts at the use and control of authority and power. In each case it is an anthropology that underlies any resolution to the question. No wonder there is an urgent need for a more systematic presentation of the Christian meaning of man.

Christian Anthropology

There are many religious or theological anthropologies. Judaism, Mohammedanism, Hinduism, Buddhism, and other religions and quasi-religions offer their particular appreciation of human life. It might also be argued that hedonism, humanism, and Marxism as philosophical movements offer what is comparable to a religious anthropology. Here, however, we are concerned with the specific Christian approach.

Certainly there are elements in the appreciation of man that must, of necessity, be common to any religious anthropology, and thus many religions can have a common ground on which they may interact. Many of these notions will be treated in the coming chapters, especially in the latter part of this work. For the specific Christian approach, it should be recalled that contact with other disciplines and other philosophies and theologies must be viewed in light of Jesus Christ.

In classical Christology the relationship to anthropology did not arise. Theologians presumed to know fully the nature of man and how he can be explained and understood. They concentrated on how to relate the divine in Jesus to the human and did not appreciate that to understand Jesus as human is to come to a better appreciation of Jesus as divine and vice versa. Jesus is clearly the manifestation of the divine Father (John 14:9), but he is also the manifestation of what it is to be human (1 Thess. 1:6). The more the believer understands himself, the more he understands Jesus. The more we understand Jesus, the more we understand ourselves. If we are to appreciate the mystery of God in man, then we must appreciate the mystery that is man.

Two affirmations of traditional Christology have influenced and even hindered the development of a truly integrated Christian anthropology. They are: firstly, if there was to be an incarnation, the Trinitarian Christian God as Father, Son, and Spirit makes possible the incarnation of Father, Son, or Spirit. There was no necessity for the Word, the Son to become man. The second affirmation is the belief that the presence of angels in Christian theology allows the possibility that God may well have chosen to reveal himself in an angel as well as in a man.[10]

For some these affirmations may appear too esoteric for consideration in contemporary theology. The implications, however, of such esoteric ideas are vast. The failure to bind together irrevocably the Word as the revealer and human nature as the means of that revelation, led to endless speculation that had little or no effect on actual human life. It is not a question of what might have been; it is rather a question of what is and what has been that should occupy the talents of theologians.[11]

If we refuse to accept these speculations and base our consideration of the incarnation on the concept of the Word of God revealing the Father precisely as Word, and if we see this revelation taking place in the life and death of Jesus of Nazareth and not in any other way, then we have the firm foundation of a Christian anthropology. The Word of God became other than God in man and not in any other way.[12] Within Christian theology, the possibility of man and the possibility of the incarnation of the Word of God in Jesus of Nazareth are not two juxtaposed possibilities. The possibility of man is rightly seen as the possibility of the more radical incarnation of the Word of God. For this reason we can say that human nature is not indifferent to the incarnation. Certainly God could have created man without any reference to the incarnation, but in fact the world, and man as in this world, can make sense only in the light of what actually has been. Man was created to be the possible expression of the Word of God. The actual enunciation of this Word in Jesus of Nazareth demands the possibility for the announcement of this Word in man himself. Christology is the most radical instance of a Christian anthropology since in the incarnation the possibility that always was is realized.[13]

One conclusion, however, that cannot be maintained as a result of the relationship between Christology and anthropology is that the study of Jesus exhausts the meaning of human life. In the past, Karl Barth seemed to have theologized to an extreme his relationship between Christology and anthropology.[14] According to this Swiss theologian, anthropology is based exclusively on Christology. Man is studied as seen in the man Jesus of Nazareth and from this point we can appreciate the nature of all men. The conclusion is that the Christian study of man is deduced from the Christian study of Jesus Christ. While Barth maintains this close relationship between the two branches of theology, he does not neglect the fundamental difference between Jesus as Son in unique relationship to the Father and all other persons. There is a different state in Jesus, according to Barth, but not a different nature, so that Jesus is able to be known as much as possible in Scripture and man is able to be known inasmuch as man appreciates Jesus.

Such a thesis is valid in its presentation of the close relationship between the study of Jesus and the study of man. It is not valid when it fails to appreciate the limitations inherent in such a principle. The event of Jesus of Nazareth is truly the absolute break in human history in which the ultimate truth of man is revealed. It remains, however, an event in history fraught with all the limitations of any event in human history. Jesus lived at a particular moment of time in a circumscribed place with the narrowness of an environment and education and tradition. He was a man and not a woman; he was celibate and lived a rather brief life. All are limitations that prohibit Jesus from being the full expression of the meaning of human life, just as his very humanity prohibits him from being the full expression of the meaning of divinity. Anthropology certainly presupposes Christology, but it can also be said that Christology presupposes anthropology. The Christian understanding of man cannot be solely deduced from the study of Jesus Christ, however fundamental he may be.

For these reasons much of what follows must maintain a delicate balance between an analysis of Jesus in the Bible and the findings of other sciences. If it is to be Christian, then this anthropology must give central place to Jesus. If it is to be anthropology and theological, then much more must be considered than the study of Jesus Christ.

The first part of this work examines Christian anthropology as theology: seeking an understanding of man in the light of the Word of God. As theology the Bible assures mankind that each individual is God's creature, precious in his eyes, created in his image (Gen. 1:27). Man is of value because he is destined to glory in Christ (Rom. 8:28-30). Man experiences in the depths of his personality an orientation to God (Acts 17:23), as well as a profound sense of alienation and sin (Rom. 7:15, 5:12). With these notions as a beginning, it is possible to study other aspects of human life, for with these biblical ideas we have the foundations of a Christian anthropology.

Notes

[1]Cf. Karl Rahner, "Man (Anthropology)," *Sacramentum Mundi* (New York: Herder and Herder, 1969), p. 366.

[2]Cf. the Outline of the *Summa Theologica* of Thomas Aquinas as found in *Summa Theologica*, vol. III (New York: Benziger, 1948), pp. 3024-3025.

[3]Cf. John F. O'Grady, "God and Man in a Changing World," *American Ecclesiastical Review*, 163 (1970), 1-10; 73-80; 175-183.

[4]Cf. John Dillenberger and Claud Welch, *Protestant Christianity* (New York: Scribner's, 1954), pp. 207-232.

[5]Cf. Karl Barth, *The Epistle to the Romans* (London: Oxford Univ. Press, 1933).

[6]Cf. Karl Barth, *The Humanity of God* (Richmond: John Knox, 1960).

[7]Cf. Karl Rahner and Angelus Haussling, *The Celebration of the Eucharist* (New York: Herder and Herder, 1967), pp. 97-99.

[8]Cf. Charles Curran, ed., *Absolutes in Moral Theology* (Washington: Corpus, 1968); Joseph Fletcher, *Situation Ethics* (Philadelphia: Westminster, 1966).

[9]Cf. Robert Johann, "Authority and Responsibility," *Freedom and Man* (New York: Kenedy, 1965).

[10]Cf. Thomas Aquinas, *Summa Theologica II*. q. 3, a. 5, a. 8; q. 4, a. 1.

[11]Cf. Karl Rahner, "On the Theology of the Incarnation," *Theological Investigations*, vol. 4 (Baltimore: Helicon, 1966), pp. 106-120.

[12]Cf. Karl Rahner, *The Trinity* (New York: Herder and Herder, 1970), pp. 21-29.

[13]Cf. John F. O'Grady, *Jesus the Christ* (Paramus: Paulist Press, 1972), ch. 8.

[14]Cf. Karl Barth, *Church Dogmatics* (New York: Scribner's, 1960), vol. III, pt. 2.

1

Man: The Image of God

When man learns who he is and what he can be, he is filled with wonder. The author of Genesis places man at the pinnacle of creation. The chaos and void of the first verse gives way to the power of the Spirit of God and there is light; heaven and earth divide; land appears with its animals and vegetation; the waters teem with creatures of the deep and God sees that it is all good. The animals receive their blessing to multiply and finally God comes to man:

> Let us make man in our image, in the likeness of ourselves, and let them be masters of the fish of the sea, the birds of heaven, the cattle, all the wild beasts, and all the reptiles that crawl upon the earth. (Gen. 1:26-27)

At the height of the pyramid stands man who is not merely given a blessing but is created according to a special plan: man is the closest to God of all creation, for he alone is created in the image and likeness of God. Man enjoys a transcendence over the rest of creation somewhat similar to that which is proper to God himself.

The Hebrew word for image *(selem)* is a concrete term that implies a strictly physical resemblance. Likeness *(demuth)* qualifies and weakens the force of the first word. *Selem* alone would suggest the carving of a statue: to look at man is to know what God is like. The addition of *demuth* implies that we cannot take completely literally the meaning of *selem*. The image of God in man is concrete but not photographic.

Nor is man's likeness to God found in the purely spiritual. For the Israelite, what we call will or intellect or spirit or soul would be expressed in the word *nephesh* and includes outward appearances and inward attitudes, the combination of the visible and the invisible. For the Israelite, the body is not distinct from the soul or spirit. There is only the totality that is man with spiritual, physical, material elements—with attitudes and appearances and actions and needs and wants. There is no foundation in Scripture for what later theology will present as the image of God found principally in the spiritual qualities of man.

The author of Genesis presents man as one with special dignity and adds that he has received dominion. Man is first called the image of God; this is softened by the word "likeness," and then developed in terms of dominion over creation. Man has dominion and consequently he is God's image. Man is the vicegerent of creation; he is to act on earth as God acted with regard to the universe and manifest the same qualities on earth that God manifested in creation. Further help in understanding the meaning of dominion is found in Psalm 8:

> What is man that you should be mindful of him; or the son of man that you should care for him? You have made him little less than the angels, and crowned him with glory and honor. (5-6)

Man shares in the glory and majesty of God because he alone is created in his image; he shares in the glory of God when he manifests this glory in his dominion over the earth. The mercy and fidelity that are the characteristic virtues of God in the exercise of his dominion must also characterize the life and activities of man. When man exercises his dominion he fulfills his destiny as one created in the image of God, only if in that exercise of power he shows the mercy and fidelity of his Creator. It is the Psalms that portray the dominion of God, just as it is the history of Israel that offers concrete signs of his dominion over Israel:

> Give thanks to the Lord of lords, for his mercy endures forever; Who alone does great wonders, for his mercy endures for-

> ever; Who made the heavens in wisdom, for his mercy endures forever; Who spread out the earth upon the waters, for his mercy endures forever; Who made the great lights, for his mercy endures forever; The sun to rule over the day, for his mercy endures forever; The moon and the stars to rule over the night, for his mercy endures forever. (Psalm 136:3-9)

Just as God concretizes his power over creation in the covenantal virtues of mercy and fidelity, so man as the pinnacle of that same creation will be the vicegerent of God, the one who takes God's place as his image, when he reflects the same qualities.

Israel's image-of-God theology is especially remarkable when contrasted with the practices of polytheism of the same period. The pagans were subservient to creation and placated the gods of nature. For the author of Genesis, there were no gods of nature. There is only the God who transcends nature and gives man control and dominion over creation. Nature is sacred not because it is divine, but because it has been fashioned by the divine.

The author of Genesis also envisaged an idyllic state of peace as the original order of things. Creation was subservient to man and man was subservient to God. Man's dominion was a reflection of divine dominion, and mercy and fidelity are the sure promise of peace. The prophets and psalmists lived with the hope that God would one day restore this harmony, for it was short-lived. The second and third chapters of Genesis offer a further elaboration of the meaning of creation with the addition of the power of evil in the world that destroyed the initial peace. Sometime in the future the original order would be restored—such was the constant hope of Israel.

After the Fall, man is deprived of his secure control over creation; he is deprived of an intimate relationship with his Creator, but he is still God's image and likeness. Though man does not have the power of creating, he does have the capacity of procreating living beings in God's image:

> God created man in his image; in the divine image he created him; male and female he created them. (Gen. 1:27)

> Adam was one hundred and thirty years old when he begot a son in his likeness, after his image; and he named him Seth. (Gen. 5:3)

Man still has the capacity of reflecting the qualities of God when he exercises dominion, even if in fact he often manifests the opposite qualities. In the ninth chapter of Genesis, the author returns to the theme of the image of God:

> If anyone sheds the blood of man, by man shall his blood be shed; for in the image of God has man been made. (Gen. 9:6)

Even if a man sins he never loses the stamp of his Creator, and never loses his dignity. Man is sacred and should not be violated.

Later in the Old Testament, the Book of Wisdom calls man the image of God:

> For God formed man to be imperishable; the image of his own nature he made him. (2:23)

Wisdom is bolder than Genesis in affirming that man *is* the image of God, rather than *created in* the image of God. In Wisdom there is also present the theme of immortality, whereas in Genesis the image of God is seen in his dominion and sharing in the glory of God. Man, according to Wisdom, is an imperfect image, but in Wisdom he is also the "spotless mirror of the activity of God and a likeness to his goodness, mercy and fidelity" (7:26).

Man's dominion and his imaging of God are seen as effects of Wisdom:

> God of my fathers, Lord of mercy, you who have made all things by your word, And in your wisdom have established man to rule the creatures produced by you, To govern the world in holiness and justice, and to render judgment in integrity of heart: Give me Wisdom, the attendant at your throne, and reject me not from among your children. (9:1-4)

If man receives and accepts the wisdom of God, then he can fulfill his destiny as the image of God in the exercise of his dominion. Always it is God who is present to man as he lives as God's vicegerent.

Christ the Image of God

The teaching of Wisdom and Genesis paves the way for the full revelation made through the perfect image of God, Jesus Christ. "Christ is the likeness of God" (2 Cor. 4:4); "He is the image of the invisible God" (Col. 1:15); "He reflects the glory of God" (Heb. 1:3); "We have seen his glory, glory as of the only Son from the Father, full of grace and truth" (John 1:14). In Jesus, the mercy and fidelity of God are made manifest; he fulfills the destiny of man to be the glory of God, to perfect the image as stamped in creation. Jesus reflects the covenantal virtues of God in a human fashion; he exercises dominion as all men are called to exercise dominion, but always in a way that reflects the activity of God in his creation. What man was called to be in creation is realized perfectly in Jesus Christ.

Christ is the new man and through him all believers are new men (Eph. 2:15), able to reflect in their lives the image that they always maintained. Through the restoration of dominion and the perfection of the image of God (Rom. 12:2, Eph. 4:23), man's understanding is illuminated by the Spirit and now man can judge according to the ways of God (1 Cor. 2:16). The irrationality of the Genesis account of man's desire to be God in judging right and wrong is reversed; man accepts his relationship to God and overcomes his sinfulness.

In union with Jesus Christ, the new man continually dies to the old man so that

> All of us, gazing on the Lord's glory with unveiled faces, are being transformed from glory to glory into his very image by the Lord who is the Spirit. (2 Cor. 3:18)

The new man must make progress in putting on the image of Jesus. The transformation is taking place now with respect to the total man. In Genesis there was no separation in man between the spiritual and the material; the same is true for the New Testament.

The believer is transformed into the image of Christ with all of the activities and qualities that are part of a human life.

The Christian and the Image of God

All these elements found in Christ Jesus, the perfect image of God, attract sinful but hopeful man. The imperfect image of God that is man needs desperately the perfect image of God in Jesus Christ before man can ever hope to rediscover and accomplish his original destiny. Under the attraction of Jesus, the Christian is transformed into the image of the Son of God who is the first-born of many brothers (2 Cor. 3:18; Rom. 8:29). Through Baptism, the Christian has put on that new man, constantly being renewed in the image of his Creator where there is no Greek or Jew, male nor female (Col. 3:10-11; Gal. 3:28). Paul does not look to the past to base his hope for the transformation of man into the image of God but looks to Jesus Christ in whom God has revealed the perfect image. When man accepts this revelation, he may be transformed into a new creation and will be the image of God, filled with the Spirit of God, manifesting the qualities of God.

A final element found in the New Testament, and affecting the understanding of man as created in the image of God, is the reality of evil and sin. Paul in particular recognizes man's sinful condition, as we have seen. It is evil and sin that mar the image of God, making us sons of wrath (Eph. 2:3) and lacking in the glory of God (Rom. 3:23). This does not mean, however, that Paul teaches a doctrine that presumes the total depravity of man and the loss of the image of God. Paul wishes only to emphasize man's need for Jesus Christ as the true image of God, and so he will propound the lack of glory in man's life. We have already seen the various passages in which Paul recognizes the inherent dignity of man who is called to be the image of God. Because man is created and destined to be the image of God, he is culpable if he refuses (Rom. 1:20-21) and always has the capacity to worship the true God (Acts 17:22-31). Man never loses his human dignity as created in the image of God even when sin mars that image, and even when he refuses to reflect that image by his sin. Conversion, a change of heart, is always possible and once again he will reflect what he can always reflect: the qualities of God.

History of the Theology of Man as the Image of God

The Bible is clear in its teaching on the meaning of man: man as a totality, male and female with all of the spiritual and material aspects, is the image of God, destined to be perfected according to the perfect image in Jesus Christ. There is no separation of man and no lessening of the dignity of the sexes. Whatever it is that adequately describes the mystery of man, it is that mystery that is created in the image of God. In Christian history, much of this teaching seems to have been lost.

The Fathers of the Church developed the same scriptural theme with much enthusiasm. The words "image" and "likeness" appeared often in Platonic philosophy, which saw the visible world as an image of the invisible and only real world. Greek dualism and the separation of the spiritual and the material formed the matrix within which the early Fathers would present their understanding of man as created in the image of God. It is no surprise that in their philosophical world the spiritual would be celebrated and the material would be downgraded. Something similar would be found in the theology of the early Fathers with regard to man as God's image.

The fundamental question that occupied the interest of many early theologians was the question of the primordial image of God after which man was fashioned. What aspect of God is the exemplar of the image of God in man? Is the fundamental reality after which man is created the Trinity itself or the Logos, or is the primordial image the Word Incarnate, Jesus Christ? The response to this question colored all subsequent attempts to formulate a theology of man.

Irenaeus of Lyons held closely to the scriptural doctrine and taught that Christ is the primordial image after which man was created. When Irenaeus spoke of the Word of God, he always meant the Incarnate Word. Before the incarnation, the Word was present in creation but not visible, and thus man who was created according to this Incarnate Word could easily go astray and mar that image. With the Incarnation, what was invisible became visible.

> When the Word became man he showed himself to man and

> man was assimilated to him and then through him who is the likeness as Son, man became very precious to the Father. In previous times it was said that man was created according to the image of God, but it was not evident. The Word was invisible and it was according to this Word that man was created. Thus the image could be easily lost. But when the Word became flesh both were confirmed: the true image was shown and the likeness was firmly restored making man conformed to the invisible Father through the visible Son.[1]

The totality that was Jesus of Nazareth was the manifestation of God's Word as well as the exemplar of man as created in the image of God. Irenaeus is concrete in his doctrine of man as well as complete. No aspect of man is lost.

Other Fathers of the Church, in particular Clement of Alexandria and Origen, held a different position in regard to the primordial image of God in man. Both of these theologians emphasized the Logos as the exemplar for man in creation.[2] Such an emphasis placed the Incarnation in an oblique position and tended to concentrate on the spiritual aspects of man as manifesting a relationship to the invisible Logos. The soul, reason, intellect, as well as the exercise of free will, bound man to the image of God with a corresponding downgrading of the role of the body of man and its participation in the image of God. In such a system, it was logical to see a thrust toward asceticism, so that the more spiritual aspect of man could more readily realize its possibility as God's image.

The third theologian who influenced the history of the theology of man as the image of God was Augustine. Unlike Irenaeus, Clement, and Origen, Augustine developed his theology of man as created in the image of God in relationship to his doctrine of the Trinity. Neither the Incarnate Word nor the Logos is the primordial image. God as Trinity is the exemplar and in particular the spiritual nature of God as Trinity.

> If, therefore, we are renewed in the spirit of our mind, and he is the new man who is renewed in the recognition of God according to whose image he created him, there is no doubt that

> it is not according to the body, nor according to any part of the soul, but according to the rational mind, where there can be the recognition of God, that man is created according to the image of him who created him.[3]

Augustine found vestiges of the Trinity in the mind of man with his division of memory, reasoning, and will. Man would reflect the Trinity in his mind when he functioned as an intellectual being.

Such teaching influenced all of Augustine's subsequent theology. Naturally the emphasis was directed to the spiritual aspect of man to the detriment of the more biblical understanding that the whole man—body, spirit, and soul—is created in the image of God.

Later theologians failed to follow the lead of Irenaeus and instead developed the insights of Augustine and Clement and Origen. All of these early Fathers concentrated on the spiritual nature of man so that the Scholastic theologians were more interested in formulating the Christian teaching of man in the image of God in terms of the soul of man. This same teaching influenced the catechisms down to the present time. The concrete vision as seen in the Bible and preserved briefly by Irenaeus was lost in favor of the spiritual orientation. An accompanying teaching on asceticism, control of the body and subjugation of physical drives and desires, has characterized all subsequent theology.

Contemporary Theology and the Image of God in Man

Today theologians have returned to the more biblical approach to man as created in the image of God. The totality of a human life in a particular concrete individual, with emotions and intellect and body and needs and attitudes and desires, is created in the image of God. There is a dignity and worth present in every individual life that ties together the spiritual and the bodily. Man is created as open to hear the Word of God in his own life, to speak the Word of God, and pronounce this Word to others. The image of God in man implies the possibility that man can manifest God because in a historical man, Jesus Christ, the Word of God became flesh.

We have already seen that Jesus is the only true and complete image of God. John assures us that: "He who has seen me has seen the Father" (14:9). Only the Word of God can reveal the Father because the Word of God is the perfect image of the Father in whom the Father necessarily and completely expresses himself.[4] It is this same Word, expressing the Father perfectly, that has become Incarnate in Jesus Christ.

Jesus Christ as the image of God in the world has two implications for man as created in the image of God.[5] First, human nature is not indifferent to the Incarnation; the possibility of man as created by God implies the possibility of the Incarnation, a radical union of God in man. Human nature is so created as to be able to pronounce the Word of God. Secondly, the meaning of a natural image of God in man makes more sense. Man as person in his unity is created in such a way that he is the presupposition of the Incarnation. Man as person is the natural image of God. We say as person because human nature is not the image of God in an abstract fashion, but is realized only in the concrete man who is personal. The natural image of God in man is something absolute, inasmuch as man is the image of God as personal; it is something relative inasmuch as this is always a possibility that is related to the actual manifestations of God in time. If God so wishes to express himself through the Incarnation of his Word, then man is ready because God has so created him. Historically this possibility was verified in Jesus Christ. The assumption of a human nature by the Word of God sanctified that humanity so that in him mankind reached the destiny toward which God had always directed it: a radical union between God and man was eternally established and verified. Jesus of Nazareth, true man, was the image of God on earth; he was the Incarnation of the Word of God and spoke that Word in his life and in his death, in the totality that makes up a human life and a human death.

Emil Brunner adds his understanding to the biblical teaching of man with his plea to the Christian to fulfill his destiny by living in the Word of God, or "Living in love."[6] He interprets the structure of man in the light of personalist categories and speaks of man as created with the possibility of responding to the Divine thou. As Christ responded to this offer of the Father and lived as the Word of God, so all Christians are called to do likewise. Believers fulfill their destiny when they live in love, or when they manifest the glory of God as seen in the manifestation of his goodness and fidelity. Christian anthropology must look to Christ as the exemplar of man himself, as one who lived in love, who responded to the invitation of the Father and manifested in the totality of his existence something of the glory of God in his efforts to show the kindness, the mercy, and the fidelity of God to his most noble creature even in the midst of that creature's failure.

For those who are called to reflect that same image, Jesus offers not only the fulfillment of what comes from creation, but the fulfillment that comes from being called to be sons in the Son. The destiny of Christians is to be conformed to the glorious image of Jesus Christ. Believers look forward to a transformation of the lowly state in which they now live to the state of assimilation to Christ. Not only is man called to speak the Word of God, he is called to be his son.

This transformation is taking place now in the lives of believers, but is completed in us only when we bear the image of the heavenly man (1 Cor. 15:49; Eph. 1:18-23), which is yet to come. Our predestination is to share in the glorious Christ (Rom. 8:29-30) in the totality of our existence: "The dead will be raised imperishable and we shall be changed" (1 Cor. 15:52).

The destiny of man involves his body as well as his spirit, and it is this destiny that has begun with the assimilation to Christ, but will be completed only when man is transfigured to be conformed to the glorious Son of the Father.

While we maintain our vision on the end of man, we can never prescind from the process that leads to that end. Redemption and salvation are not in the future alone; salvation is NOW. The conquest of evil and the participation in the goodness of God are not reserved for the eschaton; they take place where man lives his life in goodness and fidelity to his calling; they bring peace and satisfaction and contentment to man's earthly life or else they have no appeal to a man who lives in a real world.

This life in Christ that takes place now, however, cannot be considered apart from the example of the life of Christ himself who became a servant to all even to the point of death: "He humbled himself and became obedient unto death" (Phil. 2:8), so that he could experience the exaltation to the right hand of the Father and the restoration to his rightful place (Phil. 2:9-11).

If this was the fate of the man who expressed the Word of God in full measure, then believers can expect no less. If we desire to live with Christ, then we must accept a daily dying. It is Christian belief that in Baptism we die with Christ in order to live with him (Rom. 6), just as we believe that in the Eucharist we proclaim his death until he comes (1 Cor. 11:26); but the law of assimilation to Christ is not reserved to the sacramental activity of Christianity alone. In the daily lives of believers there is a dying as well as a rising. The image of God in man is not a static, once-for-all image; it is as dynamic as man is dynamic, involving a daily assimilation to the glorious Christ, and comprehends the totality of Christian existence.

Conclusion

Man is never closed to God; nor is he without his personal value and dignity. He always has the possibility of responding to a God who offers himself in love and promises him that his destiny will be realized only when in his life he offers to his fellow-man the kindness and fidelity that characterize God. Moreover, the teaching is not a spiritualism since it always considers man in the concrete and promises a destiny that involves body as well as spirit—a destiny that is not limited to some future aeon but is possible NOW, but only when man is willing to pay the cost and speak the saving Word of God to his fellow-man without seeking to serve himself.

As the first aspect of a full Christian anthropology, man as created in the image of his God lays the foundation for all future development, as well as for an optimism that can never be erased in spite of any efforts on the part of man to deny who he is by the life he lives.

Notes

[1]*Adv. Haer.* V, 16, 2.

[2]Cf. H. Crouzel, *Théologie de l'image de Dieu chez Origine*, (Paris: Cerf, 1956).

[3]*De Trinitate*, XII, 7, 12.

[4]Cf. Karl Rahner, "Jesus Christ," *Sacramentum Mundi* (New York: Herder and Herder, 1968), pp. 197-199.

[5]*Ibid.*

[6]Cf. Emil Brunner, *Man in Revolt* (Philadelphia: Westminster, 1948), pp. 98-99.

2

Predestination and Election

Christians regard the New Testament as inseparable from the Old Testament. There is a continuity that binds the covenants together as one is fulfilled in the other. What is promised to the Jewish people is fulfilled in the event of Jesus Christ; what was present in shadow is made clear in the light. One area in which the relationship between the promise and fulfillment is made evident is in the creation of the world, the future of the human race, and the person and life of Jesus Christ. All things are created for him and in him.

The principal texts of the New Testament that treat of creation in Christ are:

> In this, the final age, he has spoken to us through his Son, whom he has made heir of all things and through whom he first created the universe. (Heb. 1:2)
>
> Through him all things came into being, and apart from him nothing came to be. (John 1:3)
>
> He is the image of the Invisible God, the first-born of all creatures. In him everything in heaven and on earth was created, things visible and invisible, whether thrones or dominations, principalities or powers; all were created through him, and for him. (Col. 1:15-16)

Some have tried to explain these texts according to the distinction of natures in Christ, that is, the texts have reference to the divine nature and not to the Word Incarnate. This, however, is not accurate. The texts refer to Jesus Christ as the Incarnate Word of God. This is made clearer when we examine 1 Corinthians 15:45 (Christ is the second and last Adam); Ephesians 2:10 (we are created in Christ); Galatians 6:15 (there is a new creation in Christ). The new creation is the consummation of the work of creation begun with the origin of the world. In Jesus Christ all things have been created and through him, and him alone, all of creation will find its destiny. The future of the world and human destiny is God and his Christ, for thus it has been established. The Bible speaks of creation and the future new creation that is man's destiny and relates both to the salvation made possible by Jesus Christ.

A similar theme is present in the relationship between the covenant and the creation stories of the Old Testament. Israel first experienced the covenant with God. By his powerful Word the people of Israel were created and offered salvation. Later in her history, Israel began to see the same theme in the creation of the world. Just as God created a new people by his Word, so the same powerful Word created all of the universe (Gen. 1,2).[1] Both are saving works of God and both display his freedom of choice and his freedom of election.

As a result of her experience of the exile, Israel looked forward to a new creation. Deutero-Isaiah (42:5ff; 43:1-3; 44:24; 51:9) connects the saving power of God to the origin of Israel and of the world and looks forward to a new creation when God again will fashion out of his ruined people a more faithful remnant. To them he will offer his salvation.

For the Christian, this new creation has begun with the advent of Jesus Christ and will be perfected when there is finally a new heaven and a new earth when God will dwell with his people:

> Then I saw new heavens and a new earth. The former heavens and the former earth had passed away, and the sea was no longer. I also saw a new Jerusalem, the holy city, coming down out of heaven from God, beautiful as a bride prepared to meet her husband. I heard a loud voice from the throne cry out: "This is God's dwelling among men. He shall dwell with them and they shall be his people and he shall be their God

> who is always with them. He shall wipe every tear from their eyes, and there shall be no more death or mourning, crying out or pain, for the former world has passed away." (Rev. 21:1-4)

There is always a close connection between creation, the covenant, and the incarnation. Both creation and the covenant are culminated in Christ since through him all things have been created. To speak of human history and the future of mankind is to speak of a future that is God himself and accomplished through his Son. We are all predestined in Christ.

Predestination

The biblical teaching on predestination presupposes the actual election on the part of God of a group of people. For pedagogical reasons it is better to consider predestination of all men in Christ and then consider the election of the few. In the New Testament, Paul is the chief architect for the Christian teaching on predestination.

In the Epistle to the Ephesians, Paul presents a summary of his thoughts:

> Praised be the God and Father of our Lord Jesus Christ, who has bestowed on us in Christ every spiritual blessing in the heavens! God chose us in him before the world began, to be holy and blameless in his sight, to be full of love; he likewise predestined us through Christ Jesus to be his adopted sons—such was his will and pleasure—that all might praise the glorious favor he has bestowed on us in his beloved. (Eph. 1:3-6)

Since God has created all things in Christ, he has blessed all of his creation and has destined all people to share in the holiness of his Son; he has loved us in his Son and directs all to share in this holiness. We are not involved with some abstract decree on the part of God: we are presented with a loving direction given to each person. There is only a predestination on the part of God to a share in his glory. If we have been created in Christ and for Christ, then our future is to share in the glory that is Christ. If we accept his Son, then we share in his goodness. Our future is closely allied to the glory of God that, as we have seen, is always involved with the manifestations of his mercy and fidelity.

The Epistle continues with the concrete effects in the lives of believers as well as the future goal of the plan of God:

> God has given us the wisdom to understand fully the mystery, the plan he was pleased to decree in Christ, to be carried out in the fullness of time: namely, to bring all things in the heavens and on earth into one under Christ's headship. (Eph. 1:9-10)

Believers have actual knowledge of the plan of God that is revealed in Christ. All things have been created in Christ and he will unite all things, all people, all of human history. The future of mankind is a union established with God that will permeate all of creation. In the fullness of time, which is yet to come, there will be peace because men will be united with one another and with their God; creation will be fulfilled as it, too, finds its unity in the revelation of the sons of God (Rom. 8:19). All are destined to share in this glory and it is the Christian, the believer in Jesus Christ, who knows this secret plan of God.

In an earlier Epistle, Paul considered the same theme. In the eighth chapter of Romans he presents his thoughts on the future of mankind with a triumphal cavalcade of comforting words:

> We know that God makes all things work together for the good of those who have been called according to his decree. Those whom he foreknew he predestined to share the image of his Son, that the Son might be the first-born of many brothers. Those he predestined he likewise called; those he called he also justified; and those he justified he in turn glorified. (28-30)

There is a progression from the eternal decree of predestination of all to the actual working out of this plan through the teaching on election, justification, and glorification. God gradually unfolds his plan and reveals man's destiny leading all men to a full sharing in the love that prompted the original plan of predestination. The entire action is the work of the Father, which leads to an experience of joy as man is joined to the first-born of many brethren. Without fail, the plan will continue as the powerful work of God. The sure confidence of what we have received impels Paul to cry:

> If God is for us, who is against us? If he has given us his Son, is there anything he will deny us? (Rom. 8:31-32)

Hope, encouragement, confidence is offered to everyone. That which is most precious, his Son, God has given to the world. We can believe that all things are possible for us if the love of God is so great that he has not spared us his Son. Like Paul we should revel in the goodness of God and with full awareness of his expansiveness and his magnanimity proclaim:

> For I am certain that neither death nor life, neither angels nor principalities, neither the present nor the future, nor powers, neither height nor depth nor any other creature, will be able to separate us from the love of God that comes to us in Christ Jesus, our Lord. (Rom. 8:38-39)

Man's destiny is God; his future is the Father of Jesus Christ who has shown us a love beyond measure. No power in heaven or earth, no failure, no tragedy, no individual can take away this future. It belongs properly to this world and to the human race. God has spoken his Word and he will never rescind that Word. There is no great fear and terror with regard to the future of mankind on God's part. There is only the offering of a destiny that is none other than a sharing in the very life of God. Man need never feel ashamed of himself if he maintains his belief in his future. What he can be is always sufficient reason to rejoice.

In the biblical teaching on predestination, there must be no fear arising from the disposition of God. There is fear, however, and a significant fear. The terrible freedom that man is given allows the individual to refuse his own destiny. God forces no one but calls all to share in his life. All are destined to be his sons and share in his glory, but only if the individual freely accepts and makes his own the offer that is extended to him. The greatness of God allows man to accept or reject; the terrible power of man permits him to refuse what God himself offers. A world in need of hope, people in need of encouragement can proclaim with Paul the wonderful goodness of God and the wonderful dignity and value of a single human life because of what God has done in Jesus his Christ; but they must do so freely, without coercion.

Election[2]

All men have God as their future. There is no distinction, for all can share in the glory of God as all have been created in and through his Word. In the history of God's dealings with man, he has chosen certain people for a task. In the Old Testament, Israel is chosen from among all of the powerful nations of the world. She was without beauty and offered no reason for her selection. Ezekiel reminds his people of her beginnings:

> Thus says the Lord God to Jerusalem: By origin and birth you are of the land of Canaan; your father was an Amorite and your mother a Hittite. As for your birth, the day you were born your navel cord was not cut; you were neither washed with water nor anointed, nor were you rubbed with salt, nor swathed in swaddling clothes. No one looked on you with pity or compassion to do any of these things for you. Rather, you were thrown out on the ground as something loathsome, the day you were born.
>
> Then I passed by and saw you weltering in your blood. I said to you: Live in your blood and grow like a plant in the field. You grew and developed, you came to the age of puberty; your breasts were formed, your hair had grown, but you were still stark naked. Again I passed by you and saw that you were now old enough for love. So I spread the corner of my cloak over you to cover your nakedness; I swore an oath to you and entered into a covenant with you; you became mine, says the Lord God. Then I bathed you with water, washed

> away your blood, and anointed you with oil. I clothed you with an embroidered gown, put sandals of fine leather on your feet; I gave you a fine linen sash and silk robes to wear. I adorned you with jewelry: I put bracelets on your arms, a necklace about your neck, a ring in your nose, pendants in your ears, and a glorious diadem upon your head. Thus you were adorned with gold and silver; your garments were of fine linen, silk, and embroidered cloth. Fine flour, honey, and oil were your food. You were exceedingly beautiful, with the dignity of a queen. You were renowned among the nations for your beauty, perfect as it was, because of my splendor which I had bestowed on you, says the Lord God. (16:3-14)

Israel could lay no claim on God for her election. Among all the nations of the world, she was chosen to be his people and he was their God. Israel was blessed beyond measure and given God's Word as her own. The meaning of election, however, was not an election to leisure and self-importance. Israel was chosen by God, but specifically for a responsibility for other people. All men are destined to share in the plan of God, but it was Israel alone who knew this plan and had the task to manifest her God to the nations. Israel as God's people was to be the sign of salvation to the nations.[3] Other peoples and cultures were to recognize in Israel the presence of the only true God and stream to Jerusalem to learn of this God and share in his saving presence. Unlike other nations, Israel was to offer the true worship of the heart. God did not wish holocausts, but wanted the offering of the "humble and contrite heart" (Ps. 50:17). This is the only true worship. Sacrifices of bulls and grain offerings are pleasing only if they express in ritual form the offering of a life that is lived for God and for his people. Otherwise they are a ritual lie worthy of rejection. Israel was also to care for the poor. She was to welcome strangers and share her food and home with those in need. The unfortunate of the earth should be the special care of God's people, and the poor and those who help the poor would together live with complete dependence on the power and presence of God. If Israel fulfilled her obligations, she would be blessed and the nations would stream to her holy city and afford her the dignity and honor that is due to the nation that reveals the mystery of God's plan for his creation:

> Nations shall walk by your light, and kings by your shining radiance. Raise your eyes and look about; they all gather and come to you: your sons come from afar, and your daughters in the arms of their nurses. (Isa. 60:3-4)

The history of Israel is the history of her failure as God's chosen people. As a nation, Israel trusted more in powerful alliances than in the power of her God:

> You played the harlot with the Egyptians, your lustful neighbors, so many times that I was provoked to anger. Therefore I stretched out my hand against you, I diminished your allowance and delivered you over to the will of your enemies, the Philistines, who revolted at your lewd conduct. You also played the harlot with the Assyrians, because you were not satisfied; and after playing the harlot with them, you were still not satisfied. Again and again you played the harlot, now going to Chaldea, the land of the traders; but despite this, you were still not satisfied. (Ezek. 16:26-29)

She desecrated her worship with the introduction of false gods:

> Then I said to them: Throw away, each of you, the detestable things that have held your eyes; do not defile yourselves with the idols of Egypt; I am the Lord, your God. But they rebelled against me and refused to listen to me; none of them threw away the detestable things that had held their eyes, they did not abandon the idols of Egypt. Then I thought of pouring out my fury on them and spending my anger on them there in the land of Egypt. (Ezek. 20:7-8)

Israel also failed in her responsibility to the poor. The prophets continually judged her sins and her oppression of those who were lowly:

> Thus says the Lord: For three crimes of Israel and for four, I

> will not revoke my word; because they sell the just man for silver, and the poor man for a pair of sandals. They trample the heads of the weak into the dust of the earth, and force the lowly out of the way. Son and father go to the same prostitute, profaning my holy name. (Amos 2:6-7)

Israel misinterpreted her election and suffered the wrath of God. To be chosen by the living God to act for the sake of others is a frightening thing. Israel was called, but failed. The glories of election come only to those who fulfill the terms of the election.

It is easy enough to be critical of the failure of Israel from the distance of some 3,000 years. But it was an awesome task to which she was called and no one can claim to have done much better. In Christian history there is only one individual who was the sign of salvation to all men, who offered the only true worship of a life well lived and who had a care for the poor. Jesus Christ is the chosen one of God and he alone fulfilled his election.[4]

Jesus accomplished redemption by assuring us that evil would never triumph over good; Jesus offered salvation by giving us the promise and experience of a nearness of God;[5] Jesus offered the sacrifice of his life in love and obedience to his Father, even to the point of death;[6] Jesus loved the lowly, the poor, those who depended on God and responded to their needs with the offer of his love. The ancient call to Israel was actualized in the life and death of Jesus. Since then it is his Church that has taken up the task.

In Christianity there have been people who have been most conscious of their election and their responsibility. Paul believes that he has been chosen to preach the Gospel:

> To me, the least of all believers, was given the grace to preach to the Gentiles the unfathomable riches of Christ and to enlighten all men on the mysterious design which for ages was hidden in God, the Creator of all. (Eph. 3:8)

He believes in a similar responsibility for Christians:

> We know, too, brothers beloved of God, how you were chosen.

> Thus you became a model for all the believers of Macedonia and Achaia. (1 Thess. 1:4, 7)

The author of First Peter sees Christians with a similar responsibility and recalls the election of Israel:

> You, however, are "a chosen race, a royal priesthood, a holy nation, a people he claims for his own to proclaim the glorious works" of the One who called you from darkness into his marvelous light. Once you were no people, but now you are God's people; once there was no mercy for you, but now you have found mercy. (2:9-10)

The Christian community has the same responsibility as Israel and fulfills in history the election of Jesus. The Church is to be the sign of salvation to others, offering true worship to God with a concern for the poor. It is not without importance that the effort at renewal inaugurated by Vatican Council II should stress this responsibility. The decree on the Church in the Modern World reminds believers of their task in society to be God's holy people;[7] the reform of the liturgy tried to bind together the spiritual sacrifice of a life well lived for God and man with the ritual expression of the Eucharist and the sacraments.[8] Since that time, the Church has tried to remind herself that she is the Church of the poor.[9] Like her predecessor, Israel, the Christian Church has not succeeded in fulfilling her mission. It is not always evident that the Church speaks as God's holy people; the liturgy often lacks heart, and the Church of the poor is often identified with the wealthy and the powerful. She is the holy Church who tries to know and understand her responsibility; she is also the sinful Church who fails.[10] The biblical teaching on predestination gives hope and encouragement; the teaching on election strikes at the very heart of the believer and the Church. Failure on the part of Israel led to the wrath of God. There is no election without responsibility. If the Christian Church continues to fail in her responsibility, she can expect to suffer the wrath of God.

Christianity and Judaism

The question that immediately comes to mind when the doctrine of election arises is the relationship between the elect of the Old Covenant and the elect of the New Covenant. In the history of Christianity there have been various interpretations of the relationship between Israel as God's elect and the Church as God's elect. In certain periods of history, the pogrom characterized the attitude of the Christian; in more recent years, the Vatican Council declared the Church's attitude toward Israel in the decree on non-Christian religions.[11] The Council takes its cue from the doctrine of Paul who sees Christians indebted to Israel for her faith.[12] Like the Council, we too must turn to the Bible to determine the relationship between Israel and the Church in the doctrine of election.

In the Epistle to the Romans, Paul presents his full thought on Israel in chapters 9-11.[13] He begins with an attestation of his personal interest. He was joined to this people and is prepared to give himself for the sake of this people:

> There is great grief and constant pain in my heart. Indeed, I could even wish to be separated from Christ for the sake of my brothers, my kinsmen the Israelites. Theirs were the adoption, the glory, the covenants, the law-giving, the worship, and the promises; theirs were the patriarchs, and from them came the Messiah (I speak of his human origins). Blessed forever be God who is over all! Amen. (9:2-5)

The existence of Paul as one who is chosen is an existence for the sake of others, just as his Master existed for the sake of others. In this case, Paul wishes to exist in favor of the Jews because they are God's chosen people. All that Paul will say of the Jews in these chapters rests upon the basic assumption that the Jews are still God's chosen; if man is unfaithful, that never means that God is unfaithful: "It is not as though the Word of God failed" (Rom. 9:6). If God promised, then he will remain true to his promise. God has promised Israel to be her God.

In verses 20-24, Paul presents his teaching on the vases made for beauty and the others made for menial tasks.[14] Such a doctrine should not be interpreted as predestination of some to glory and others to damnation. Rather, it is clear from the verses that follow that Paul sees the vessels made for menial tasks to be made of Jews and Gentiles alike, and in both cases the mercy of God is made manifest. God endures the vessels made for menial tasks, but made so by their own choice and not by the choice of God. Even those who made themselves so will not experience the wrath of God immediately, but are present as a manifestation of the judgment of God, while the vessels for beauty are the manifestation of the mercy of God. The resolution of both will be realized only when the mercy and judgment of God are resolved in the Kingdom yet to come. What Paul presents is an aspect of temporal reprobation to manifest that the divine judgment is subordinated to the divine mercy, which is mirrored in those who have accepted their destiny in Christ.

In the tenth chapter, Paul presents a very negative picture of the Jewish people. They are not enlightened (10:2); they are ignorant of the righteousness found in Christ (10:3, 13); they have not heeded the Gospel (10:16); they are disobedient and contrary people (10:21). Paul returns to his fundamental optimism in regard to the Jews in the following chapter: "I ask then, has God rejected his people? By no means!" (11:1). Paul recognizes a function in the rejection of Christ by Israel. Now, the hope of the Christians is tied to the future of Israel. The original root is holy (11:16); Israel has made a false step. But if by such a false step blessings have come to the Gentiles, blessings beyond expectation are yet to come: "What will their acceptance mean, life from the dead" (Rom. 11:15). When the fullness of Gentiles has entered the Church, then Israel will recognize her Savior in Christ and she, too, will take her rightful place as God's holy people. The promise of God remains: "For the gifts and call of God are irrevocable" (11:29). Somehow God will bring good out of the failure of Israel. Paul reminds the Gentiles that they have little of which to boast; they are the wild branches and must remember that it is Israel who belongs and it is only through her failure that the Gentiles are able to have a part in becoming God's elect.

The chapter ends with another of Paul's hymns of ecstatic praise that are ever wonderful and ever mysterious:

> How deep are the riches and the wisdom and the knowledge

> of God! How inscrutable his judgments, how unsearchable his ways! For who has known the mind of the Lord? Or who has been his counselor? Who has given him anything so as to deserve return? For from him and through him and for him all things are. To him be glory forever. Amen. (Rom. 11:33-36)

Paul does not give praise to a God who issues absolute decrees of glory or reprobation, but an adoration of a God who is love and whose ways are ultimately merciful and very faithful to his promises. The Jews are God's chosen people and they will remain so because what God has so spoken, he does not deny.

Conclusion

Both predestination and election are rooted in the eternity of God in which God chooses man to be his partner in creation and his partner in mediating his saving promises to others. As in the doctrine of the image of God in man, this adds to man's value and dignity.

The New Testament adds that this predestination and election are made in Christ. He is the first-born of many brethren; he is the first to be predestined as he is the first to be elected for the sake of others. In him the judgment of God is sustained so that all sinners might be justified (2 Cor. 5:21; Rom. 11:32; John 1:29). We cannot understand the meaning unless we see it in relationship to the life, death, and resurrection of Christ as both the predestined and the elect.

Election and predestination are made according to a plan that includes the whole history of man. Somehow in the dialectic between the offer of salvation and man's ability to refuse or accept there is accomplished the plan of God to restore all things through his Son. His ways are not our ways, nor his thoughts our thoughts. In history his mercy will be fully and finally manifested. The final key to understanding human history lies with God and includes the mystery that is man who is not only created in his image, but is predestined to glory through his Son.

Finally, the doctrine of predestination and election both involve a social and an ecclesial dimension. Each man is predestined; some are elected for responsibility. The call is made as personal and involves free personal existence, but man's vocation always involves a fuller and social context. It is man as a community of men who is predestined to be conformed to the image of Christ; God calls the individual but only as a member of the community of man. If we are to share in the glory of God through a manifestation of his goodness and fidelity, this implies a social dimension, since there is no share in the glory of God unless this glory is communicated and part of a community.

A similar meaning is present in the notion of election. Both in the Old Testament and in the New Testament, God's people live for the sake of others. This "existence for the sake of others" reaches its climax in the offering of his life by Christ that we might be justified. The same law, however, is valid for the whole of salvation history. Paul always is willing to give himself for the sake of his fellow Jews (Rom. 9:1-5), as he is willing to give himself for the apostolate among the Gentiles. In the Old Testament, Israel was called to give herself for the sake of the nations; the Church is called to do likewise today. Such a teaching is equally valid for the life of the individual, who is called to give of himself in the service of others, and in this fulfill his responsibility as one who is called to manifest in his life the goodness and fidelity of a God who has predestined him, as he has predestined all men, to share in the glory of his Son, through the restoration of all things in heaven and on earth. The biblical understanding of predestination and election is the second basis for a Christian anthropology.

Notes

[1]Cf. Gerhard Von Rad, *Old Testament Theology* (New York: Harper and Row, 1962), vol. I, pp. 139-146. *The Problem of the Pentateuch* (New York: McGraw-Hill, 1966), pp. 131-143.

[2]The biblical teaching on election is closely allied with the meaning of predestination. In the thought of Paul it is not always evident whether he is speaking of the two as applied only to believers. In this study, I follow the general conclusion that in the undeveloped thought of Paul in this matter, it is possible to speak of all people predestined to share in the glory of God with a special group given the responsibility to lead others to their destiny. Cf. H. H. Rowley, *The Biblical Doctrine of Election* (London: Lutter-

worth, 1950); G. E. Mendenhall, "Election," *The Interpreter's Dictionary of the Bible* (New York: Abingdon, 1962), pp. 76-82; J. L. McKenzie, *Dictionary of the Bible* (Milwaukee: Bruce, 1965), pp. 227-228.

[3]Cf. Gerhard Von Rad, *Studies in Deuteronomy* (London: SCM Press, 1953), Chapter I.

[4]Cf. John F. O'Grady, *Jesus, Lord and Christ* (Paramus: Paulist Press, 1973), ch. IX.

[5]*Ibid.*, Chapter VI.

[6]Cf. Karl Rahner, *On The Theology of Death* (New York: Herder and Herder, 1961), pp. 70-71.

[7]Cf. "Constitution on the Church in the Modern World," No. 43, *Documents of the Vatican Council II* (New York: Guild Press, 1965).

[8]Cf. "Constitution on the Sacred Liturgy," Nos. 10-11, *Documents of the Vatican Council II* (New York: Guild Press, 1965).

[9]Cf. "Constitution on the Church," No. 8, *Documents of the Vatican Council II* (New York: Guild Press, 1965).

[10]Karl Rahner relates the holy Church to the sinful Church in "The Church of Sinners," *Theological Investigations*, vol. VI (Baltimore: Helicon, 1969), pp. 253-269.

[11]Cf. "Declaration of the Relationship of the Church to Non-Christian Religions," *Documents of the Vatican Council II* (New York: Guild Press, 1965).

[12]*Ibid.*, No. 4.

[13]Cf. Johannes Munck, *Christ and Israel* (Philadelphia: Fortress, 1967).

[14]*Ibid.*, pp. 58-71.

3

Man Ordered to God

The Bible speaks of man as created in the image of God, predestined to share in the glory of Christ as God's Son. This implies a dignity and value for man that can never be denied him. It also implies an orientation to God. If man is so created, then the very dimensions of his being must call out for God and for the experience of God. Everyone has to have a religious dimension, even those who seem to deny its possibility. For the Christian there is no such thing as an individual who is not blessed by a creating and supporting God. However hidden, this religious aspect of man is as natural as the air he breathes.

When Paul climbed the Areopagus, he appealed to the human instinct to build altars to unknown gods and proclaimed that: "What you worship as unknown, this I preach to you" (Acts 17:23). This same belief that man is religious prompted Paul to declare that the Gentiles were culpable in their denial of worship to the true God: "Although they knew God, they did not honor him as God or give thanks to him" (Rom. 1:21). For all of the New Testament writers as well as the Old Testament writers, the existence of God is self-evident:

> "O Lord, you have probed me and you know me; you know when I sit and when I stand; you understand my thoughts from afar." (Ps. 139:1-2)

The need for man to acknowledge and worship this God is equally evident. The Bible considers man as religious because the Bible offers the belief that man is created in God's image and destined to share in his glory.

In the history of theology, the orientation of man to God, or his proper religious aspect, has been the subject of heated debate. Fathers of the Church, theologians, official teaching declarations, catechisms, sermons, and religion classes have offered some understanding, but greater confusion. If man is oriented to God, why is this not the common experience of all men? If we can find happiness only in God, as Augustine reminds us ("You have made us for yourself, O God, and our hearts can never rest until they rest in you!"), how is it possible to speak of God's *free* communication of himself to man? If man finds his happiness only in God, how is he free?

Scripture offers very little help to solve this problem. The Bible is not an answer book; it presents the facts of belief and encourages man to use his intellect to study and develop the meaning of those facts. Theology, the human effort to understand the revelation of God in Jesus Christ, must offer help in resolving these questions of man's orientation to God.

When we move into the realm of systematic theology and beyond the scope of the theology of the Bible, further limitations impose themselves. Theology is always under the control of those who are the theologians. Like everything that man does, it is always imperfect and incomplete. Faith assures us that man is ordered to God and is somehow culpable if he refuses that orientation; faith also tells us that God is good and gives himself in total freedom to his creation, and he respects the freedom of his creature. The resolution of these aspects of Christian faith gathers together all the knowledge that man has acquired and is a never-ending search. Thus far we have concentrated on the experience of the Bible as our guide. Before examining the question of nature and grace, it is helpful to study the meaning of religious experience from a philosophical and anthropological point of view.

Philosophical Meaning of Man as Religious

The core of religion is always religious experience. Religion involves a human response to the world as we experience it, but only if in that experience of the world we experience the divine, the transcendent. This is the first requisite for religious experience. There is a second requisite as well that is not always present. Part of the experience of the transcendent must include the experience of God as personal. Without this latter, worship, which has been carried on throughout history, would not be possible. Specific examples of religious experience help clarify its meaning.

Freidrich Schleiermacher (1768-1834) is usually regarded as the theologian of romanticism and religious experience.[1] He lived in a time when Germany was under the influence of the romantic movement and during which religion was considered as a remnant from a past age, a more primitive development in the history of man. It was a period of liberation and discovery when men sought to explore their undeveloped potentialities and achieve new and exciting levels of human fulfillment. People were cultured and full of ideas, aesthetic and even moral, but not religious. Schleiermacher sought to show that religion was a necessary part of human life. Those who ignored it did not liberate themselves, but foreshortened their experience and truncated their lives. Since the romantics paid attention to experience, feeling, and imagination, Schliermacher emphasized these in his presentation on the meaning of religion.

For Schleiermacher, religion must have its empirical basis. It is found in the ordinary areas of life, the common affairs of every day, rather than in the obscure and the extraordinary. For him all feelings are at least potentially religious and give man the possibility of accepting his need for God:

> The common element in all howsoever diverse expressions of piety by which these are conjointly distinguished from all other feelings, or in other words the self-identical essence of piety is this: the consciousness of being absolutely dependent, or, which is the same thing, of being in relation with God.[2]

Schleiermacher tried to show that the experience of life, contact with being, is an experience of God. When man accepts his sense of dependence, which is evident enough in every life, Schleiermacher found an empirical basis for religion and worship. The question that his critics have asked Schleiermacher is: "Does the experience of dependence demand an acceptance of dependence on a reality that is personal?" And, "Is religion of necessity more than feeling?" The value of Schleiermacher's thought for our purposes is that he pointed to dependence as a sign of the transcendent. This is as true today as a hundred years ago.

Rudolf Otto offered another attempt to ground religion in human experience.[3] He criticized Schleiermacher's analysis of dependence, which does not safeguard the qualitative difference between the experience of God and other experiences. What characterizes the true experience of God is "creature-consciousness."[4] For Otto, the experience of God as *Mysterium Tremendum* evokes a double response: one of awe and fascination and one of fear and terror. In the presence of the Totally Other we are filled with dread, yet drawn by wonder.[5]

Otto's analysis of the experience of the holy has rightly attracted much attention and is continued today in the writings of many cultural anthropologists.[6] It is part of human experience. We are all familiar with it in varying degrees. Otto calls it an experience of creature-consciousness that in turn prods us to think of the possibility of a Creator. The experience of dependence in Schleiermacher makes us aware that a Creator is possible. Both thinkers tried to root religion in the experience of man.

A third philosopher who dealt with religious experience is William James.[7] James was a pragmatist, more interested in the effect of religious or mystical experiences on people than in its meaning. He recorded several examples of mystical experiences and tried to systematize them under four headings:

1. Ineffability: only those who have had the experience can understand it; it cannot be "named."

2. Noetic quality: the experience not only concerns emotion, but also yields insight.

3. Transiency: the experience not only lasts for but a short time, it is not subject to accurate recollection or recall.

4. Passivity: although the state can be induced and may require careful preparation beforehand, the experience itself involves a sense of passivity.[8]

The contribution of James is his ability to examine the various possibilities of religious experience as a philosopher and as a pragmatist, pointing to the relationship of man to the transcendent, and the need for man to experience the religious.

In each case of the preceding thinkers, there is an acceptance of the religious dimension of mankind and an effort to explain the place of religion by founding religion in the experience of man. There are experiences of dependence, creaturliness, and finally there is the mystical experience, some awareness of a closeness of a transcendent one. When this experience includes an awareness of a personal God, then there is human homage and worship. This is religion. Everyone is religious at least in the respect that part of human experience is the experience of the transcendent one. Such is the conclusion from the works of Schleiermacher, Otto, and James.[9]

Traditional Philosophy of Man's Nature

There are numerous philosophers and thinkers who have witnessed to the presence of a religious dimension in man. What must be examined now is the more precise relationship between man as oriented toward God and the actual communication of God in grace. An examination of the meaning of nature as it was understood in the past, as well as in the present, will offer more precision in the quest for an understanding of man's religious nature.

Until very recently, much of Western Christianity accepted a very static notion of man's nature. Within an Aristotelian-Thomistic framework, it was easy to believe that nature could be accurately defined and limited. Most theologians and philosophers assumed that the nature of man was well known. A careful study of the meaning of the term "nature" discloses however that the concept is fraught with ambiguity.

For Aristotle and Thomas Aquinas,[10] the meaning of "nature" originated in the ambit of living things. Nature signifies the generation of something living. Later the idea was transferred to mean the principle of that living thing; then any intrinsic principle was called "nature," and finally it signified the reality or the essence of something, e.g., the nature (essence) of a chair, or man, or God. That which makes something what it is, and not something else, is the "nature" of the object. As is evident, the meaning of "nature" is not totally clear. Even on a philosophical plane it can mean too many things. The confusion is compounded when it is used to apply to God, to man, to a tree, and to a chair. At the very least, the use of the word nature is analogous and not univocal. The nature or inclination of a spiritual being is not the same as the nature of a nonspiritual being.

A further development in the meaning of nature is given by the Scholastic theologians and philosophers when they see nature in a theological sense. There is a purpose involved; nature is dynamic and oriented toward a goal. It is of the nature of birds to fly, not in an abstract sense, but actually to fly. Nature is oriented toward a concrete goal and the being is affected and changed as it moves toward that goal.

In the epochs that followed Thomas Aquinas, the emphasis fell more on nature as well-defined and nature as static and permanent. Theologians and philosophers knew the nature of man; his nature was unchanging and beyond development. His genus was animal and his specific difference was rationality. With this as an established fact, all the questions of the meaning and purpose of man and his life could be answered.

Since nature could be clearly delineated and it remained static, the meaning of grace could equally be isolated and defined. Grace was defined as that which is not due to nature, neither as constituting a part of nature, as flowing from nature, nor as demanded by nature. Within such a system, the relationship between man's nature and grace is easily established: there is none. The best that theologians would admit was an "obediential potency,"[11] that is, a nonrepugnance of man for God. If God so wished to communicate himself to man there was nothing in man that was opposed. Such a position seems a rather strange one for Christian theologians to espouse, especially when we consider that non-Christian thinkers such as James or Otto would admit more than a nonrepugnance of man for at least a religious experience.

The problem with such a traditional system is its simplicity. Grace is defined or described in a negative way based on a meaning of man's nature that is at best unclear. When we examine more closely the meaning of man's nature and come up with rational animal, then it is not so clear what grace is. If man has a religious orientation, then there should be some evidence of this in the meaning of man; his nature should be affected. If we can work within our own experience and accept the findings of Schleiermacher, Otto, and James, then there must be another understanding of human nature that will be of greater help in our effort to understand more thoroughly our relationship to God. Contemporary philosophers offer us this new meaning of nature by speaking of man as transcendence.

Contemporary Philosophy of Man's Nature

In more recent philosophy, the nature of man is clearly distinguished from the nature of other creatures. Man is not just another of God's creatures among many; rather there is a clear difference between him and all other creatures. In an effort to delineate this difference, philosophers will speak of the nature of man as transcendence, and include in this notion the tension between existence and person, as well as the basic historicity of man.[12]

Man is transcendence—even the most humble of men dream the impossible dream. The slumdweller rises to the roof of the tenement and gazes at the stars, oblivious of all else. He senses the infinite and knows that things can be different even though there is little possibility of that now. Education, family background, opportunities, personal talents—all limit a man, and yet man is without limits. The man teetering on the moronic can still learn something, just as the genius can still learn; the man who loves and loves deeply can still broaden his love and deepen his love. When we move in the area of love and knowledge, man appears almost infinite in possibility; he is not closed, but is open to all of reality because he can grasp reality. A child is born and all can ask: "What manner of man will this child be?" We do not know what man will be for we do not yet know the limits of his knowledge and love. Whatever makes a man a man, he is transcendent, able to become more able to break the bonds of time and space.

Nature as existence—once we accept the notion that the nature of man involves transcendence, we face the problem of existence. Transcendence is the foundation of that mode of existence in which man sees himself in relationship to himself. This can be expressed in the tension between nature and person—between what man can be and what man is.

Man has been given many talents and many possibilities. In his freedom, he is called to integrate these possibilities and in that integration the person develops. In life there is always this tension. How does the housewife resolve the tension between her possibilities of a brilliant career in teaching or administration, and her possibilities as a mother of children and wife to a man? If she resolves the tension, she becomes the integrated individual and her personhood achieves another plateau. The artist is drawn between the need to communicate and the need to express his feelings; resolution contributes to the development of the person. In a real sense, man makes of his life what he wants; it is his most precious possession and that which is most properly his own. To choose one possibility excludes another; to choose and integrate possibilities causes tension but brings maturity and the achievement of personal existence. Man makes himself a man.

Nature as History—if man is transcendent and is offered possibilities beyond number, then man is never completed; human nature is not fixed in itself, perfect once and for all, but is open to a future that is present almost without limits. Julian Huxley remarks that man is the small being in whom "the vast evolutionary process . . . is becoming conscious of himself . . . the torchbearer of advance in the cosmic process of evolution."[13] Man then does not see himself as something that is given but as something to be accomplished in history. What becomes is surely always the resolution of the tension between nature and person and is based on human transcendence, but can be understood only when history and its dimension is considered as part of what makes a man a man. Man never commits himself totally and completely at one moment, just as he is never perfected at one moment, but is caught in history and in history he becomes what he must become.

When man's nature appears as open to an ever-developing knowledge and love, with possibilities beyond measure that can be realized and spread out in history, then the question of grace as the gift of God himself to man, fulfilling man in the depths of his personality, becomes more involved than the earlier statement: grace is that which is not due to nature, neither as constituting an aspect of nature, as flowing from nature or demanded by nature.

The Meaning of Grace

Just as nature is confused in its precise meaning, grace too is equally confused. Christians refer to grace as a gift, friendship with God, help of God, power of God, and proceed to speak of actual grace, sanctifying or habitual grace, sacramental grace, and finally created and uncreated grace. With such an array of terms, no wonder that people are confused.

In this study, grace will be used in the sense of the self-communication of God to man; grace is God himself entering into a relationship with man (uncreated grace), bringing about a change in man (created grace), which is both the result of this self-gift of God and the change in man so that he can receive this communication. The graced man is the man who has accepted this self-gift of God and allows God to permeate all of the aspects of his personality so that there is not any aspect left hidden and closed off from the powerful presence of God. Any other consideration of grace must be viewed in light of this fundamental outlook.[14]

Nature is seen as an openness to the transcendent; man is becoming and never limited by what he is at one moment, but rather always open to become more than what he is. There is always the possibility of growing in love and in knowledge. Human nature is also seen as yearning for the religious, for a philosophy of life that will make sense of a human life. Mystical and religious experiences are part of the human condition. Human nature cries out for the transcendent, for the religious, and is satisfied only when this dimension of man is realized.

Grace is the gift of God himself. Grace is a relationship that makes a person different; grace is experienced as all relationships are experienced; grace is the result when a person gives himself into the mystery of the transcendent and finds himself; grace is the changed person who fulfills himself in finding his destiny in God.

To understand the meaning of nature and grace, however, is not to understand their relationship. Man seems to be ordered to God because he is so created. Yet the gift of God to man is a free gift and man must freely accept what is offered. Theology tries to integrate the findings of psychology, as well as the faith of Scripture, with the traditional understanding of the freedom of God and man. There must be an effort to spell out in greater detail the meaning of man created in the image of God and predestined in Christ. To understand the position of contemporary theology on the relationship of nature and grace, some consideration must be given to the history of the question from the time of Thomas Aquinas to the present day.

Natural Desire to See God

The theologians of the high Middle Ages accepted the distinction between natural and supernatural, as we said before, but at the same time they continued to debate the meaning of the axiom "grace presupposes nature," and the more particular question of man's natural desire to see God. The question was usually posed in relation to the created intellect tending to God as its object, but in reality the problem was the relationship of the spiritual nature of man and the supernatural order of grace.

Frequently enough the question of man's desire to see God in his essence was answered in the affirmative with the restriction that this end is possible only through grace. Thomas Aquinas defended this position, which was related to the Aristotelian principle that our natural desire for knowledge can be fulfilled only when it knows its first cause:

> Any man is naturally inclined to his ultimate end, but he is not able to reach that end except through grace, and this because of the eminence of the end.[15]

Thomas held a strong position in regard to man's natural desire to see God: for him the created intellect ontologically tends to the vision of God in its essence.[16] Once this is accepted, the problem of the relationship of nature and grace is clearly presented: Can there be a supernatural order of grace undue to man when the intellect has a natural desire for the vision of God in himself? No one should be surprised that since the time of Thomas Aquinas theologians have argued intermittently over what Thomas meant.

What must be maintained is that Thomas taught an ontological natural desire of the rational creature for the immediate vision of God. He personally held a certain middle position inasmuch as he inherited a doctrine of man from the Fathers of the Church, with one concrete supernatural end, and he transposed these ideas into Aristotelian categories. His synthesis includes a certain problem that is still in need of further development today, but his teaching merits more respect than that of many of his successors. Thomas taught the transcendence of the human spirit and thus indicated the structure of the human spirit in which the natural desire for God could be inscribed.

The Formulation of the Double System of Nature and Grace[17]

At the beginning of the fourteenth century, some theologians taught that God was able to create a man without an ordination to the beatific vision. This was the foundation for the system of pure nature.

In the sixteenth century, Cajetan offered more thought that would contribute to the formulation of pure nature with his teaching on man in a double fashion. He considers man first in an absolute way inasmuch as he is ordered to happiness. In this sense he can have a natural desire to attain that happiness. But in another fashion, he cannot have a natural desire for something that transcends his nature. In this sense man does not have a natural desire for the vision of God. He further proposes that human nature has a proper natural happiness and natural friendship as a natural end.[18]

The thesis of Cajetan was not universally accepted, but many theologians did accept his fundamental outlook and continued to direct further investigations into the question. Suárez notes: "It is necessary that every natural substance have a certain natural end which is co-natural and toward which it tends."[19] Suárez develops his thought by noting that if man has another and supernatural end, then this must be added to man as a distinct end.

At this same time a system of theology developed at Louvain in accord with the general tendencies of Cajetan and Suárez. In the presence of such a theology, Michael Baius reacted by a return to what he considered the Augustinian doctrine and conceived human nature related to grace, inasmuch as grace fulfilled the most profound aspirations of human nature. In 1576 certain of the propositions of Baius were condemned. The reaction was the blossoming of a double system of nature and grace. On the natural plane man has a natural destiny, has natural virtues and natural means to attain this destiny; to this fully developed system there is added another supernatural system with a supernatural end, supernatural virtues to correspond to the natural virtues, and supernatural means to attain this end. There is no relationship between nature and grace because both are completely separated.

In the years that followed the condemnation of Baius and the development of a system of pure nature, the ordinary believer accepted a concept of nature that was closed and completed, fixed and permanent. Grace became reified as something that was added to man and to which man was indifferent. In such an appreciation of the meaning of nature and grace, theology had come a long way from the doctrine of the Bible which saw all men ordered to God. Lost was the notion from the Fathers that man existed in one concrete order in which his destiny was God in himself. Overlooked was the doctrine of Thomas that saw man with a natural desire to see God in himself. Theologians affirmed strongly the doctrine of the gratuity of the gift of God himself, but in this affirmation forgot the orientation of man toward the self-communication of God.

Today the problem has not changed. How can contemporary theology come to a resolution that preserves the profound insights of the Fathers of the Church and Thomas Aquinas in regard to man's positive orientation to God, and at the same time preserve the total freedom of this gift of God himself? How can we express the relationship between nature and grace and at the same time preserve the transcendency of God and the immanence of grace that perfects man in his concrete existence?

From Blondel to Rahner

Toward the end of the nineteenth century, Maurice Blondel laid the foundation for a return to the earlier understanding of nature and grace with his efforts to construct a new apologetics.[20] Traditional apologetics presupposed an abstract image of man to whom the Catholic religion offered arguments of credibility in regard to the divinity of Christ and the acceptance of the Catholic Church as coming from Christ. Once man was presented with the motives of credibility the arguments moved toward credentity with the observer apparently learning impelling reasons to accept and believe. The entire process was somewhat abstract and outside the ordinary experience of man. Christianity met a need in man in much the same way as Madison Avenue might convince modern man that he needs the second car.

Blondel was a man convinced of the import of Christianity for his contemporaries and tried to show that the Christian faith is not something extrinsic to man, but a reality that corresponds to his most profound aspirations. There is no need to propose reasons for credibility and credentity in the same way that a man hears the salesman talking about the new car; what is necessary is to have man experience that in Christianity he finds what he has experienced in himself long before he ever came to the study of Christianity. Blondel wanted an apologetics in the concrete so that the supernatural could be assimilated by man, because the supernatural and grace agree with the nature of man. He did not develop a strict metaphysics of the nature of man, but through a phenomenological analysis of concrete man he detected what he considered a natural desire for the supernatural, a discovery not unlike the opinion of the Fathers of the Church and Thomas Aquinas. Humanity, according to Blondel, is orientated to the supernatural because man has no other concrete end than heaven, salvation. The providence of God affects all men because the will of God is a saving will for all men.

In the beginning of the twentieth century, the doctrine of Modernism and the period of integralism following the publication of *Pascendi Gregis* and *Lamentabili* nipped the theology of Blondel before it ever had a chance to develop. Certain aspects of his doctrine were similar to that proposed by George Tyrrell, Alfred Loisy, and other Modernists. With the Church condemnation of Modernism, all theories that in any way hinted of grace as due to man were immediately suspect. For almost the next forty years, Blondel's attempt to return to a more primitive understanding of the relationship between nature and grace was forgotten with the reascendancy of the more traditional apologetics and the system of pure nature. Another attempt to change the situation arose in the late forties with the publication of *Surnaturel* by Henri De Lubac.[21]

De Lubac returned to the study of the medieval question of man's natural desire to see God as well as the position of the Fathers that saw man created in relationship to grace. In his book he tried to show that this one concrete end is profoundly inscribed in the nature of man; it is not something that is added; nor does it change nature. He compared the work of grace to the work of creation so that in this elevation in grace there is a personal communication of God which is prepared for in the positive orientation of man toward this elevation. At the same time he insists that grace is received only in the manner of a gift:

> The spirit in effect does not desire God as an animal desires its prey. The spirit desires God as a gift. It no longer searches to possess an infinite object but wishes a free communication, a gratuitous communication with a personal being.[22]

De Lubac insists that this desire is an absolute desire that nevertheless does not signify a demand because man cannot demand something of God. If man is understood intrinsically, however, the desire cannot be denied, not because man can place necessity on God, but because God must respond to the demands that he has placed on himself:

> If there is in our nature the desire to see God, that is possible only because God wishes to give us a supernatural end which consists in seeing him.[23]
>
> That is not to say that man because of this desire demands that it be fulfilled, but on the contrary, it is because God wishes to give to man this fulfillment that man is obliged to tend to possess it.[24]

He concluded that the natural desire of man for God is an expression of the exigency of God in relationship to man, and moreover is well in accord with traditional theology both of the Church Fathers and such medieval theologians as Thomas Aquinas.

Surnaturel appeared at a time when man needed to believe in the possibility of man as a religious creature with the possibility of a supernatural destiny. Europe was still torn apart as the result of the War and it was encouraging to find a theologian who believed in man and his future destiny involved with God. Some agreed with his basic approach, but in general the reaction was swift and severely critical. The controversy centered on the level of history and De Lubac's interpretation of the doctrine of the Fathers, as well as Thomas Aquinas, and on the level of strict doctrine. The basic objection launched against his thesis was that it destroyed the gratuity of the supernatural order. If God created man with an ontological desire for himself, then this desire had to be fulfilled; if grace is due to nature, then it is no longer grace. Theologians once again affirmed the theology of pure nature with the teaching of "obediential potency": there is nothing in man opposed to grace and if God so wishes, he can communicate himself to man. The final blow came with the publication of *Humani Generis* in which Pope Pius XII stated that God could create intellectual creatures without ordering them to a supernatural end.[25] De Lubac and his ideas entered under a cloud that was to remain until the convocation of the Second Vatican Council more than ten years later.

Vatican II and the Doctrine of Karl Rahner

The Second Vatican Council takes as its starting point for the consideration of man the calling of all men to glory. In the decree on the missions, the Fathers state:

> Freely creating us out of his surpassing and merciful kindness and graciously calling us moreover to communicate in life and glory with himself, he has generously poured out his divine goodness and does not cease to do so. Thus he who has made all things may at last be "all in all" (1 Cor. 15:28) procuring at one and the same time his own glory and our happiness.[26]

The Council considers all men concretely as ordered to the one end which is their happiness in sharing in the life of God.

In the same decree on missionary activity, the Council fathers quote Acts 17 in the context of man's orientation toward God:

> This universal design of God for the salvation of the human race is not carried out exclusively in the soul of a man with a kind of secrecy. Nor is it achieved merely through those mul-

> tiple endeavors, including religious ones, by which men search for God, groping for him that they may chance find him.(27)[27]

Similar statements scattered throughout the decrees permeate the Council's understanding of man.[28]

A more careful analysis of the mentality of the Council fathers reveals an acceptance of the basic thesis of Blondel as well as the theories of De Lubac. The system of pure nature that appeared obliquely in the First Vatican Council has ceased to be the context of the Second Vatican Council. Rather, man is seen as ordered to the vision that is God, and because of this ordering, the Fathers appeal to many aspects of contemporary man's desires as signs of his destiny to be realized only in God.[29] The Council accepts this teaching but does not present a fully developed theology. For such a synthesis, believers today can turn to contemporary theologians who have benefited from the study of the doctrine in the previous years and offer their own explanation of the relationship between nature and grace. The following presentation is based on the teaching of Karl Rahner, Juan Alfaro, as well as Henri De Lubac and George Tyrrell.

Contemporary Doctrine of Nature and Grace[30]

Whenever a theologian is involved in the question of man's orientation to God, he is face to face with the mystery that is God and what is equally wonderful, the mystery that is man. The two doctrines are not disparate. We cannot speak of God unless in relationship to a concrete man, Jesus of Nazareth, who has revealed God; nor can we speak of man unless we see him as related to the same God who has communicated himself in Jesus of Nazareth. The future of God involves man as the future of man involves God. No explanation will adequately express the mystery that is God and man, but some explanations will offer more understanding than others.

The foundation of any presentation must not be some hypothetical order. We do not live in possible worlds but only in a concrete world in which man's destiny is God. Moreover, this world itself is involved in man's future, as Paul notes in Romans: "Creation awaits with eager longing for the revelation of the sons of God" (8:19). The destiny of man is not separated from his world, nor is it something that is added to him outside the context of creation. If the end is first in intention, then creation is possible only in relationship to grace as the self-communication of God. This concrete end that God has proposed should also be inscribed into human nature; it should not be extrinsic to man and his world, but should correspond to his deepest aspirations. The whole world in the concrete is ordered to the supernatural: to share in the blessedness of God.

This teaching is especially important for the understanding of the relationship of Christ to human nature. If man is created in the image of God, then human nature is so constructed that it can pronounce the Word of God. In Christ, human nature reached the goal toward which it always tended because man himself can speak the one Word of God.

We cannot speak of man being indifferent to the communication of God and seriously accept the doctrine of the image of God in man. Nor can we seriously speak of a predestination of man to glory and maintain that the destiny of man does not flow from an intrinsic orientation.

These considerations lead to a rather profound impasse. According to early Christian tradition, the ultimate supernatural end of man is inscribed in his nature; man is positively ordered to the life with God because man in the concrete has an absolute, ontological supernatural and natural desire for the vision of God. At the same time, we still maintain that grace is a free gift. Is there any hope of reconciliation?

Karl Rahner responds that in man there is an element that is not constitutive of nature as such, but which is always a determination of human nature. This determination "bases" the desire of man for God. He calls this determination of man a supernatural existential.

In the Romance languages, there is a difference between *existential* and *existentiel* in philosophy. *Existentiel* within this philosophical system is that which arises as a result of a free decision of man. *Existential* signifies that which antecedes the free decision of man as a given.

Rahner speaks of a supernatural *existential* inasmuch as the ordination of man toward God is a determination of man that is given to him and which precedes the actual decision of man to accept or reject this determination. He can refer to this as a *supernatural* existential inasmuch as this determination is not constitutive of human nature as such, though it is always present (hence it is also natural), and orders man to the vision that is God himself. This supernatural existential is not the same thing as the self-communication of God to man, or grace, since God communicates himself to man only when man freely accepts this relationship. Man is ordered to God, which explains the search for meaning in life, but an ordering to God is not the same thing as the actual acceptance of this ordination and the self-communication of God. Rahner holds a position similar to that of De Lubac, but preserves the free communication of God with his doctrine of the supernatural existential.

Certainly such a doctrine is not perfect. There are many questions that Rahner leaves open to criticism. In a sense it almost seems that he proposes the same ideas as De Lubac, with the addition of his supernatural existential in an effort to preserve the theological notion of the gratuity of the supernatural order. This, however, should not be final reaction to Rahner's thought. What Rahner does is propose a theological analysis of a relationship that man experiences. Man in the thought of many contemporary philosophers is transcendent; he experiences himself drawn beyond the limits imposed on him by space and time that in some way makes him a man and not an animal. He is at home in this world because it is his world, and yet at times he seeks to escape from the limits of his "home" and experience a total joy and peace that obliterate all time and space; he seeks to penetrate the mystery of the universe and with others to find repose. It is possible to conceive of man without this experience, but it is not real. Rahner has taken this experience and seen it in terms of a relationship to God as mystery that fulfills man as mystery[31] and calls this a determination of man or a supernatural existential. If his doctrine helps us to understand the mystery that is man communicating with the mystery that is God, then he has fulfilled his task as a theologian and we could want little more.

A fitting conclusion for this chapter on nature and grace

would be an analysis of the axiom: grace presupposes, extols, and does not destroy but perfects nature.

Nature and Grace on the Existential Plane

The careful analysis of the doctrine of nature and grace often leaves the reader with a sense of confusion and a question of relevancy. In reality, the relevancy is considerable on the plane of human existence, as well as on the level of theory.

The understanding of nature and grace influences the religious aspect of man as well as his religious institutions. In the history of Western society, philosophers as well as literary men and artists have proposed a return to nature as necessary for man. Rousseau, Thoreau, and others have reacted against a society that is "thing" oriented, as well as a society that is "other-world" oriented and lacking in an appreciation of this world. A false supernaturalism can easily rob man of his destiny as the one who creates his world; a religion that offers this sense of supernaturalism does not appeal to the mature man, and cannot long survive. If all that matters is grace and the spiritual life, then man who is rooted in the earth (Gen. 2:7) will not find enthusiasm for grace and the spiritual life.

Today the danger to religion appears to have shifted away from a false supernaturalism, which seems to have characterized recent religious history, to an equally false naturalism. If all that matters is man and what he wishes, without any reference to such questions as evil and sin and the need for a responsible exercise of power and dominion, then man can never develop his talents as one given spirit in matter and not just matter. False supernaturalism prevents man from developing and finding his place in this world; false naturalism leads man to destroy his earth. Every understanding of nature and grace has its repercussions on the level of practical human existence.

Grace Presupposes Nature

In a real sense this axiom could be reversed. If grace, the self-communication of God to his creature, was the first intention of God, then nature is directed to grace and might be termed: nature presupposes grace. Creation, as we have seen, is ordered to the covenant between God and man. The axiom, then, cannot signify that nature is prior to grace.

Nor can we say that nature is the measure of grace. In the Gospel narratives, it becomes evident that often those who were least endowed were closest to God: "God chose what is foolish in the world to shame the wise" (1 Cor. 1:27). Oftentimes it seems that individuals who have more native ability find themselves tempted with a false autonomy, while those who are in need turn more characteristically to their God. At least it is not evident that nature is the measurement of closeness to God.

What then can be said of the axiom? In the self-communication of God to man, human nature is always presupposed in its totality. There can be no dialogue unless man is able to enter that dialogue; there can be no enunciation of God's Word unless man is capable of speaking that Word; there can be no exchange of knowledge and love unless man is able to know and love. Grace is not a self-gift of God unless man as man is involved with all his hopes, desires, intellect, will, emotions, relationships, and projects in his world. Real men are the basis of this possible self-gift and not abstract men.

Grace Extols Nature

Man is always able to transcend his possibilities and add newness of life. By grace man is ordered to share in the mystery that is God, beyond what might be considered his normal possibilities. Grace as the self-gift of God signifies that in the center of man and his possibilities lies the destiny of one ordered to God. The possibility of man, as the man fully developed and perfected, intertwines with the possibility of God who gives of himself to his creation. The gift of grace realizes the profundity of man's transcendence; it is not something that is imposed from without; grace is seen as the flowering of what is possible because of the transcendence of man that his Creator has given to him. In such a treatment we are immediately influenced by the scriptural doctrine of man as created in the image of God and predestined in Christ. In the acceptance of this offer by God, man reaches the point toward which he was always directed.

Grace Does Not Destroy Nature

Even with the self-gift of God, man remains man and God

remains God; the distance between Creator and creature may be narrowed, but it is not obliterated. Grace touches us where we are, with the failures as well as the successes: the joys as well as the sorrows, the experiences of unity as well as the sense of alienation. Man is still very human with the acceptance of his relationship to God. There can be no false supernaturalism that tends to make man an angel. Nor can there be an immediate perfection of man through the acceptance of the gift of God. Man does nothing totally, at once, but spreads out the meaning of his life in a span of years and decades. Grace causes no miracles if those miracles rob man of his nature. Grace is as real as man; it does not destroy man.

Grace Perfects Man

Through grace we will be ourselves. The offer of God leads man beyond his possibilities, but presupposes those possibilities as rooted in transcendence so that man's transcendence reaches a stage of fulfillment in the actual permeation of himself by the gift of God. Grace perfects man by drawing him on into a future, and in this, grace perfects man by overcoming evil in man's life. Man finds himself today in an ambiguity; he senses himself alienated from his God, from his fellow-man and even within himself. Simultaneously he longs for a state of peace and harmony. When man accepts the offer of God, he is on the way to overcoming this sense of alienation and disharmony and to finding his fulfillment. The life that a man lives is totally his in a fashion that relativizes any other possession. He can make of his life what he wishes but will find his life only when he finds it in relationship to his God: "He who loses his life for my sake will find it" (Matt. 10:39). Man will be perfected in himself when he is willing to pay the cost of accepting his relationship to his God. There can be no perfection of man without the element of human suffering, or without the cross of Christ. The man who is in sin needs to die if he is to rise to perfection. There is a synthesis of nature and grace, but this is found only in Jesus of Nazareth and in those who follow his route.

In Jesus of Nazareth, the Word of God presupposes a concrete human nature with all the hopes, desires, feelings, emotions of any concrete man. Nothing is eliminated. What is human is assumed and becomes the expression of the divine. In him grace extols nature inasmuch as in him human nature reaches its highest possibility: man is the expression of God's Word. Nor is human nature destroyed in Jesus. The Word of God became incarnate in sinful flesh to redeem sinful man. What is lacking is sin, but what is present is suffering and death. Through his suffering and death, he becomes "Lord," empowered to perfect us as he himself was perfected in his acceptance of his death. In Jesus of Nazareth nature and grace are present in harmony without any false supernaturalism that leads man away from his world and without any false naturalism that denies the condition of man alienated from God and himself. In Jesus, the most profound aspirations of grace are realized. For all who await the full harmony of what we are and what we can be and hope to be, there is a continual struggle to harmonize nature and the gift of God that is grace. In this struggle we believe that we are aided by the powerful presence of God. This is what the life and death of Jesus of Nazareth has told us.

We have spoken of man created in the image of God, or predestined in Christ to glory, and as oriented toward God as a gift. With all of this given, man has great value and a dignity that can never be completely lost. The section on man's orientation toward God briefly mentioned the reality of sin and evil in the world. This must now be considered as basic to any Christian understanding of man. Evil and sin are too much a reality to be overlooked. What has already been said, however, must always be the context within which we also speak of sin. There is always a fundamental biblical and Christian optimism:

> We know that God makes all things work together for the good of those who have been called according to his decree. Those whom he foreknew he predestined to share the image of his Son, that the Son might be the first-born of many brothers. Those he predestined he likewise called; those he called he also justified; and those he justified he in turn gloried. (Rom. 8:28-30)

Notes

[1]The phrase comes from R. R. Niebuhr in his introduction to Friedrich Schleiermacher's *The Christian Faith* (New York: Harper and Row, 1963), p. xii.

[2]F. Schleiermacher, *The Christian Faith*, p. 15.

[3]Cf. Rudolf Otto, *The Idea of the Holy* (New York: Oxford Univ. Press, 1958).

[4]*Ibid.*, p. 24.

[5]*Ibid.*, p. 42.

[6]Cf. Mircea Eliade, *The Sacred and the Profane* (New York: Harcourt, Brace, 1959).

[7]Cf. William James, *The Varieties of Religious Experience* (New York: Random House, 1929).

[8]*Ibid.*, Lectures 16, 17.

[9]In contemporary psychology there are several noted psychologists who point to a deeper dimension in human life that can be related to the need and search for transcendence and eventually to what the Christian faith regards as the need of man for God. Cf. Abraham Maslow, *Religion, Values and Peak-experiences* (Columbus: Ohio Univ. Press, 1964); Victor Frankl, *Man's Search for Meaning* (Boston: Beacon Press, 1962); Rollo May, *Man in Search of Himself* (New York: Norton, 1953).

[10]Cf. *Summa Theologica*, III, q. 2, a. 1.

[11]Cf. Peter Parente, *Anthropologia Supernaturalis* (Rome: Marietti, 1943), pp. 151-152; Reginald Garrigou-Lagrange, *Grace* (St. Louis: Herder, 1952), pp. 306-308.

[12]The brief philosophical presentation here is based almost entirely on the philosophy that underlies the theology of Karl Rahner. No effort to present a complete justification is intended. For further development, see Joseph Maréchal, *Le Point de départ de la Métaphysique* (Paris: Desclée, 1947); Karl Rahner, *Spirit in the World* (New York: Herder and Herder, 1967); Karl Rahner, *Hearers of the Word* (New York: Herder and Herder, 1969); Joseph Donceel, *Philosophical Anthropology* (New York: Sheed and Ward, 1967).

[13]Cf. Julian Huxley, "The Future of Man—Evolutionary Aspects" in G. Wolstenholme, ed., *Man and His Future* (New York: Little, Brown, 1963), pp. 1, 22.

[14]Robert Gleason, *Grace* (New York: Sheed and Ward, 1962).

[15]*In Boet. de Trinitate*, q. 6, a. 4, ad 5.

[16]*Contra Gentiles*, 5057; Cf. also: *Summa Theologica*, I, q. 12; *Compendium Theologiae*, pp. 103-106.

[17]The history of this question is taken from Henri De Lubac, *Surnaturel* (Paris: Aubier, 1947); De Lubac, *The Mystery of the*

Supernatural (New York: Herder and Herder, 1967); Henri Rondet, *The Grace of Christ* (Westminster: Newman, 1967).

[18]Cf. *In Primam Secundae*, q. 99, a. 9, n. 3.

[19]Suárez, *De Ultima Fine Hominis*, diss. 18, section 2, n. 11.

[20]Cf. Maurice Blondel, *The Letter on Apologetics, and History and Dogma*, (New York: Holt, Rinehart, Winston, 1965). *Le Procès de L'Intelligence* (Paris, 1922) pp. 217-206; *Qu'est-ce-que la Mystique* (Paris, 1925) pp. 1-63.

[21]Cf. De Lubac, *Surnaturel* (Paris: Aubier, 1947).

[22]*Ibid.*, p. 483.

[23]*Ibid.*, p. 489.

[24]*Ibid.*, p. 486.

[25]Pius XII, *Humani Generis, Acta Apost. Sedis*, 42 (1950), p. 570; *The Catholic Mind*, vol. 48 (1950), p. 695.

[26]"Decree on Missionary Activity", No. 2, *Documents of the Vatican Council II* (New York: Guild Press, 1965).

[27]*Ibid.*, No. 3.

[28]Cf. "Constitution on the Church in the Modern World", Nos. 10, 14, 18, *Documents of the Vatican Council II* (New York: Guild Press, 1965).

[29]*Ibid.*, No. 10.

[30]The following section is based on the theology of Rahner, Alfaro, and George Tyrrell. Cf. J. Alfaro, "Person and Grace," *Man Before God* (New York: Kenedy, 1966); Karl Rahner, *Nature and Grace* (New York: Sheed and Ward, 1965); Rahner, "Concerning the Relationship Between Nature and Grace," *Theological Investigations*, vol. 1 (Baltimore: Helicon, 1961); J. F. O'Grady, *The Doctrine of Nature and Grace in the Writings of George Tyrrell* (Rome: 1969).

[31]Cf. K. Rahner, "The Concept of Mystery in Catholic Theology," *Theological Investigations*, vol. 4 (Baltimore: Helicon, 1965).

4

Evil and Sin

Christianity has a basic optimism about the future of man. God has spoken his Word and that Word is good. There is worth and value in any human life and the destiny of the human race is God himself. It is good to be optimistic about yourself and about the future; optimism helps to overcome the great threat to optimism: the presence of evil.

To look at man with a critical and careful eye, however, involves looking at the unseemly aspects of human life, as well as the destructive forces that are periodically unleashed in the universe. No road map is needed if one wants to find evil and sin. Little wars and big wars dot the history of our race; death and sickness and destruction may have become more sophisticated in the twentieth century, but their force is without change. How beautiful to think of man as created in the image of God and predestined in Christ with all of his being crying out for God. Would that this was the only thing one saw in the search for the meaning of man and the search for understanding human life!

Christianity is realistic. It admits of sin and evil and acknowledges that sin and evil have no favorites; no one is preserved from their influence. Christian anthropology is realistic since it too attests to the presence of evil in man and in his world. We begin with the meaning of evil and then ask the ancient question: how did it all happen?

Evil and the Power of God

The frequent use of the words "evil" and "sin" often confuses their meaning. The death camps of Nazi Germany, the massacre of My Lai, cancer, mental retardation, death, earthquakes, hurricanes, segregation, war, malaria, are all evil and all tragic. Yet there is a remarkable difference between the murder of Vietnamese civilians at My Lai or the destruction of life at Auschwitz and the sting of a malaria-carrying mosquito. War and segregation are not in the same category as hurricanes and earthquakes. In spite of the dissimilarity, there is a common element in all of these diverse evils. Each is part of the world but each might not be; the world is out of line, or man is out of line; things and people are not as they should be.

In human history many have attempted to offer a response to the general condition of evil in man and in his world. None have been successful. The Bible treats of the problem of evil in the Book of Job, which concludes with the mystery of God (Job 38-42).

The Book of Qoheleth continues with the same theme and concludes that it is better to eat, drink, and be merry since in the end we will all die. Even Jesus Christ seems to accept the presence of evil in the world and tells his disciples to have courage because he has broken its power, even if he has not eradicated its presence: "Be of good cheer, I have overcome the world" (John 16:33).

Philosophers have also tackled the problem. Some settle for a dualism: spirit is good and matter is evil. Seek to overcome the control of matter and you will be liberated from the power of evil. Other philosophers have blamed evil on man in a total sense. Contemporary existentialism seems to accept the reality of evil and offers the injunction to try to lessen its power and learn to settle for the absurdity of human life that inevitably ends in death.

Theologians have tried, philosophers have their responses and all agree that evil exists in man and in his world. On this there is agreement, even if the solution to "why" defies an easy answer.

With such a long list of previous attempts that have failed, no one should think that we will ever solve the question of evil: what does it mean and how did it originate? What is offered here is a different approach that may be of assistance in trying to move towards a better understanding of a thorny question.

To understand the difference between evil and sin demands an analysis of both, as well as an examination of the context in which both are possible. When this is treated, the question of the origin of evil and sin must be faced. Were things always as they are, and will life always be a mixture of evil and goodness, sin and virtue?

The Problem of Evil

Today we live in a world in which everyone is conscious of evolution. It is not a perfect world, but a world that is being perfected and developed. Things are not always the way they should be. Anything that is changing and becoming is still "on the way" to perfection. This is the context within which we will discuss evil.

Evil involves more than man and his world; it also involves God, who has been recognized as a good God, as someone who loves and cares for his creation and loves and cares for man. In trying to study the meaning of evil and sin, these are the two principles that must be recalled:

1. The world is evolving; it is not perfect but a perfecting world. This is the context for any resolution to the question of evil.
2. Evil involves more than man and his world; it also involves God who is presented to man as a good God.

With these two notions, we might be in a better position to understand evil and sin. Since moral evil (sin) causes more difficulties for man, we will treat this first followed by a presentation of natural disasters, or physical evil.

Moral Evil and Its Possibility

The reality of moral evil in the world often impinges on the credibility of the "good" God, and leads some to deny the existence of God. If God exists and if he is so good, why do men seek to destroy each other? If God is good and powerful, why did he not change the trajectory of the bullet that killed John Kennedy? Why did he allow the massacre at My Lai and the thousand other acts of man by which he destroys himself? How can we reconcile moral evil with a God who is good?

The response to these questions depends on our understanding of the meaning of the power of God and how God acts in his creation.[1] If God's power is conceived within the confines of efficient causality, the problem is more acute than when God's power is conceived in terms of transcendent causality.[2]

Traditional theology presents the power of God in such a way that he is responsible for everything, for all that happens and precisely how it happens. God is an efficient cause working in the universe and doing things through the instrumentality of objects and man. God is the primary cause and man and other objects are secondary instrumental causes. In this way he is all powerful since he can do all things and does all things. With such a belief the question of evil causes difficulties.

If God is responsible for all things and evil exists in the world, then he is responsible for evil as well. Traditionally, theologians have responded by ascribing the existence of evil to man's power and not to God. God is responsible for everything but only permits evil. Often enough, such mental gymnastics freed God from responsibility for evil, but caused confusion by leaving the impression that God has all control over good but little over evil. This reduces his power to the near vanishing point.[3] All such explanations presuppose that the power of God is the ability to determine what is to be and how it is to be, within the framework of efficient causality. This, however, is not an adequate response to the question of moral evil; it raises more questions than originally presented. This idea of the power of God, fortunately, is not the only possibility.

People often measure power by the incapacity to resist. The analogy used is the potter and the clay. The only limits imposed on the potter is the amount of clay and the quality of the clay; he can do whatever he wills with the lump, and the lump can offer no resistance. Such an analogy fits authoritarian personalities as well as dictatorial regimes, but certainly not a God who reveals himself as a Father.

In reality the potter, the dictator, or the authoritarian personality exercises very little power. Pop posters say it well: "Because you have silenced me does not mean you have conquered me." Where there is no competing power, or where this power is unable to be exercised, omnipotence will last as long as there is an army or a police force, or until the competing power is free to respond. Then omnipotence will topple. A child has power over tin soldiers just as the physically powerful or the politically powerful control their subjects. In both cases the power is very small.

Real power is the power to influence the exercise of the power of others. Totalitarian regimes will remain in power as long as they maintain political control, but the man with ideas has power that will outlast any totalitarianism. As long as man is man the only real power is the power of persuasion. To influence a man's mind is more lasting than the twisting of an arm.

If we choose to apply any notion of power to God, then it should be the effective power of persuasion rather than the power of a dictator or a potter. The real analogy is the wise parent who exercises power in persuading his children rather than the weak potter who exercises power over an object that offers no resistance. As the man with ideas, or the parent, leads those who listen to think, so God leads man to think and accept the values that bring life. God persuades man to choose and is powerful in his persuasion.

In the light of this appreciation of power, the question of evil becomes more intelligible.[4] God places man in a situation in which he is capable of freely choosing significant values; God draws man to these values and persuades him that in the acceptance of these values he will find personal happiness. He may even entice man but does not force. The chosen values are man's personal option.

Man is free in his choice but not free in the consequences of that choice. If he accepts the values presented, he grows in his humanity and goodness increases; if he rejects the offer he fails in his search for happiness and evil increases. Because God persuades and man is free, then man has the possibility of destroying his fellow-man or the possibility of committing moral evil.

Some might complain about a situation in which God insisted on judging man harshly everytime he refused the values as presented. Such is not the case. God offers a fresh possibility to man again and again to find happiness. Man need never judge God harshly for allowing him to fail, for the possibility of failure is also the possibility of growth, and God holds no grudges.

In this view God is responsible for evil just as he is responsible for everything that man does. God places man in a situation in which moral evil is possible and thus is responsible for the moral evil when it arises. The responsibility, however, flows not from efficient causality, but from transcendent causality.

Transcendent causality is a supportive causality.[5] God does not intervene in his creation but sustains, encourages, and persuades his creation to develop according to its own capacity. God allows for the potential in man and supports him in the exercise of that potential. With transcendent causality evil is possible, for man often fails to realize his true potential. As long as God chooses to support man and to persuade him to choose values, God is responsible for evil as well as good for he has created the context in which evil is possible.

This understanding of the power of God as the power of persuasion allows us to recognize the existence of moral evil without limiting God's goodness; it respects the ability of man to choose for himself in freedom; it is totally Christian since it presents God as he is, a Father leading man freely to accept his offer of himself and happiness, but not forcing him. Certainly this appreciation of moral evil can help us to understand why there are wars, why there is prejudice, why man chooses to be a wolf to his fellow-man.

Natural Disasters: Physical Evil

The second question in regard to evil in the world drives to the heart: Why do children suffer? The classical modern presentation of this question is raised by Albert Camus in *The Plague*. Both priest and atheist doctor witness the ravages of the plague; the priest calls for repentance; the doctor works to alleviate human suffering; both witness the suffering of children and the priest loses his faith. How can God be good and powerful if children suffer, if earthquakes devour thousands, if life is snuffed out at its peak? The power of persuasion within an evolving and imperfect world may help us to understand these questions.

The power of God as sustaining Creator of the world is meaningful only when we include the idea that God calls his creation to greater perfection. As we have seen, God sustains and protects his creation as it develops on its own powers. His power of persuasion and his transcendent causality is not limited to man but includes the totality of the universe. Moreover, he exercises this power in the world according to the stages of the world's development. In an evolving universe not everything is possible at once.

The movement to life and values was slow, always sustained

by God who gradually led his creation to greater perfection. For billions of years the earth was devoid of life and in such a world the possibility of value is rather limited. Movement came in the direction of life but only when physical conditions could support life. As the movement continued with ever-richer varieties of life, the possibility of values increased and reached an apex with the advent of man. The whole process is the response to a God who is luring his creation into greater self-actualization.

In this evolutionary world the question of natural disaster or physical evil is not acute, at least on a theoretical level. The destruction of life through earthquakes and hurricanes and sickness could have been avoided only by a postponement of human life to the period when the physical universe had reached its own stage of perfection. Such a desire, however, fails to understand the evolutionary process as well as the close tie between man and his world. An evolving world in which there is loss of life as well as a struggle for survival in its movement toward perfection is of greater value than a world devoid of human life. The presence of man, even in an imperfect world, makes the free acceptance of values possible, which is a perfection greatly desired. Perhaps we can imagine a world in which there would be no struggle for existence nor loss of life through natural forces, but it has never been an actuality and seems to be reserved for the end of time. Nor should we lament its absence. The struggle for life and the conquest of all evil makes possible the realization of greater values and growth for man, as Christianity teaches.

The Christian Attitude toward Evil

An evolving world does not limit the task of the believer, nor of any man, to suffer the pain of evolution passively. Nor can man accept the inevitability of moral evil in the destruction of persons. The Christian is told explicitly to do something about the presence of evil. Jesus never gave a clear answer to the question of evil but he did charge us to struggle with evil and overcome it just as he overcame its power (John 16:33). The basic Christian attitude is to make progress over evil and its power.

In regard to moral evil, the believer seeks a love of God that promotes the well-being of other persons. The love of neighbor, not his destruction, is the goal of Christianity. Christians must overcome the evil in themselves and then help others in overcoming the power of evil in their own hearts. Progress is the hope of the Christian. Political progress must overcome injustice and prejudice and bring nations to peace rather than to war; society must progress in its structures to protect men against the power of evil and use law to preserve man from his inclinations to tear down rather than build up. There is no complacency in Christianity even as it accepts the doctrine that God forces no one to accept the values that promise life. The same attitude characterizes the Christian in the face of natural disaster and physical evil. Progress in medicine must overcome the ravages of sickness. The control of the environment with its proper use will lead to a lessening of physical evil in the world with the further advance of the universe toward its final perfection. As the believer works to overcome moral evil in the love of the neighbor, so he overcomes physical evil in the fulfillment of his vocation to subdue the world.

At a period of history when we are conscious of the presence of evil in the world made vivid with the graphic display of war and death in Vietnam, riots in the cities, and with the usual share of natural disasters, it takes more than faith to affirm the goodness of God, of man and of the world; it takes hope. If man could project into the future only the world that he knows now, with its mixture of love and hatred, Peace Corps and Vietnam, Head-Start programs and race riots, and suppose that the world will ever be so, then there would be little enthusiasm for life or for a Creator. The possibility of a better future alone can give meaning to the present struggle against the forces of destruction. Truth, justice, peace, openness, and the celebration and enjoyment of life will eventually lead to a better world in which what now appears in shadows and in forms struggling to survive will overcome, despite all setbacks and the power of their opposites. At least the hope of a better future redeems the suffering that man experiences now from all horror and uselessness. An evolving and imperfect world in which man must choose personal values may always involve evil and suffering, but that suffering can always be less.

Such a picture is existential and perhaps offers some understanding of the world in which we now live and some encouragement to continue. It does not, however, respond to the "why." Was the world ever so and will it be ever so? The Christian teaching on Original Sin is the response to these questions and offers man a further explanation of his world in which evil seems to prosper easily while goodness struggles for survival.

The Origin and Condition of Evil and Sin

The meaning of the Christian doctrine of Original Sin has undergone considerable development in recent years. How much reality is present in the teaching and how much outdated myth is a question for all Christians. Since the meaning has its roots in the Jewish as well as Christian tradition, we will trace its beginning in the Bible through the history of Christianity and conclude with an attempt at a presentation consonant with the general condition of man today.

Original Sin in the Bible

An effort to base Original Sin in the Bible causes hesitation. Nowhere in the Bible are there such terms; rather the words themselves convey an understanding that is more the result of Christian history than its biblical origins. What Scripture emphasizes is the force of sin in the world not only in regard to the sins of individuals but as an element in the whole history of salvation. Secondly, the Bible concentrates, especially in the New Testament, on the superabundance of God's goodness and not the condition that demands this redemptive activity. As we analyze both Old and New Testaments, these presuppositions must be recalled.

Sin in the Old Testament

The classical text in regard to the origin and power of sin is the third chapter of Genesis:

> The woman saw that the tree was good for food, pleasing to the eyes, and desirable for gaining wisdom. So she took some of its fruit and ate it; and she also gave some to her husband, who was with her, and he ate it. Then the eyes of both of them were opened, and they realized that they were naked; so they sewed fig leaves together and made loincloths for themselves. (Gen. 3:6-7)

Woman is tempted by the serpent; she and man transgress the command of God; they are questioned by God, sentenced and expelled from the Garden. This is the story: the theologian asks what does this narrative mean?

Recent exegesis and theology conclude that the third chapter of Genesis is not an attempt to present the actual historical circumstances of man's origin. The theologian considering Genesis instead seeks first to present a mirror to his contemporaries and through this mirror lay claim that the present condition of man reflects a previous condition in his history.[6]

The condition of God's people at the time of the writing of Genesis was a condition of infidelity and temptation in the presence of their God. Israel always felt drawn to the fertility cults of her neighbors and failed frequently in her commitment to her God. God had entered into a covenant with Israel in which he promised to be her God on condition that she worshiped him alone and accepted her dependence on him. In the story of Genesis, man and woman stand for Israel who is tempted to ignore the commitment to God and instead follow the claims of the serpent (in Canaanite religion the serpent was the sign of life and fertility), and refuse to accept her dependence on God by desiring to decide for herself what is good and what is evil. The text concludes with the results of man's action. Disillusionment sets in and man receives less than what he had expected. Instead of independence and life, man receives servitude and death. What the serpent promised is never realized just as what the fertility of Canaan promised to Israel was never realized. The author of Genesis took some ideas from his own ambit and used them in a polemical way to indicate the reality of Israel's temptation as well as the continual state of decision in which Israel finds herself. At the same time, the text is a warning to Israel: all that she thinks she will find in forgetting her commitment to God will not be realized.

If this chapter of Genesis is a mirror of contemporary Israel, and for that matter a mirror for all men, does it have any relationship to the actual historical condition of man's origin? Karl Rahner uses the concept of historical aetiology[7] to describe the same chapter of Genesis. There is a relationship between the events as narrated and the original condition of man's origin.

Aetiology is the science of causes in which the present situation is understood by examining the contemporary condition and positing causes for the condition present now, as well as present in the remote past. If man is tempted to deny his relationship to God today through a false sense of independence, then this is the cause of man's initial failure of commitment to his God.

Psychologists speak of the first five years in a child's life as greatly influential and determinative of the entire life of the individual. What a person is today depends on what he was and in particular what he was as a child. The theologian examines Genesis in much the same light. What mankind is now is influenced by what happened in the beginning.

The writer of Genesis is moved by the question of the origin of evil and division in his world. He is aware of the hatred and evil that characterizes his society; he knows how men seek to destroy one another, to exploit the weak and the poor and to fail to live up to their commitment to one another and to their God. He sees as well the accomplishments of man and his good qualities and concludes that things need not have been as they are today; he posits at the origin of man's history the same refusal to accept dependence on God as he experiences in his own society. Man is alienated within himself, alienated from woman and from his fellow-man and alienated from his God. Instead of living according to his commitment to his God, man turned to a false sense of independence that has characterized his life ever since. What the human race is now depends on what the race was at the beginning; man transgresses now as he did at the origin of his history. This is the teaching of Genesis 3.

The rest of Genesis continues the theme of evil in the world with the narration of fratricide:

> Cain said to his brother Abel, "Let us go out in the field." When they were in the field, Cain attacked his brother Abel and killed him. (4:8)

The law of blood:

> "If Cain is avenged sevenfold, then Lamech seventy-sevenfold" (4:24)

and the general corruption that preceded the flood:

> When the Lord saw how great was man's wickedness on earth, and how no desire that his heart conceived was ever anything but evil, he regretted that he had made man on the earth, and his heart was grieved.
>
> So the Lord said: "I will wipe out from the earth the men whom I have created, and not only the men, but also the beasts and the creeping things and the birds of the air, for I am sorry that I made them." But Noah found favor with the Lord.
>
> These are the descendants of Noah. Noah, a good man and blameless in that age, for he walked with God, begot three sons: Shem, Ham, and Japheth.
>
> In the eyes of God the earth was corrupt and full of lawlessness. When God saw how corrupt the earth had become, since all mortals led depraved lives on earth, he said to Noah: "I have decided to put an end to all mortals on earth; the earth is full of lawlessness because of them. So I will destroy them and all life on earth." (6:5-13)

The rest of the Old Testament presents a general condition of evil and sin for man: "Behold I was brought forth in iniquity and in sin did my mother conceive me" (Ps. 50:5); "And enter not into judgment with your servant, for before you no living man is just" (Ps. 143:2); "Can mortal man be righteous before God?" (Job 4:17); "I am a man of unclean lips and I dwell in the midst of a people with unclean lips" (Isa. 6:5). Certainly the references of Genesis to Adam are most rare in the rest of the Old Testament,[8] which further emphasizes that the sin of Adam was not central to the faith of Israel, but the condition of evil and sin was accepted as the condition in which man lives. There was a consciousness that man is a sinner from his origin, and although this is not usually reduced to the sin of Adam, at least it is related to the sins of the ancient fathers of Israel. The Old Testament accepts this condition of evil as part of man's experience and at least one individual (Gen. 3) related this to the condition of man's origin.

Sin in the New Testament

The teaching of the New Testament maintains a continuity with the Old Testament in regard to the power of evil and sin in the world. Man lives in a condition of perdition or nonsalvation, or in the shadows of darkness that are overcome only in Christ.

Darkness and Evil in John

The author of the fourth Gospel begins his prologue with the Word coming into a world of darkness. Whenever the author speaks of darkness, he seems to present it as a condition of mankind:

> The judgment of condemnation is this: the light came into the world, but men loved darkness rather than light because their deeds were wicked. Everyone who practices evil hates the light; he does not come near it for fear his deeds will be exposed. But he who acts in truth comes into the light, to make clear that his deeds are done in God. (John 3:19-21)
>
> Jesus spoke to them once again: "I am the light of the world. No follower of mine shall ever walk in darkness; no, he shall possess the light of life." (John 8:12)

He further emphasizes his theme when he presents the cure of the blind man in chapter 9 with his characteristic irony. Those who are supposed to see (Jewish leaders) are in darkness, while he who appears to be in darkness (the blind man) in reality sees and walks in the light. The same theme is subtly present in the departure of Judas from the supper-room: "and it was night" (John 13:30).

The idea appears also in the Epistles of John:

> Here, then, is the message we have heard from him and announce to you: that God is light; in him there is no darkness. If we say, "We have fellowship with him," while continuing to walk in darkness, we are liars and do not act in truth. But if we walk in light, as he is in the light, we have fellowship with one another, and the blood of his Son Jesus cleanses us from all sin. (1 John 1:5-7)

What the author seems to presuppose is a general condition of darkness that all men experience and in which men live. This darkness is the opposite of the God who is light. If men choose to follow Christ then they no longer walk in darkness and no longer walk in evil and sin. John makes no reference to the origin of this darkness in man and his world, but presumes its presence. It will explain the obdurancy of the Jews in the acceptance of Jesus as well as the difficulty in believing in Jesus, common to all men. In the midst of darkness Jesus promises life to those who will throw off the power of darkness and walk in the path that he has brightened. This theme in John corresponds to the basic theme of evil in the Old Testament.

The Condition of Nonsalvation in Paul

Paul presents a similar idea in different images. In the Epistle to the Romans, Paul opens his letter with a presentation of the universal need for salvation. Pagans and Jews are found in a condition of alienation from God (1-3) and in need of the justice of Christ. In the Epistle to the Ephesians, Paul remarks that "We are all sons of wrath" (2:3). He concludes in Romans that: "All have turned aside, together they have gone wrong, no one does good, not even one" (3:12). Paul sees all mankind under the condition of nonsalvation and in need of the one saving power of Christ. To this condition of nonsalvation, or power of evil in the world, he adds his teaching on personal sin.

In Romans 5:12, Paul joins the power of evil under whose dominion man lives with individual sin and intertwines their effects.

> Therefore, just as through one man sin entered the world and with sin death, death thus coming to all men inasmuch as all sinned.

Paul relates the presence of evil and death in the world to the actual contribution of all men to this condition by their personal sin. Both death and sin appear as independent powers that determine the existence of the individual. In the presence of such powers the individual sins and is responsible for his sin. Paul will not excuse a single individual by recourse to Adam.

In Christian tradition, Augustine, following Ambrosiaster, interpreted this verse differently. The last clause of the verse is causal in modern translations: *because* all men sinned. Augustine interpreted this clause as a relative clause so that he accepted the translation: "death spread to all men, *in him* all men sinned." All participated in the sin of Adam and so all are involved in the sin of Adam. This verse of Romans became the classical text of Original Sin in the New Testament. Philologically, the interpretation of Augustine cannot stand.[9] The clause is causal and has no reference to the more traditional teaching on Original Sin. All Paul wishes to establish here is the relationship between Adam and all men; personal sin is the manifestation of the sin that entered the world through Adam. All other notions of a hereditary sin transmitted from one generation to another must be excluded.

A study of Pauline thought discloses several basic attitudes of Paul in regard to sin that form a basis for the Christian tradition on Original Sin. Sin is a power in the world: in Romans 5:12-21, Paul presents sin as present in the world, which accounts for death in the world; man is in some sense under its power and suffers from its influence.

Sin is culpable—throughout his Epistles Paul reminds his readers of their responsibility for sin in their lives and exhorts them to live a life according to the grace they have received. If they do not live in this way, they must accept the consequences of their sin (Rom. 1-3; 5:12).

All men are in a condition of nonsalvation; Jews and Gentiles are alike under the wrath of God and in need of salvation in Christ. All men are under the dominion of death (Rom. 1-3).

This condition antecedes man's free decision; Paul sees man as a sinner from the beginning and contributing to his personal sinful condition by his own sin. The concrete man is born in a state of captivity and in need of liberation through Christ (Eph. 2:1-5).

Sin entered the world through one individual; Paul compares the salvation for all men through one man with the origin of sin in one man (1 Cor. 15:21). Sin had to have a beginning for Paul as it had to have a beginning for the theologians of the Old Testament.

The final aspect of Pauline doctrine is his emphasis on salvation and not on damnation. Paul does not present a clear picture of sin and alienation from God. His intention is to offer man an awareness of the salvation that has already taken place in Christ, a salvation that signifies a superabundance of grace as the gift of God himself to man. Since salvation depends on a need of salvation, Paul must present his understanding of man's condition of alienation, but this is the secondary concern. His accent is always on the positive: grace and man's salvation, and not on the negative: sin and man's damnation.

When we seek to discover the roots for the Christian meaning of Original Sin in the Bible, we must not expect to discover a fully developed understanding. Questions and problems of the fourth or twentieth century cannot be read into a mentality of the first century. The Bible asserts the presence of evil in the world and seeks to explain this presence in the light of man's understanding of himself and his world at that time. Later generations can offer their own explanation of the origin of sin and evil in the world without detriment to the Bible. Each age has its contribution to make to the understanding of evil, and provided Christians maintain their belief in the need of man for salvation and the origin of moral evil in man himself, any effort to delve deeper into the reality of sin and evil is welcomed.

The Bible knows of the sinful condition of man and of man's need for God; the Bible knows that man contributes to the power of evil in the world by personal sin; the Bible also knows that in the midst of evil and sin God has manifested his goodness and mercy with the sending of his Son. With Jesus Christ the control and power of evil and sin is broken. With this as a foundation, Christian theologians can formulate and make more precise the relationship between the power of evil, personal sin, and man's alienation from God.

Original Sin and the History of Theology

Frequently Augustine of Hippo is given the title of the father of the teaching on Original Sin. Certainly the thought of that great bishop influenced later generations of Christians in their understanding of Original Sin, but Augustine was not the originator of the teaching. The reality of sin in the world and the need for God and his gift of himself in grace was a constant teaching of the early Church.

The first centuries and the early Fathers could not be faithful to Scripture without some understanding of the power of evil and sin. It is true, however, that the early Greek Fathers did interpret the presence of evil and sin in a more functional sense as a presupposition of the redemption. This does not mean that they overlooked its reality and force. In their opposition to a Greek dualism, many of the Fathers emphasized the goodness of human nature and, in particular, the goodness of matter as created by God. This does not mean that they taught a human self-sufficiency. They often extolled the possibilities of man and did not speak of the power of evil and sin. Following the lead of Paul, they concentrated on the meaning of the redemption that took place in Jesus Christ. It should also be recalled that usually Baptism in the early Church was for adults and not infants. This practice would tend to point out the reality of personal sin rather than the power of evil in the world. Irenaeus, Cyprian, Origen, and other Church Fathers spoke of Original Sin before Augustine and the Pelagian controversy, but it was the latter that brought the fuller understanding of its meaning to the Christian Church.[10]

Pelagius[11]

Pelagius was a monk from Britain who came to Rome during the fourth century to study Scripture. During the barbarian invasion he migrated to North Africa and began teaching his interpretation on the meaning of sin and the meaning of Christian man. Shortly afterward, he left for Palestine while his disciple Coelestius stayed behind in North Africa. Coelestius propagated the teaching of Pelagius with certain exaggerations and drew severe criticism. The Synod of Carthage condemned the teaching of Pelagius and Coelestius. Shortly afterward the provincial Council of Jerusalem came to the defense of Pelagius, which in turn only angered the bishops of North Africa. With Augustine as leader, the bishops again condemned Pelagius in 416. Pelagius sought and received after his second condemnation the approbation of the new Pope Zosimus. Finally, for the third time the teaching of Pelagius was condemned by the Synod of Carthage in 418. This condemnation was approved by Pope Zosimus: "Roma locuta, causa finita."

On the level of ecclesiastical teaching, the controversy was resolved. The same was not the case on the level of theology. It is difficult for us to reconstruct the thought of Pelagius today since we know his teaching only through the works of his adversaries. An added difficulty is distinguishing the more moderate view of Pelagius from those of some of his disciples. Some explanation of the teaching of Pelagius is necessary.

Pelagius was a rigorist who reacted strongly against the corruption of Rome. He emphasized strongly the sense of sin and personal responsibility. Man was able to do good or evil. He too easily chose evil. God had given man a free will, which was the great gift of God. In liberty man could choose to live according to the example of Jesus Christ and make progress in his spiritual life. Man needed to know what were his possibilities and needed to be prodded into achieving what was possible for him.

Much of what Pelagius said was true. Unfortunately some of the conclusions of his teaching were not in accord with Christian tradition. Too often Pelagius interpreted the work of Christ in terms of example for us. His understanding of Christ's life and death seemed to overlook the power of the redemption and the liberation from sin and evil. Pelagius particularly reacted against the understanding of Baptism given to infants "for remission of sins." He was not opposed to infant Baptism, just to the aspect of sin involved. It was this particular idea that drew the criticism of Augustine and other North African bishops.

From the writings of Augustine we learn that Pelagius also taught that Adam would have died whether he had sinned or not. The sin of Adam harmed only himself and did not affect the human race; infants are in the same condition as Adam before he had sinned; Baptism is only a consecratory rite of the Church.

As is true for all theology, explanations are necessary to understand exactly what a theologian is trying to say. The great tragedy of the Pelagian controversy was the misunderstanding and thus the failure of correction for Pelagius, as well as for Augustine.

Augustine[12]

Augustine of Hippo was a churchman who always placed the teaching of the Church first. He jumped into the Pelagian controversy with a fierceness that consumed most of his energies. The reward for his effort was his influence on Church teaching on sin and grace for the next 1,700 years. In a dialectic, there is often the resolution that combines the best of the two positions. This is not the case with the dialectic between Augustine and Pelagius. The result is more Augustinian with many of the insights of Pelagius lost in the battle. The teaching of the Catholic Church on Original Sin is fundamentally the teaching of Augustine. But the teaching cannot be simply identified with Augustine. Many of the affirmations of Augustine are part of his personal synthesis and have never been accepted by the official Church, even if they have been accepted by subsequent theologians. This is particularly true with regard to Augustine's thought on predestination, on the explanation of the relationship between Original Sin and concupiscence and the affirmation of the fate of infants who die without Baptism. Today the original position of Augustine is to be preserved inasmuch as it contains the basic affirmation that man in his world is a sinner and in need of being liberated from the power of sin through Jesus Christ.

Augustine was not happy with the teaching of Pelagius on free will. Left on his own, man could not attain to the good. Man was a sinner in need of the power of God. Personally, Augustine knew of the sinful tendencies of man and cried out passionately for the power of God to help him. Man was dependent on God if he was to accomplish any good.

With regard to Original Sin, Augustine interpreted Romans 5:12 in terms of Original Sin influencing all generations. All men are included in the seed of Adam, and so Original Sin is transmitted through generation to posterity. Augustine insisted strongly on the culpability that belonged to all men. The sin of Adam was not just a process of nature, but was made freely. And so the transmission of Original Sin implied a voluntariety that is seen in concupiscence, which is present in every act of generation, even with regard to Christian parents. This concupiscence comes from sin and is the punishment of sin. Original Sin is taken away through Baptism, but an infirmity of man still remains. Death for Augustine is also the result of sin. As the sin of Adam is present in infants, they are damned if they die without Baptism.

Today, as we study Augustine, it is evident that his affirmations are in need of critical evaluation. Only what is fundamental must remain as the firm teaching of the Church: man is not self-sufficient before God, but in need of God if he is to become what he is called to be. The man who lives by his own powers and seeks only to affirm himself is the man who is lost in the sight of God.

The Council of Trent[13]

The Council of Trent treated the teaching on Original Sin in its fourth session and sought to reaffirm the conclusion of previous Councils. The Fathers also sought to add their own ideas according to the needs of the Reformation struggle. Above all, the Council wished to avoid the accusation that it was Pelagian in its outlook. The conclusions were not always the clearest nor the most thorough. The differences in teaching in the reformers did not help the task of the Council Fathers. Zwingli held a position close to Pelagius. This was due in part to the controversy in exegesis wrought by the humanists and in particular by Erasmus of Rotterdam. Romans 1:12 was not interpreted in the Augustinian sense, but rather in terms of the relationship between the sin of Adam and the personal sin of believers. Based on this interpretation Zwingli insisted that culpability could be present only in an actualization of Original Sin through personal sin. Luther insisted on the corruption of man. Original Sin is a habit that is the root of all sins and remains even in the baptized.

The Canons of Trent[14]

The first two Canons of Trent (788-789) form a unity. The first treats of the sin of Adam, and the second, the result for his posterity. 788: Adam lost the state of sanctity and justice in which he was created. The consequences of this for Adam were the anger of God, death, and captivity under the power of the devil.

789: The sin of Adam has consequences for his posterity. Death is the common lot of men; Original Sin is transmitted to all. Adam lost justice and sanctity for all others. All experience the results of the sin of Adam.

790: Original Sin is by origin one and is proper to each person and is transmitted through propagation and not imitation.

791: Infants even of Christian parents contract Original Sin and should be baptized. This Baptism is a true remission of sin and not just a consecratory rite.

As a result of Trent, the problematic of Original Sin is made evident. We deal with Original Sin as true sin, by origin one, proper to each person who comes into this world. There is a solidarity of sin for all men, involving Original Sin and personal sin. Further confusion comes in the consideration of the universality of Original Sin and the connection between generation and transmission.

In conclusion it can be said that the Roman Catholic Church teaches that man, even before personal decision, is found in a state of nonsalvation and in need of the grace of Jesus Christ. The Church reacts strongly against any form of Pelagianism or rationalism; man is a sinner and affirms his sinfulness by his personal sin. The further questions of universality, by origin one, and the meaning of transmission are part of the theological construct that surrounds the thinking of the Council Fathers. Further development in an understanding of anthropology today necessitates a restudying of the meaning of Original Sin while preserving the basic meaning of the Christian teaching.

Meaning of Original Sin

In the history of theology there have been many theories with regard to the essence of Original Sin. What exactly does this teaching mean? Augustine taught that the essence of Original Sin is concupiscence with the corresponding inclination to evil. It was a positive reality, almost a sickness of the soul. Anselm of Canterbury rejected the theory of Augustine since Baptism was supposed to take away Original Sin and Baptism did not take away concupiscence. To him, the essence of Original Sin was a lack of due justice. Man does not have what he should have: the grace of God.

For Thomas Aquinas Original Sin is a combination of the two ideas. Formally, Original Sin is the lack of grace; materially, it is the disorientation of powers within man. Man finds himself in disharmony within himself and inclined to evil through concupiscence. For Thomas, this is the material element of Original Sin.[15]

The thorny question in the theology of Original Sin is voluntariety. How can Original Sin be part of the human experience, but not something personal? How can Original Sin be voluntary in every man? The position of Aquinas is terminative voluntariety.[16] Just as it is the will that decides to commit murder but the hand that actually fires the gun, so Adam as the head of the human race influences and affects all his posterity. Thomas relates this to generation since what is generated is lacking grace. As Original Sin is a sin of nature, and a concrete human nature arises only through generation, so Original Sin is transmitted through generation.

How valid such theories remain is questionable. What is noted is the influence of classical teaching on all subsequent Church teaching. Often enough Original Sin was seen as something with which we were all born: it was taken away in Baptism but the inclination to evil remained. Infants who died without Baptism went to Limbo as a place of natural happiness; somehow Original Sin was connected with generation, and so sexual relations were at least shameful, if not venially sinful, even for Christian parents. There is little doubt that the meaning of Original Sin is in need of reinterpretation.

Contemporary Thought[17]

Simplicity is usually seen as a virtue. When applied to Original Sin a simplistic understanding is devastating. Somehow the contemporary theologian must integrate the teaching of Scripture, the insights of classical theology, the teachings of the official Church, and the knowledge gained through the behaviorial sciences in the past fifty years. Evolution, monogenism and/or polygenism, free will, the power of evil in the world, personal sin, and a lack of grace must somehow fit together and make sense if we are to remain faithful to the Christian tradition. If anything, complexity is the context of Original Sin and not simplicity.

Central Affirmation

From Scripture we know that Original Sin is functional. What Christianity teaches is redemption and not fundamentally sin. Redemption can make sense only if man is in need of redemption. This is already evident. Man is in need of being saved from himself, in need of overcoming the disharmony in his relationships, in need of being freed from powerlessness and given a purpose and meaning to his life. People are alienated in the worse sense of that word, full of cynicism, estranged from others, pessimistic and searching for meaning. People need salvation, need to experience the peace and harmony that only a God can give; people need redemption, need to be assured that evil will not ultimately triumph; in spite of all of the setbacks and problems, there is a future that is better than the past and the present. Original Sin means that we begin where we are: situated in an evil world and in need of some direction and some healing of our divisions.

The second note of a central affirmation is the firm Christian belief that things need not have been this way. The condition of alienation should not be identified with creation on the part of God. Only a sadistic God would create man with the sense of alienation and sin and suffering that has characterized human history. Man is alienated; things need not have been this way. Such is the central affirmation of the Christian teaching of Original Sin.

Personal Sin, Sin of the World, Lack of Grace

To try to understand the human condition involves the state or situation in which all men find themselves, their personal contribution to evil, and their lack of grace. Original Sin involves all three.

Personal sin: When Scripture speaks of the condition of non-salvation, it especially considers the personal sins of men. Paul in Romans 1-3 treats of the sins of the pagans and the Jews. In Ephesians, the context is also personal sin, and even in Romans 5:12 it is personal sin that manifests and concretizes the sin that is already present in the world. People actually tend to destroy one another, to make one another suffer. Jealousy, pride, envy, lust, avarice are all sins that are part of the life of every individual. They are as real as the birds of the air and the flowers and the trees. On the corporate level, we have war and crime and destruction of life that are equally real.

Sin of the World: There is a solidarity in sin that can be called the sin of the world. Evil exists as a powerful force around us. Scripture often sees the world as evil. John in particular uses the term "world" in a perjorative light (1:10; 12:31; 14:19). There is a force that exists and to which individuals contribute by their own personal sin. The question is how can we explain this reality that seems to be more than just the sum total of personal sins? The *situation* of man in his world is not good and this situation influences man's decisions. An examination of the meaning of the term "situation" will clarify the sinful condition of man in his world.

We can distinguish between situation taken actively and passively. Actively taken, the situation is something outside of man pertaining to his ambit. Passively, it is intrinsic to man and affects the person who is so situated. As is evident, both aspects are closely related. Man cannot exist in an artificial way separated from his environment. The environment has its influence over a person and no one can live without this influence. If there is evil in the environment, then the person is infected by that evil and the situation is not merely extrinsic to the individual. What is called the sin of the world is more than the human condition. It is a complex reality that entails a powerful force for evil surrounding man and influencing him. This is particularly evident when the individual contributes to the power of evil by personal sin, which only adds to the force of evil that in turn makes its influence more powerfully felt on the individual's life. So the circle continues.

Lack of Grace

The third element to be integrated in any understanding of Original Sin is the actual absence of grace in the life of an individual. We have already seen that man is created in the image of God, able to take the place of God in this world, manifesting the qualities of God, mercy and fidelity. Man is so created that he can speak the Word of God and pronounce it with his being, and not with just his mouth. When man lives without the presence of God, there is something lacking. What he is called to be is not present and there is a need that must be satisfied to fulfill the complete plan of God. The powerful presence of God in any person's life is an integrating element. It helps to actualize the possibilities that are given; the resolution between nature and person can find a support and there can be the healing that is so necessary. Original Sin implies a lack of something that should be. The supernatural existential, the determination of man that draws him toward God, should be fulfilled and when it is not, then man suffers severe consequences. God freely called man to enter into a relationship with him that was beyond man's given potential, but when this is given and then not accepted, there is a deprivation of a perfection that should be part of every human life. Man ought to respond to God on a level of personal communication because God has spoken to man on this level. The lack of grace signifies that man has refused to respond, has denied the call to communicate on a personal plane. Original Sin cannot be understood apart from an alienation from God, as well as an alienation from man. Grace, as the self-communication of God to man, is not present and it should be present.

When we put these ideas together, the meaning of Original Sin is that man is without God; he lives in a sinful world and is influenced by the evil that surrounds him; finally, as a result of his lack of grace and the influence of his situation, he himself contributes to the evil of the world by his personal sin. It is a terribly vicious circle that grows in force and control. Once sin entered the world, it spread until all were under its control.

The Plan of God and Original Sin

God has always worked through mediators. He comes to us not in an inhuman fashion, but always through his creation and, in particular, through his highest creature. Grace as God's gift of himself is mediated humanly. It was God's plan that man would mediate the presence of God to his fellow-man. Instead of passing on from one generation to another the presence of God in grace, and mediating this presence through the goodness and fidelity present in human life, people could mediate only what they had. We are not sure whether the first conscious act of man was a rejection of God through the rejection of his neighbor, but we do know that evil and sin were introduced into this world by man himself and once present, what was mediated was a sinful condition and not a grace-filled condition. Children are born into this world which is sinful and will quickly learn of the power of evil; children are born into this world alienated from God in the sense that they are not filled with the presence of God, but in need of a personal acceptance of God through the acceptance of Jesus Christ as their Savior. Parents generate children and offer them what they themselves have: a share in a sinful life and a share in a sinful world.

The Origin of Evil

Genesis offers us insights into present times as well as into the history of man. We all suffer the temptation to live as separated from God, seeking a false autonomy; we have our fertility rites that are a constant temptation. What Genesis says is that man has been this way for a long time. Somewhere in our distant past, man started the strife that has characterized human life ever since. There was an origin of evil when man turned against his fellow-man. That period of history is unknown to us. Perhaps in the movement from consciousness to self-consciousness, there was the first human act that sought to destroy. From that time on the evil spread until all men came under the influence of evil. We will never know whether the origin of mankind involved a single couple or many couples; we will never know when man first began to destroy his fellow-man. We only know that in time the power of evil was among us and has continued to be with us.

When we consider the possibility of evil and sin, perhaps it was inevitable that sin would come. If man is given the possibility of choosing good and refusing evil, then the time would surely come when he would refuse the good and choose the evil. The universality of Original Sin may have taken some time to be realized, but in the history of mankind, it was inevitable and quickly became the condition for all.

The Future of Man

We have already seen that the future of man is good because his future is God. Often the paradise stories of Genesis were judged to deal with the origin of mankind. They might more accurately deal with his future. The vicious circle of sin begetting sin has been broken in Jesus of Nazareth. He was born into a sinful world but was not without the presence of God. He was the Word of God Incarnate. Through him man was able to begin the reversal of the process. Instead of being influenced by evil and contributing to evil, Jesus was free from sin and repaid good for evil. The vicious circle has been broken in him. The control of evil could be diminished because of Jesus Christ. Man was in need of someone to reverse the process of evil and make it possible to reintegrate himself in the light of God. This Jesus accomplished. The future of mankind must be a good future in which the power of evil will be overtaken by the power of good. Paradise was not something that necessarily was, but it is something that must necessarily be in the future.

Baptism and Original Sin

Christian tradition has always associated Baptism with Original Sin. In this new interpretation, the two are still closely related, but not in the sense that Baptism is a magical washing. Baptism is the end of an initiative process by which the individual commits himself to Jesus Christ and seeks to overcome evil. Baptism is the entrance into the community of Jesus that will find its full meaning only when the individual has reached the term of his Baptism in his death. Baptism is an ongoing sacrament calling the individual to overcome evil and be holy; Baptism calls the believer to contribute to the holy community that is the Church and strive forward to the time when the holy community will be the only community. Baptism is the expression of faith and makes a person holy because now God mediates himself through his Son and through the Church that his Son has established. The baptized individual is graced, is holy, and begins to allow the presence of God so to permeate his personality that in time, and finally in death, every aspect of his personality feels the influence of God.

Nor should Baptism be limited to adults. Children need the influence of a holy community in their growth. When they come to their personal acceptance of Jesus Christ, they need to have had the guidance and help that only the Church can give. Baptism is the beginning that reaches a personal acceptance when the individual is capable of making his own the faith that was expressed by the community when he was welcomed into the Church. Baptism will find its final resolution in death when the individual chooses finally and irrevocably for the power of good and for the presence of God.

Conclusion

Original Sin is as real today as ever. It is a powerful force that is present in all of us. When viewed in the light of what has already been said, however, it is relativized. Man is created without God, but is created with a powerful orientation toward God, as he is created in his image; man is also destined to share in the glory of God through his Christ. Original Sin is surely real but fits in the broader picture of man who has already been blessed in creation and is already destined for God. It is a matter of personal acceptance, and in this acceptance the individual believer is aided by the holiness of the community of which he is a member through Baptism. No one is totally deprived of God even if everyone enters this world without grace and comes into a sinful world. Original Sin in the sense of *the* Original Sin is the entrance of moral evil into this world which need not have been so, even if it was inevitable. Original Sin as present to us is the lack of grace and our human situation of living in a sinful world to which we contribute our own evil by our personal sin. It is universal since it touches us all. But it is fundamentally overcome because of the redemptive life and death of Jesus the Christ.

Original Justice

One of the most remarkable and lasting features of the popular story in Genesis is the vividness of description of the garden of Paradise. God was present to man and he was at peace and in harmony with all of creation. It was an idyllic type of life with all pain and suffering conveniently excluded. For believers today it is impossible for us to discover how this meeting between God and man actually happened in the beginning of human history. What the Bible wants to emphasize through the image of a beautiful garden is that the presence of God was true. Adam and Eve reigned over the animals and other creatures and were therefore different from the animals. How man came to receive this relationship and how long it lasted is not part of the perspective of Genesis.

As we struggle today to understand our origins, it is a fundamental belief that God's grace reaches man as he is—in the actual situation in which man finds himself. Grace is given, as a real capacity for faith and love. But grace is given for a real and historical pilgrimage toward God, a pilgrimage that would last for centuries. Humanity was at the beginning of its history in Genesis, and therefore grace could be given only as an initial growing and expanding familiarity with God in this world.

Modern theologians differ in their opinion with regard to the actual acceptance of this offer of God. Some feel that the grace was offered but immediately refused. As man moved from consciousness to self-consciousness, the first human act was a rejection of God through the rejection of the neighbor. This is a possible opinion and certainly not against faith. The theologians hold this position because cultural anthropology offers no evidence or relic of a deeply religious attitude at the beginning of human history. A differing opinion is also possible.

The beginnings of mankind need not have been characterized as a full deployment of spiritual experience and knowledge. Language was still being shaped, forms of human behavior and interpersonal relationships were just being discovered. All we have to believe is that this was a beginning in the fullest and most radical sense of that word. It is quite possible to accept that first man lived in harmony for some period of time, growing according to the light and inspiration of God's gift of himself in grace. At least both positions are possible.

With these opinions, however, we come face to face with the question of preternatural gifts. Did not Christian theology teach that the first man was endowed with the gifts of immortality, integrity, knowledge, and freedom from pain and suffering? Was not the first man so graced that he was given additional gifts that he lost with the Fall? It is surely true that this has been part of Christian tradition, and like much of traditional theology, it is in need of reexamination.

Serious theologians readily admit that these gifts do not possess the same theological value. Immortality is witnessed in the Bible, and in some sense, the gift of integrity is also present. The gift of knowledge comes from a misinterpretation of the biblical images and teaching and there is no foundation for a kind of freedom from suffering and pain. Adam would have been vulnerable if he was human. If a tree fell on him, he was hurt. God does not show off by unnecessary miracles.

There is no difficulty in believing that immortality and integrity are consequences of the gift of God in grace. The Greek Fathers characterized grace by its two fundamental properties: immortality and incorruptibility. The New Testament holds this opinion when it speaks of never dying for those who believe (John 11), and becoming incorruptible (1 Cor. 15). But if grace was given as a beginning, both these gifts would have to share the same fate: they were present in an initial stage.

Our picture is based on the supposition that no sin had yet appeared in human life; it was a primitive type of existence; man was limited and a limited being who was also bodily. Finitude and bodily existence tend to break down and hinder the human effort to realize itself in its full relatedness to others. Man always lags behind his possibilities; he realizes himself in that he is ever falling short of self-actualization. The bodily aspect necessitates the actualizing of man through limited, particular, and multiple symbolic activity. As part of the biological world, he shares with all plants and animals the fate of corruption and death. He would not have been human is this were not true. If all this is accurate, what of the gifts of immortality and integrity?

Grace as the gift of God himself is a dynamic presence bringing about a change in man. If grace is allowed to develop, man can overcome some of his limitations, he is able to master and rule his finitude and overcome the resistance of a bodily existence; man would have been able to integrate the possibilities that are offered him and become a being in harmony. The graced man is also the man who will never die; he will be so involved with the mystery of God that he will share in the immortality of God. The preternatural gifts of integrity and immortality tell us much more about what might have been and what might be in the future than what actually was. What belongs to human existence, natural and supernatural, personal and corporate, spiritual and corporal, is necessarily and inevitably and fundamentally in evolution, and thus aimed at its full realization in God through a long history. The gifts of immortality and integrity show us the end-process of this evolution.

Man finds himself concretely in a state of alienation within himself and with all of reality, including the fullness of reality which is God. He is influenced by the power of evil in the world and contributes to this power by his personal sins; he finds himself lacking in what he should be. Original Sin is real because it is clearly seen. Any discussion of humanity and human nature must always include this unseemly and unhappy aspect. For all his glories, man still has the narrowness of sin and evil.

Foundations for a Christian Anthropology

Man is created in the image of God, is able to exercise dominion, and fulfills his vocation when, in that control of this universe, he manifests the qualities of God: mercy and fidelity; man is predestined in Christ. The future of the human race is a good future because it is God. No tragedy, no power or force can rob the human race of its future because God has so determined. Individuals may rightly refuse to accept this future; it is their pleasure, but no individual can hold back the superabundance of God's grace that is bringing human history to himself. Of the vast numbers of people, some have been chosen for the sake of others; it is an election to responsibility and not leisure and carries blessings as well as accountability. Man can always be more than he was and is at any moment; he is oriented to God and his whole being cries out for God as he strains forward to go beyond his possibilities and find a newness and a richness in life. Man needs God and will rest only in God. Man is of value and of great worth and most precious because man is of God. Even the lowest of the lowly can dream the impossible dream and believe that it is possible because of God's great gift. And man is a sinner, living in an evil world, making that evil more powerful by personal sin. Man is glorious and he is narrow; he is richly endowed and impoverished by his sin; man is noble and seeks the true and is petty and seeks himself; man is gracious and gives as he is stingy and hordes. He has vast possibilities and casts them to the ground; he can build magnificently and more easily he can destroy; he gives life and takes it away. In all, he still remains God's noblest and highest creature, of infinite worth, possessing the greatest gift of all: life.

Notes

[1]Cf. *God and the World* (Philadelphia: Westminster, 1965), ch. 4.

[2]We have grown accustomed to thinking of God's causality in regard to creation and man in terms of what the Scholastics call "efficient causality": "that which by its activity or exercise of power produces existence of change in another" (B. Wuellner, *Dictionary of Scholastic Philosophy* [Milwaukee: Bruce, 1956], p. 19.) God is seen as an agent outside of creation producing through his power effects that in this case are the actual world and all that is part of this world. Today, certain theologians are conceiving of God's causality in regard to the world as more intrinsic to the world and speak rather of his transcendent causality that does not overlook efficient causality, but adds a further dimension to the causality of God in regard to the world. K. Rahner remarks: "God is the transcendent ground, sustaining everything, but not a demiurge whose activity is carried on inside the world. He is ground of the world, not a cause side by side with others in the world." (*Hominisation* [New York: Herder and Herder, 1965], p. 95.) Throughout this work Rahner emphasizes the presence of God as cause in the world but always as sustaining and supporting his creation, rather than interfering from without. At the same time he will exclude the notion that God is just a cause among causes in the world, but is the ground for all causality that exists. This distinction should become clearer in the actual application to the question of evil in the paper.)

[3]Maritain's is surely the most comprehensive effort to present this position. In the opinion of this author, however, it labors under an inadequate notion of power. Cf. J. Maritain, *Existence and the Existent* (New York: Doubleday, 1956), pp. 101-109.

[4]Cf. Cobb, pp. 90-41.

[5]Cf. K. Rahner, *Hominisation* (New York: Herder and Herder, 1965), pp. 81-86. Tillich's doctrine of "Ground of Being" is similar to Rahner's doctrine of transcendent cause.

[6]Cf. A. Suelzer, *The Pentateuch* (New York: Herder and Herder, 1965), pp. 24-32; J. Plastaras, *Creation and Covenant* (Milwaukee: Bruce, 1968), pp. 36-64.

[7]Cf. Karl Rahner, *Hominisation* (New York: Herder and Herder, 1965), pp. 36-44; "Aetiologie," *Lexikon Für Theologie und Kirche*, 2nd ed., 11 vols. (Freiburg, 1957-67).

[8]Sirach 25:33; Wisdom 2:24.

[9]Cf. Stanislaus Lyonnet, "Le Péché Originel et L'exegese de Rom. 5:12-14," *Recherche Sciences Réligieuse*, 44 (1956), pp. 162-196.

[10]Cf. *The Teachings of the Church Fathers*, ed. John R. Wills (New York: Herder and Herder, 1966), Nos. 513-535.

[11]Cf. "Pelagius," *New Catholic Encyclopedia* (New York: McGraw-Hill, 1967); E. A. Mann, *Dictionnaire Théologie Catholique*, vol. 12, cat. 678-683; G. de Plinval, *Pelage, Ses Ecrits, Sa Vie et Réforme* (Lausanne: Payot, 1943).

[12]Cf. Eugene Portalie, *A Guide to the Thought of Saint Augustine* (Chicago: Regnery, 1960), pp. 177-229.

[13]Cf. A. Vanneste, "Le Décret du Concile de Trente sur le Péché Originel," *Nouvelle Revue Théologique*, 87 (1965), pp. 669-726; 88 (1966), pp. 581-602.

[14]Cf. *The Teaching of the Catholic Church*, ed. Karl Rahner (Cork: Mercier Press, 1966), p. 137, par. 221, 222, 223. "If anyonc does not confess that Adam, the first man, by his transgression of God's commandment in Paradise immediately lost the sanctity and justice in which he had been constituted, and by the offence of this sin drew upon himself the wrath and indignation of God and the death with which God had threatened him, and with death captivity in the power of him who had the empire of death, that is to say the devil (Heb. 2:14), and that the whole Adam by the offence of this sin was changed in body and soul for the worse, anathema sit (par. 221).

If anyone assert that Adam's sin harmed himself alone and not his posterity, and that the holiness and justice received from God which he lost, was lost for himself alone and not for us too; or that stained by the sin of disobedience, he passed on to all mankind death and bodily punishment but not sin as well, which is the death of the soul, anathema sit. For he contradicts the Apostle who says: "Wherefore as by one man sin entered into this world, and by sin death; so also death passed upon all men, in whom all have sinned" (par. 222).

If anyone assert that this sin of Adam's which was one in origin and is passed on by propagation not by imitation, and is in each and proper to each, can be taken away by the powers of human nature or by any remedy other than by the merits of the one mediator our Lord Jesus Christ who reconciled us to God by His blood, "made unto us . . . justice and sanctification and redemption" (1 Cor. 1:30) or deny that this merit of Christ Jesus is applied, to adults and to children, in the Sacrament of Baptism duly administered in the Church's form—anathema sit. "For there is no other name under heaven given to men, whereby we must be saved" (Acts 4:12). Hence the words: "Behold the Lamb of God, behold him who taketh away the sins of the world" (cf. John 1:29) and "As many of you as have been baptized in Christ, have put on Christ" (Gal. 3:27) (par. 223).

[15]*Summa Theologica, I, II,* a. 81-83.

[16]*Ibid.*, q. 81, a. 1.

[17]It is difficult to sort out exactly what ideas come from what author. The following ideas are a combination of thoughts from Rahner, Schoonenberg, Hulsbosch, Barth, Tillich, and the reaction of students, particularly at the Seminary of Our Lady of Angels, 1969-1970. The bibliography connected with this chapter offers to the reader ample means for further study.

5

The Origin of Mankind

Where did it all begin, or how was it all possible? A world teeming with human life needs a beginning. To understand where we are now demands that we know something of where we began, as we struggle to discover where we are all going. The origin of the human race has fascinated more than its share of thinkers. Christian anthropology must make its response to the question of human origins and must respect the responses of other sciences.

Evolution has been with contemporary man for so long that it is taken for granted. Things develop and change; thus it has always been and so it will continue. The twentieth century has not only accepted biological evolution, but looks to find evolution in every aspect of human life. Even theologians speak freely today of the development or evolution of doctrine,[1] words carefully avoided until very recently. Sociology, psychology, and even politics and economics have their evolutionary theories. It is no great surprise to live with biological evolution.

Evolution is the theory that holds that living species that are true species, and not just variations of the same species, can be reduced to a common root from which others are derived through change and mutation.[2] Evolution is affirmed for all living things. All life came from more primitive forms, back to the most primitive of all; all life came from the sea and developed and changed and mutated until this earth was populated with the myriad species known today. The development was gradual and plotted, yielding to ever-greater organization and complexity until at the pyramid of life stood *Homo sapiens*.

The question of interest in this study is not the evolutionary theory but anthropological evolution. How can theology explain the origin of man? Traditionally the explanation of human origin centered on what might be called an anthropological fixism: all forms of life, each species was directly created as was man. This is the theory based upon a fundamentalist interpretation of Genesis 1-2. God created all living things, each according to its kind, and finally created man. Every species, as we know it now, comes to us directly from the powerful presence of God in creation. This is one extreme viewpoint on the origin of mankind. There are other extremes as well.

Twentieth-century man has also learned of the possibility that there was no divine force in the origin of mankind. Human life, as is true for all matter, has evolved according to its own intrinsic principles. There is no appreciable difference between the origin of animal forms from lower species and the origin of mankind from a highly developed simian form.[3] As must be evident, behind such a system there is more of a world outlook than the mere facts of science. One extreme is to trace everything as it is back to God; the other is to deny any influence of a God.

Christian thinkers often try to steer the middle course between the two extremes and hold that there is a real connection between man and the animal world, but there is a distinction as well. A creative power of God is postulated with regard to the origin of mankind. How this action is conceived is another question.

Scriptural Considerations

> The Lord God formed man out of the clay of the ground and blew into his nostrils the breath of life, and so man became a living being. (Gen. 2:7)

The author of Genesis expresses in his poetic form that God created man from the earth. For centuries this text was interpreted as immediate creation by God of man from inorganic matter. Certain other texts affirmed that the first woman was created immediately by God from Adam:

> So the Lord God cast a deep sleep on the man, and while he was asleep, he took out one of his ribs and closed up its place with flesh. (Gen. 2:21)

> Man was not made from woman but woman from man. Neither was man created for woman, but woman for man. (1 Cor. 11:8-9)

When the theory of evolution first appeared in the middle of the nineteenth century, many thought that such a thesis had to be denied by believing Christians because of this affirmation of Genesis. In light of interpretations of Genesis today, this opinion is no longer necessarily maintained.

The author of Genesis was not interested in presenting a theory opposed to, or in favor of, evolution. What he wanted to do was to teach something about the meaning of human life and used the ideas of his own time to express his thoughts. Scientific affirmations about the origin of the world or the origin of the human race are matters for science and not for faith. Whether man was created from organic or inorganic matter, whether he arose monogenistically or polygenistically are questions for science and not for the Bible. Evolution in Scripture, its presence or absence, is an open question to which Scripture can make no response.

The author of Genesis, however, as expressing the faith of a people, does make some affirmations that are germane to the question today. The text states that man arose from the earth. All of human life is somehow determined by its origin which is from the earth. Clear limits of man's existence are presented. No person can live as if he had no relationship to the earth; all that a man is, even on the most profound of human levels, is somehow affected by his earthly origin. The bodily life, the emotional and psychological life, and even the spiritual life that is man is limited and influenced by the world of which he is a part and to which he is inextricably tied. Man is earthly and the author of Genesis is most emphatic about this earthliness.

Although earthly, man has a special relationship to God. Other creatures receive their blessing but man alone is created in the image of God (Gen. 1:27). Man is different from all other creatures and this distinction precedes even his free decision. Man is constituted in creation with a special possibility with God; man can enter into a dialogue that is never able to be overlooked and is present even when man chooses to deny this offer of dialogue (Gen. 3:8). Man is from the earth, but has more than earthly possibilities.

The text of Genesis, unlike much of the Old Testament, places woman on an equal level with man; she too is created by God and has a special relationship to God. She is created, in poetic form, from the rib of the man. Far from manifesting a subservient role, this enhances man's need for woman. The rib is closest to the heart and man will never find his heart unless he finds someone whom he can love. There is a moral union established between man and woman; together they are the image of God and will be so in actuality only when they are united by a union of love. The "helper" of Genesis 2:18 is not a servant; she is a companion who is like man and whom man needs for his own sake. The complementarity of male and female is summed up in the closing verses of chapter 2:

> The man said: "This one, at last, is bone of my bones and flesh of my flesh; this one shall be called woman, for out of her man this one has been taken." That is why a man leaves his father and mother and clings to his wife, and the two of them become one body. (Gen. 2:23-24)

In summary it can be said that the first chapter of Genesis should be used to interpret the second chapter, and not vice versa. The possibility of evolution is outside the ambit of scriptural consideration. What is affirmed is man's origin from the earth, his special relationship to God, and the equality of the sexes.[4]

Church Teaching

The official teaching of the Roman Catholic Church recognized the value of the theory of evolution only gradually. At first, like most Christian bodies, there was a negative reaction. Scripture taught the creation of man by God directly and evolution could not be reconciled with this belief. Gradually the interpretation of Genesis favored a lessening of opposition to the theory of evolution. In 1950, Pope Pius XII in *Humani Generis* allowed the discussion of the possibility of evolution, but urged caution and reserved the final decision to the official teaching office.[5] In the text of the encyclical, the Pope affirmed the immediate creation of the soul by God.[6]

In 1966, Pope Paul VI addressed theologians gathered in

Rome and offered greater encouragement to the study of evolution and added the possible study of the theories of monogenism and polygenism.[7] The institutional Church had gradually learned the value of the use of science in its theological explanation, and from that encouragement various opinions have developed that are based on evolution as a valid hypothesis.

The Origin of Mankind

The theory of evolution has clear consequences that affect Christian anthropology. Theologians must respect these findings of science and preserve the affirmations of Christian Scripture and tradition. Only if the contemporary theologian can maintain a relationship between science and theology has he fulfilled his responsibility. The following presentation aims to relate science to theology and to make sense to the ordinary believer who has grown up in an evolutionary world.

Catholic theologians often seem to think that the relationship between theology and evolution can be solved according to the lines indicated in *Humani Generis*, with the distinction between body and soul: the body arose from prehuman organic matter, with the soul directly created by God. The organic forms evolved to that point at which time God created the spiritual soul, and so established the first man. Such an explanation is not, however, acceptable.

The Bible affirms that *man* arose from the earth, not the *body* of man; moreover, Scripture affirms that man has a special relationship to God, and not just his soul. A subtle form of dualism is always latent in such a theory: God is concerned with the soul and so is theology; God is less concerned with the body, and so the theologian gives the body of man to science. But man is totally from the earth and is totally from God; there is no separation in Scripture.

Further difficulties evolve with regard to the action of God. When the evolution of the human body is accepted and the immediate creation of the soul by God is affirmed as bringing about the first man, how can this intervention of God be understood? Such an explanation has God intervening miraculously as a demiurge, rather than as the transcendent God of Christian tradition. God has intervened in human history but always in the context of salvation. It is no majestic enhancement to affirm that God intervened in the origin of mankind apart from his initial creative act, nor, as we shall see, does the origin of individuals, after the initial presence of man on this earth, by a similar action add much to the power of God. How can we understand hominisation so that the activity of God is preserved and the evolutionary theory is also affirmed as preserving human dignity and divine power?

Scripture presupposes the profound unity of man, which is equally affirmed by the teaching office of the Church. There is no teaching on the soul of man or the body of man. The distinction between body and soul must be based on an understanding of the body as the symbol of the soul and expressing the spiritual aspect of man. Any explanation of man's origin must be based on the affirmation that man is from the earth and is unified. One possible theory depends on the meaning of becoming, or transcendence, and the understanding of cause and operation.[8]

Becoming is not the same as change; becoming signifies a newness of life or being that was not present previously; becoming is not superficial and profoundly affects the totality of the being. Becoming involves an overreaching, an extension of the being, a growth and development that significantly alters the being through the addition of that which is new. Examples clarify the difference between change and becoming.

People can change the color of their hair; it is a true change but is not a development. Christianity can change its outward appearances, and not at the same time effect a development. Becoming on a human level signifies a newness that is present now which was not present before. A person has undergone an attitudinal development and somehow it is the same person, but also someone who has a newness and a richness that was not present before. Maturity in life is a development, a becoming, and need not be present even when the individual has gone through the accidental changes of adolescence to adult life. To become more is to move from one threshold to another level, while maintaining continuity with the previous level of existence.

Becoming is possible because man is open to transcendence. Everyone can be more than he is at any one moment in life; there is always the possibility of knowing more, of loving more deeply, of going beyond the limits of space and time and reaching out for the experience of that which transcends space and time. The limits of man's endurance are unfathomable; the powers of man's spirit are still unknown; the possibilities of any human life are still present as long as there is life. Transcendence is not a passive quality of man; it is an active motion based on man as spirit in the world. As long as man has spiritual qualities, the material can never fully express the richness of those spiritual powers. The body falls short of manifesting the expansiveness of the human spirit; it is always possible to discover another way, another medium through which the spiritual can be expressed. Nor can we ever reach the point in believing that all of the possible expressions of spirit have been exhausted. Becoming and human transcendence form the basis for all of the creativity in life.

Transcendence need not be limited to human transcendence. Infrahuman creatures do not have the reference to the totality of reality as does man, but matter is never totally matter. There can be a transcendence present in all creatures that is a transcendence of essence. The world in evolution can be conceived as a world that is becoming through the transcendence of itself. All of creation is striving to outdo itself as it leaps forward with an excitement that adds ever-new possibilities to the universe. Animals perform feats of marvel; plant life is fascinating under close scrutiny; the most primitive forms of life capture the attention of the lifetime of scientists. All of creation is in motion and is adding to itself new possibilities and new forms.

The third element in the theory involves cause and operation. How can we explain transcendence? There is the active transcendence in which the creature operates and develops. But philosophy seeks an explanation of this newness of being that results from self-transcendence. Is it possible to conclude with more than what was present initially? If so, how can this be explained? The ultimate reason for creative transcendence in the universe has to be related to the absolute infinite cause, the power of God, which offers existence to all reality and sustains the transcendence of creatures.

Traditional philosophy regarded God as the final cause of creation, as the goal of creation, and as the efficient cause, as the one who began the operation and is responsible for all that happens and precisely as it happens. We have already seen that another possibility is open to us. Instead of conceiving God as an efficient cause, it is proper to consider the transcendent God as the transcendent cause who gives to his creation the power to become, and supports his creation and sustains his creation in its ever-developing journey to perfection. God is the dynamic transcending cause who is truly present to the universe, but who gives to the universe its own powers to develop.

The relationship between God as transcending cause and the creature as transcending can be conceived as follows: the finite created being can transcend itself only when the infinite cause pertains to the constitution of the finite cause. The operation of the finite cause, however, is able to transcend itself only when the infinite cause is not an intrinsic element of the created cause. Otherwise the created cause would have already within itself what is becoming and would not experience transcendence. The creature that is becoming through transcendence is to be conceived as a cause to which the infinite reality of God pertains as a constitutive element, but not that this reality of God becomes an intrinsic element of the cause as such. The causality of God is not an operation on the part of God that goes beyond the operation of the creature or which does something that the creature does not do. It is the created reality that actually transcends itself and adds a newness of being, but this is possible only because the transcendent cause supports and sustains the operations of the finite cause. God gives to his creation the power and possibility of becoming more than it is and makes this possible because he is present to this creation, not as efficient cause intervening but as transcending cause supporting, sustaining, and encouraging.

Hominisation can be conceived as follows: in the origin of the first man (or men) there was a becoming through the transcending of the infrahuman organism to an organism endowed with spirit as self-consciousness. There was a movement from consciousness to self-awareness that was the passing of a threshold. This process was not the result of the proper powers of the organism alone, but was truly the result of the powers of the organism sustained by the transcending power of God. God acted through the powers and possibilities that he has already given to his creation. God created the first man, inasmuch as he supplied the secondary causes with the possibility of transcending themselves. Nor was it a combination of partial categorical causes such as principal and instrumental cause. The organism itself was the total cause of the result through its power of transcendence, just as God was the total cause present as transcendent cause.

This explanation has great advantages. It excludes a radical evolutionism that denies all cooperation between God and man, and excludes a totally materialistic approach to human origins. There is a difference between matter and spirit that must be preserved. It also renders the more moderate theory of evolution more intelligible and maintains the unity of man. Man is totally from the earth, but man is also totally from God. Nor does the theory propose that spirit evolved from matter. God as spirit is present in all of his creation and has given to his creation the power to become more than what it is. The leap from consciousness to self-consciousness is surely a dramatic development but not nearly so dramatic as the gift of God himself in grace, clearly attested as part of Christian belief. The origin of mankind is the domain of science as well as theology. In the previous explanation, the effort to relate both disciplines can bring advantages to scientist and theologian. To the believer, it offers a possible explanation that is in accord with a more scientific approach to life. At the same time, it enhances the goodness of God who has given to his creature the possibility of sharing in creative activity by always calling and enticing man to become more than what he is, and add a new richness to the already wonderful gift of life.

Monogenism and Polygenism[9]

To treat of the origin of mankind also involves the scientific question of the origin of the human race from one initial couple (monogenism) or the origin of the human race from many couples (polygenism). For centuries this question was never discussed. Adam was the presupposed father of the whole human race with all people descending from him. Within a literal interpretation of Genesis, this was the only possibility. In the seventeenth century the theory of pre-Adamites was proposed. According to this opinion, there were men before Adam who lived in a state of pure nature. They died off before Adam, and Adam could still be considered as the father of the human race as we know it. Such a theory did not gather much support. The question today is more from science than from mere speculation.

Since the origin of the human race is a subject for science and lies in the field of observation, what does present-day biology state with regard to human origins and how is this to be related to theology? A major part of contemporary scientists hold to a doctrine of polygenism. The transition from inferior forms to higher forms was made on a population level and not on the level of individuals. The same theory is proposed with regard to the origin of the human race. The movement from consciousness to self-consciousness was made not by a single individual or pair, but on the level of several or many couples. The passing of the threshold was extensive. Whether this transition was made at more or less the same period at different places in the world is a further area for investigation. What does theological anthropology say to such a theory?

If we are dealing with a scientific fact, then theology must simply recognize the fact. If we are dealing with a hypothesis, then theology must proceed more cautiously. Up to the present time, a monogenistic approach to the origin of mankind has been prevalent in Christian theology. But it must be remembered that such a problem is not fundamentally a theological problem, but a biological and zoological question. Theology cannot give answers to questions outside its competence. Nor can theology dismiss the problem as being a mere hypothesis. It must be agreed that even though polygenism is a hypothesis, it is quickly gaining as much support as the hypothesis of evolution. Science may never prove either theory, but for the present, both theories offer more solutions to difficult problems than any previous theory, and there are no great hopes for the toppling of the theory on the horizon. What does the theologian say?

The great obstacle against polygenism in Christian tradition is the belief in the universality of Original Sin. Monogenism more easily explains the universality of Original Sin in the more traditional explanation of the meaning of Original Sin. In contemporary thought, however, the universality of Original Sin is seen much more in the communication of the power of evil and not in the biological transmission of an inherited sin. In the explanation of Original Sin previously presented the Christian can believe in a true universality of the power of evil in the world and, more importantly, in the condition of man being in an ungraced situation, and still accept the hypothesis of polygenism. Original Sin need not be seen as one sin, but as a beginning of sin which in time influenced and affected the whole of the human race. Even if we hold to polygenism in different parts of the world, we can still see the origin of moral evil beginning in time and even in different times and places, and once invited into human history, increasing its power. The first sin or sins need not be thought of as the greatest sins. They were great in the sense that they began a situation that would culminate in the evil situation of the world in need of redemption. With the reinterpretation of Original Sin, the question of monogenism or polygenism is not greatly urgent for the theologian. The scientists are given the task to continue the study of human origins. The theologian will be satisfied whether science holds a theory of monogenism or polygenism.

The Origin of the Individual

The origin of the human race can be explained through the theory of becoming based on transcendence and God as transcendent cause. Something similar can be said of the origin of the individual. In the history of theology, the origin of the individual has been a study on the origin of the soul. Such a position is rather limited since in theology we treat of the origin of the individual as a whole, and not just part. Before dismissing this traditional approach, it is necessary to understand its meaning. According to Christian faith, the individual man has immense value because he is created in God's image and is predestined to share in the life of God. God refers to this man as person in dialogue, called to enter a community with God. It is true that the individual, through the process of generation, is inserted into the general biological context that will determine his existence, but in this lies the mystery of the origin of the individual who is more than a moment in the flux of evolutionary forces. For biology, the origin of the individual is casual and without great significance. For Christian theology, the origin of the individual is of profound meaning because such an individual has a destiny that surpasses his biological origin. When Christian theology centered on the origin of the human soul, it was an effort to preserve this profound value that is present in every individual. If today this theory is reinterpreted, it includes the belief in the intrinsic value of the individual.

Traditional theology taught a theory of creationism to explain the origin of the individual: God created the soul as the parents generated the body.[10] This theory preserves the value of the individual, as the individual man has an immediate relationship to God and is of special value because the soul is immediately created. The difficulty of the explanation is that this intervention on the part of God does not really add to God's power and dignity and does not enhance man's power to participate in the creativity of God. The same objections to the general theory of the origin of mankind are present in the origin of the individual through the direct creation of the soul by God.

Becoming, based on human transcendence supported by God as transcendent cause, can adequately explain the origin of the individual and preserve the unique value of the person. There is no great difference between the question of hominisation of man in general and the origin of the individual. Both involve becoming and transcendence. In the origin of the individual, however, it is not a question of the infrahuman to the human, but a transcendence of the human couple. Parents in the act of generation truly transcend themselves, add a newness of being, express their love for each other in a physical way, and in more than just a physical way. We conclude that the parents are responsible for the child and not just for the body of the child; it is their flesh and blood and it is the individual who is endowed with spirit that is the result of their union. Whatever is the result belongs properly to them. It is equally true that God is responsible for the child and not just for the soul. As transcendent cause, he has supported and sustained and encouraged the parents to express themselves in love and transcend their own existence by the presence of new life. Together God and parents create the great gift of human life.

Conclusion

This chapter has discussed the origin of the human race and the origin of individuals within an evolutionary framework. The ideas presented are theories—good theories that still remain on the level of opinion. Theology seeks to help explain faith and help man to live in the real world. The theory as presented here tries to preserve the best of Christian tradition and make sense to modern man who lives and is affected by a scientific world. Theology cannot live with its head in the sand. Science has much to offer that cannot be dismissed. The final proof of the value in this theory lies in its ability to help believers understand something more about the origin of human life, within a Christian framework. If it helps, then the theological enterprise has accomplished its task as it awaits new and further developments in the behavioral sciences and continues to respond with a firm Christian faith.

Notes

[1]Cf. Avery Dulles, *The Survival of Dogma* (New York: Doubleday, 1971).

[2]Cf. Robert Johann, "The Logic of Evolution," *Thought*, 36 (1961), pp. 537-554; Raymond Nogar, *The Wisdom of Evolution* (New York: Doubleday, 1963), pp. 27-31.

[3]Cf. Desmond Morris, *The Naked Ape* (New York: McGraw-Hill, 1967).

[4]Cf. H. Renckens, *Israel's Concept of the Beginning* (New York: Herder and Herder, 1964), pp. 227-230.

[5]Pope Pius XII, *Humani Generis, The Catholic Mind*, 48 (1950), p. 698.

[6]*Ibid.*

[7]Pope Paul VI, "Original Sin and Modern Science," *The Pope Speaks*, 11 (1966), pp. 229-235.

[8]Cf. Karl Rahner, *Hominisation* (New York: Herder and Herder, 1965). Much of what follows with regard to the theory of human origins is taken from this work by Rahner, as well as from J. De Fraine, *The Bible and the Origin of Man* (New York: 1962); J. De Fraine, *Adam and the Family of Man* (New York: 1965); The thought of the movement from consciousness to self-con-

sciousness is based on the writings of Teilhard de Chardin, especially *The Future of Man* (New York: Harper and Row, 1964), ch. 6, 10, 13, as well as *The Phenomenon of Man* (New York: Harper and Row, 1961).

[9]Cf. Karl Rahner, "Monogenism," *Sacramentum Mundi* (New York: Herder and Herder, 1969); Rahner, "Evolution and Original Sin," *Concilium*, 6 (1967), pp. 30-35.

[10]Cf. *Summa Theologica*, I, q. 118, a 2, a 3.

6

Man as Person in Dialogue

Somehow the complexity that makes up any human life has its center and its unity. The Bible speaks of man as flesh *(basar, sarkx)*, which expresses that man is from the earth; he is weak and fragile. He is also alive *(nephesch, psyche)*. When God withdraws his breath from man, then man dies. He does not have life, he is life. Man is also spirit *(ruah, pneuma)*. It is the spirit that gives or communicates life and is related to God. It is not easy to sort out the various expressions used for man and for human life in the Bible. The nuances are not always evident to a twentieth-century mentality. At one moment, man as bodily and frail is emphasized to give way to man as spirit-filled. There is no complete and accurate biblical anthropology; there is only a picture of man that is unified and complex.[1]

The Bible takes its cue from life. Any attempt to express the meaning of man, to capture his nature, is doomed to failure. Man never knows his full possibilities until those possibilities are actualized and that is yet to be accomplished. Many expressions are needed to manifest the reality that is just one human life; how much more so when there is an attempt to understand the nature of man and the possibilities of mankind. Human life is fragile, but also mighty; it is hard to let go of life and it is clung to with all the control of the spirit. Man is alone and yet related to others; he cannot live without others; he is free, yet must of necessity enter into dialogue; he is a thinker and a feeler; one who can be elevated to the heights and cast down to the depths. The Bible does not and cannot offer the full picture. What is believed is that somehow in the complexity that is a human life there is a richness and a unifying element. The Bible calls this God.

The nature of man calls for the search for unity. Person, freedom, sexuality, individual, community, history, time, space are all aspects of human life and human nature. What man does—thinker, player, controller, worker, creator—all flow from what he is. And so the list continues. Certain aspects of man's nature seem more fundamental than others. Since it is impossible to treat completely the nature of man, some selection is necessary as we move through the complexity in search of the unity. Man is person: he is self-conscious and free; this is the beginning.

Man as Person

Person, personality, personalism, have become clichés in recent thought. The terms are not new but in the course of time have suffered interpretations that often obscure their meaning; at the same time, the terms manifest the wealth of meaning they contain. The age of personalism has dawned again. Writers and thinkers are all hurrying to express what the new age may mean. To understand the richness involved required an understanding of the history of the term "person" and its meaning.

The word "person" has been recognized since ancient times as indicating man's own mode of being. Thomas Aquinas explained the meaning of person by relating man as person to his understanding of all reality, and in particular to his understanding of substance. For Thomas, a substance subsists in itself as a whole, and not part of a whole, and is distinct from everything else.[2] Person is substance with rationality. Being a person is a special way of existing in itself, as a whole, and distinct from everything else. These ideas from classical philosophy tell a great deal about person even today. A person is independent, distinct from all other persons with an individuality that cannot be duplicated. As helpful as this description of person might be, however, it is not what we usually mean by person today.

Contemporary philosophy, which is the spirit that has affected society, sees person as characterized by self-consciousness and freedom.[3] Self-awareness with the possibility to become are the two great qualities of person today. The individuality of Aquinas remains, but the emphasis is on the qualities of this individuality and not the quality of rationality as previously envisioned. Person is unique and never again repeated. What a person becomes is properly that person's alone, and without that person the being that is present would never exist. What the individual person will become through self-awareness and freedom always remains a mystery. Animals are individuals and come into existence apart from others, but animals are finished at birth. No one wonders: "What manner of dog will this be?" But people do wonder at the birth of a child: "What manner of child will this be?"

The individual who is person builds up human capital using effort and planning. All man has from nature becomes the material out of which he fashions himself. Man is a project; he has a task that gives him responsibility to accomplish that task.[4] To be a person means to be called to be more and more of a person. Through openness, through the vocation to full actualization of potential, man is more than just an individual, more than just a natural whole distinct from others; he is a person. Person is the whole of man considered as a vocation to freedom and development and implies a commitment to that development. How man achieves his personhood, or becomes a personality, is an arduous process.

Personality

Some philosophers distinguish between person and nature in their effort to explain human life. Nature is that which is given and person is the integration of the given qualities of a human life. Man learns about reality and thus reality is personalized. At the same time he accepts reality, and reality as it is manifested, so that the person is realized. In the first case an object is brought into subjectivity, while in the second case a subject is objectivized, with both states tending toward a state of complete correspondence between person and nature. The acceptance of reality is part of the development of personality.

Sometimes reality should not be accepted. And so the rejection of reality is also significant for personality development. An acceptance of reality causes a certain identification of the person with the reality. Revolt achieves a positive disassociation from something that is, but should not be. There is always the possibility of a noble refusal to accept certain aspects of life. This refusal can enhance the person.

A man can revolt and change things and this type of revolt is necessary for life. Man can also revolt against something that he cannot change and this, too, may enrich personality. If a man sees absolutely no good in children suffering, and yet he knows this is something that he in no way can completely change, then he is in a position to accept reality or revolt. A firm nonacceptance of this reality is a noble attitude. Albert Camus expresses noble revolt in *The Plague*: "Until my dying day I shall refuse to love a scheme of things in which children are put to torture."[5]

Revolt is often seen in a strictly negative framework. This should not be. Again it is Camus who asks: "What is a rebel? A man who says 'no,' but whose refusal does not imply a renunciation. He is also a man who says 'yes'."[6] It is a passionate commitment to human life that makes a man refuse to accept what seems to be in discord with life. Revolt and revolution are part of the dialectic that is present between nature and person, between what is given and what becomes. To achieve personality demands an acceptance of reality, and at other times a refusal to accept reality. Both are essential and both aid in the growth of the person.

We all know people who seem to have achieved a high level of personality, who have successfully mixed the acceptance and rejection of reality and have accomplished something with themselves. The man with the strong personality knows who he is; he has strong convictions about himself, and knows his talents and weakness; he executes well what he believes without the strain of worry and indecision; he has himself in hand with ideals to be realized as well as actualized. The individual with the strongly developed personality has unified the multiplicity that makes up the complex person and has bound together all the gifts of nature so that they are all personalized. "A mind will be more fully personal, the more completely its contemporary states are united with each other to form a single total state, and the more completely its successive total states are united with each other to form the history of a single mind."[7]

Achievement of Personality[8]

Psychologists and philosophers are quick to point out the need for the development of personality. They speak of the task that is given and offer some helpful suggestions on the mode of achievement of personality. The encouraging note is that the achievement is termed a process that engages a lifetime, and involves the acceptance of limitations, making one's nature, accepting and making the earth, the world, the fullness of reality and other people.

Acceptance of limitations and creatureliness: Man must learn to accept himself for what he is—a creature with limitations. It is necessary to identify with the limitations and not live as though divorced from them. No one person is the most talented or most intelligent or most beautiful or most creative person in the world. Everyone has strengths and weaknesses. To deny the latter is to fail to fulfill the former. Perfection is not present in any life. Even the high and mighty have their closeness to the earth and so have limitations. If nothing more, sickness and the inevitability of death should make a man conscious of his imperfection and finitude and open to accept their presence. For the achievement of any degree of personality, this is fundamental: accept yourself as you are.

Man makes his own nature: Each man must accept himself for what he is and then believe that he can make his own nature. The possibilities that are given are beyond the realm of complete achievement. To choose one is to exclude another. Man must make the choice of what qualities to actualize; he must decide what combinations will bring him what he desires. In spite of the presence of determination through heredity and environment, there is much in man that is undetermined. Form an idea of what might be; work toward the resolution of that project. The difference between a free and nonfree being is here. In a nonfree being, the nature always precedes and determines the actions. The free agent has a nature that partly precedes and is partly determined by the activity of the individual. The making of the self is the natural follow-up of the acceptance of the self.

Man accepts and makes the earth: This refers primarily to the physical universe that is given to man. Man is of the earth and is at home on this earth. There is no aspect of the earth that cannot add to an individual's life. Every exclusion will only detract from what might be. The sea has its healing effect, as do the mountains. The smallest flower has a power that is to be accepted and blessed; animals are part of creation and so related to man; sunshine and rain, snow and hail, wind and fire are all part of the earth and are all part of any human life. Achieving personality demands that the earth be accepted with no part left out or overlooked. If man is truly from the earth, there is no part of creation that is foreign to him, no part of creation that does not offer its healing balm and soothing presence. The individual who is achieving personality knows the magic and delight of creation and takes every opportunity to revel in its pleasures, gaining powerfully from its nearness. The earth is man's and man is of the earth. It belongs to him in his goal of development.

Man accepts and makes the world: This refers more to what man has accomplished in the universe, the world of man with its cities and towns and art and language and customs and laws. There is a beauty about the city of Paris or a fascination present in New York that are part of life. There is freshness about a New England town or a rural community in Greece. These are what man has done, and in spite of problems what man has done is good. It is marvelous to have large cities or small towns, and each has its charm. Music and art are man's accomplishments and are part of human development. All music has value from the classical of Beethoven and Bach to the electronic music of the Beatles. Art is always liberating in any form and it is as much a part of man as eating and sleeping. The same is true for language and customs and laws. Each has its noble quality and each has its place in the development of the person. Anyone who excludes himself deliberately from any aspect of human life is already dead in that regard. To be alive is to be open to all that man has done and welcome its presence in life.

Man accepts the fullness of reality: Personal life includes the fullness of being that is beyond the earth and this world. Man cannot say no to being. Life has its mystery that can be found only in the presence of the mysterious and transcendent One. The religious dimension of life is not just one more ingredient in a human life; the religious is that which permeates what has already been described. Man is religious not as a component, but as a dimension of all human life. The achievement of personality implies the acceptance of God.

Man accepts and loves others: We can consider people as part of the earth, as a given or part of man's world. The task is separated and placed at the end because it is the chief means of integrating all others. Even the religious dimension of life is mediated humanly. Man is a being with others and this is based as much on his spirituality as on his materiality. Somehow in the struggle of interpersonal relationships the possibility of a human life blossoms and grows. We learn to love others; we learn to allow others to be different, even when we cannot understand them; we learn to think well of others and promote their well-being, and offer them the most precious gift that we can: ourselves. There is no possibility for a development of personality without the acceptance and honoring of others. Communication as the union with others binds irrevocably the myriad dimension of human life and unifies the complexity that characterizes man. Man is dialogical, open to others and open-ended.

Personality means "the highest acceptance of human self-possession and the most free self-commitment; inner independence and moral involvement; concentration on one's own hands and surrender to an ideal and worthwhile task."[9]

Christian Personality

The resolution of the relationship between nature and grace already responds to the possibility of Christian personality as distinct from the achievement of personality. There is no great gulf between what is possible for man on a psychological level and what man is called to become on a theological or spiritual level. Christian personality and its achievement is none other than the realization of what the psychologists offer with the one additional feature of a Christian God who is Father of our Lord Jesus Christ, in place of the acceptance of a transcendent reality. There is some advantage, however, in examining the same psychological elements within a strictly Christian interpretation.

Man accepts limitations and creatureliness: Within the Judaic-Christian tradition, the acceptance of limitations and creatureliness is the meaning of what the Bible calls truth. Man must seek and live the truth: he is dependent on God who is his Creator, and must respond to that dependence by offering homage and worship. The truth that will make us free (John 8:32) is the realization that we come from God and move in him with all of our weaknesses as well as strengths. The Bible always calls for the acceptance of man with limitations and then adds that in spite of those limitations and man's creatureliness, the God who is without limitation has entered into a covenant with man and offers him more than the limited and finite creature could ever hope.

Man makes his own nature: What man is called to become in a Christian perspective is none other than a child of God, a sharer of God's nature:

> Dearly beloved, we are God's children now; what we shall later be has not yet come to light. We know that when it comes to light we shall be like him, for we shall see him as he is. (1 John 3:2)

This is the vocation to which man is called. Each man is predestined in Christ to glory and to live in the glory of God. But each man makes of himself what he wants and even specifies how he will live this divine vocation. There are no set paths that God has mapped out for the individual. There is the offer of possibilities that man freely chooses as he makes his nature and fulfills his destiny as one called to share in the life of God. Each man is to be holy—but to be holy as he chooses to express that holiness. God offers many possibilities and will support man in any choice, even if that choice is in reality the rejection of his future. Saint or sinner are parts of life. Whether they express the totality of a human life is given to the individual to decide.

Man accepts and makes the earth: We have already seen just how much man is of the earth (Gen. 2:7); he is united to earth and sun and moon and together they form part of God's creation (Gen. 1-2). Man is also responsible for this earth and stands as God's vicegerent for creation. He is to rule with the qualities of God and bring forth the richness that is hidden in the earth (Gen. 1:26-30). No part of creation is foreign to man and each helps man exercise his power of dominion.

Man accepts and makes the world: What man brings forth is to manifest the qualities of God. Mercy and fidelity are to characterize human life. His most noble accomplishments only add to man's dignity. God has given man the ability and talent, and man must exercise that talent with the same deliberateness and concern with which God has begun the creative activity. Man shares in the power of God in bringing creation to perfection and completion.

Man accepts the fullness of reality: This dimension of human life is specified in the acceptance of God who is Father of our Lord Jesus Christ. Man as Christian man believes in a God who has manifested himself through a covenant, offering more than man could demand or expect. He has shown his goodness and his faithfulness and man is called to accept this kind and gracious Father who has not spared us his only Son (Rom. 8:31).

Man accepts others: It is the Gospel that tells us that we cannot love God, whom we do not see, if we do not love our neighbor, whom we do see (1 John 4:20). To love man is to love God; to accept man and to enter into dialogue with man is to accept God and to enter into dialogue with God. The Gospel of Matthew expresses very well the need for man to accept others:

> The king will say to those on his right: "Come. You have my Father's blessing! Inherit the kingdom prepared for you from the creation of the world. For I was hungry and you gave me food, I was thirsty and you gave me drink. I was a stranger and you welcomed me, naked and you clothed me. I was ill and you comforted me, in prison and you came to visit me." Then the just will ask him: "Lord, when did we see you hungry and feed you or see you thirsty and give you drink? When did we welcome you away from home or clothe you in your nakedness? When did we visit you when you were ill or in prison?" The king will answer them: "I assure you, as often as you did it for one of my least brothers, you did it for me."
>
> Then he will say to those on his left: "Out of my sight, you condemned, into that everlasting fire prepared for the devil and his angels!" (Matt. 25:34-41)

To achieve a Christian personality involves the acceptance of ourselves for what we are; the acceptance of the task to become what we can be: children of God; the acceptance of the earth, the world and other people. In all, it demands the acceptance of God who has manifested himself to us in the life, death, and resurrection of Jesus of Nazareth. It is a great vocation and an exciting task.

Freedom

The presupposition that has underpinned the foregoing thoughts on person and the achievement of Christian personality is human freedom. Unless there is a possibility for man to choose to develop and "become," it is useless to talk about the achievement of personality. Freedom is as much a characteristic of person as self-awareness, and it is only the combination of the two qualities that will accomplish the perfection that man seeks.

Modern man is still discovering the implications of human freedom. The very confusion in the meaning of the word testifies to that. The French Revolution may have liberated man from the *ancien régime*; psychology may have liberated man from servitude to instincts; modern technology may have freed him from drudgery, but the constant call for freedom NOW from political, social, psychological, and even religious quarters gives ample proof that freedom is still to come.

The challenging feature of modern times is freedom and its possibilities. In spite of the French and American revolutions, we still suffer from the evils of capitalistic liberalism and totalitarianism. We are threatened by the abuse of psychology and the disintegrating effects of analysis and sensitivity sessions. Automation may eventually enslave man to the machine. Even within Christianity we have still to learn what it means to live in the royal freedom of Jesus Christ. There is an urgent need to understand more accurately the meaning of freedom.

Almost everyone knows what freedom means: freedom is the capacity to act or not to act, to do this or to do that. Precisely because everyone knows this description of freedom, the meaning of freedom is misunderstood. This is really a very superficial image of freedom. According to this image, freedom is a neutral power by which every person at any given moment is capable of picking out from an infinite variety of possible actions, whether good or bad, heroic or petty, the one that suits his fancy. This is wrong. A man is never free to do exactly what he wants at every moment of his life. Our lives are conditioned by environment, heredity, and education. We are not the totally free people we pretend to be. The image is wrong on a more fundamental level. True freedom involves the whole person and is not a neutral but a positive act. Freedom in its most fundamental sense is the ability to commit oneself to an ideal, to actively give oneself over to the fullness of reality and thereby achieve liberating and peace-giving effects.[10]

From the depths of one's creativity, every person must commit himself to outside reality as a whole. This is a fundamental choice between love and selfishness, between ego-centeredness and thou-centeredness. The person either radically agrees to the whole, the fullness of reality outside himself in a spirit of openness, service, respect, and love, or he radically refers everything to himself. Freedom is the ability a person has to reject or accept God.[11] The freedom of choice, to do this or that, is not worthy of consideration in the presence of the true and ultimate freedom of the acceptance or rejection of God.

Freedom in Scripture

The Gospels present Jesus of Nazareth as a free man. Jesus knew and loved the traditions of his ancestors; he respected the Sabbath but always within bounds. He cured on the Sabbath (Luke 6:7), allowed his disciples to pick grain on the Sabbath (Luke 6:1). He fulfilled the demands of the law when the law helped people, but would not worry about eating with unclean hands, especially when people fulfilled this prescription but left their hearts unclean (Matt. 7:1-23). He accepted social customs and told the leper to show himself to the High Priest (Luke 5:12-14), but broke social customs when they were inhuman. He gladly spoke to sinners and ate with publicans (Luke 5:30). For Jesus, the law was the expression of the love of God and neighbor:

> This is the greatest and first commandment. The second is like it: "You shall love your neighbor as yourself." On these two commandments the whole law is based, and the prophets as well. (Matt. 22:38-40)

This was his basic law with every situation and interpretation founded on the love of God and neighbor. Jesus was free in regard to law and social custom because he interpreted the law in light of the love of God and neighbor.

The Gospels present Jesus as the man who was free because he had given himself to his Father, had actively disposed of himself in the presence of the fullness of reality that is his Father, and with all of his being committed his life and eventually his death to the will of his Father. Jesus was free because he loved God and loved men.[12]

The second spokesman for freedom in the New Testament is Paul.[13] He developed Christian freedom in terms of freedom from sin, from law and death. What Jesus had manifested in his life was now possible for the lives of believers if they accepted the royal freedom of their Master.

Freedom from sin is the heart of the redemption as accomplished in Jesus. This is freedom from the state of estrangement from God and freedom from the wrath of God that man had merited. Paul knows that for the believer sin and evil will not prevail; the power of sin is broken and man is now under the more powerful influence of good, but only if man accepts the offer (Rom. 6:1-4, 14, 20-23).

The second expression of freedom is freedom from law. The law for Paul is good in itself, but it had never given man the strength to avoid sin. With its commandments and prohibitions it had succeeded in giving man an appetite for sin. Law brought sin into experience. With Jesus, man is no longer bound to the law since he is beyond the law with the presence of the Spirit (Rom. 7:4-11; Gal. 2:4; 4:21-31; 5:1-15). The relationship between law and spirit is treated by Paul in the seventh and eighth chapters of Romans. The basic conclusion reached by Paul is that the Christian needs no law as long as he lives the life of the Spirit. There is no place for legalism in Christianity. Christian man is to live by the Spirit.

The third freedom is freedom from death, which for Paul is always a consequence of sin. Paul speaks of eternal death since only then would sin claim its decisive victory (Rom. 6:8; 1 Cor. 15:20-22, 55-57).

This threefold freedom from sin, law, and death is realized in three stages. Fundamentally it comes from the cross of Jesus. Through his act of obedience and his death, he won freedom for us. The sign of Christian freedom is the sign of the cross of Jesus (Rom. 6:6-7). This freedom becomes a reality for us inasmuch as it is offered to us as a call from God:

> My brothers, remember that you have been called to live in freedom—but not a freedom that gives free rein to the flesh. Out of love, place yourselves at one another's service. (Gal. 5:13)

We become free when we accept the gift of God as seen in the life, death, and resurrection of Jesus. Christian existence is a constant call to freedom from sin, law, and death, begun in Baptism.

Paul's third stage is to live in love: "Since we live by the Spirit, let us follow the spirit's lead" (Gal. 5:25). The new law of love fulfills our call to freedom as we learn to bear one another's failings (Gal. 6:2). Full freedom is what Paul expresses to the Galatians:

> The life I live now is not my own; Christ is living in me. I still live my human life, but it is a life of faith in the Son of God, who loved me and gave himself for me. (Gal. 2:20)

Finally, in Paul we must see that Christian freedom is never complete until the experience of death. The final freedom is the freedom of the sons of God when we will share in the glory of God, through the sharing of his life. Scripture sees freedom as the ability of man to dispose himself to the love of God that is perfected in death, but present in the expressions of the love of neighbor. We are free from sin and law and death, which was begun for us in Jesus Christ and his death, and is offered to us as a call. Freedom is the ability to accept or reject God through the acceptance or rejection of the neighbor in life and in death, which will sum up what was previously expressed in life.

Theology of Freedom[14]

When the Word became flesh we reached the highest point of

the self-realization of human freedom. By this act a man was called and responded to give himself completely to the mystery that is God. In the incarnation, a human being was called to communicate with God to the greatest depths of possibility, and this human being responded in freedom in the life that he lived and the human death that he accepted. The Word became man and fulfilled the possibilities of human freedom. The life and death of Jesus of Nazareth explains the possibility of human freedom.

The freedom of Jesus was possible because man is spirit in the world, able to transcend the possibilities of his space and time and enter into communion with his God. Human transcendence is directed to the mystery of God because God has so created man with an orientation and a possibility for communion with himself. The conclusion of such thinking is that God, as the foundation for transcendence and for freedom, is willed in every act of freedom, whether this is conscious or not. Man is not forced to accept his transcendence; there is always the possibility of consent or refusal and it is this possibility that constitutes his freedom. The Christian theology of freedom always relates man and his transcendence to God.

To speak of freedom as directed toward God does not imply, however, that freedom is divorced from this world. Freedom always presupposes the object that is in the world. Even the most profound acceptance of God in freedom is mediated in creation. We meet God in the most radical way everywhere and in the most powerful way in the presence of the neighbor. The free man is one like Jesus Christ who has given himself to his God through the giving of himself to others.

Finally, freedom is a trustful creative task that is given at every interval of life. It is trustful because it calls man to give up himself in order to find himself; it is a leap in the darkness of life which believes that man will find what is liberating only when he turns over himself in an active availability to a mystery that he can never fully understand. Such trust is frightening, but necessary if man is ever to realize his basic freedom.

Freedom is a task because it is never given at one moment in full measure. Freedom is a gift, but a gift that is never-ending and never complete in life. Freedom is earned and becomes operative only when the responsibility of life and to all creation is accepted by the individual. Freedom is the constant call to allow the presence of God's grace as the gift of himself to so permeate the human personality that no area is not affected by the goodness of God.

Freedom is creative since it is never tied down to a system or to categories. The bonds of space and time are broken in the free man as are the confines of a narrow approach to life. The free spirit is the person who glides through life discovering the richness hidden in the ordinary; creativity flourishes as the free person explores the possibilities that are his and the potential of the world of which he is a part. Freedom offers a newness that is hidden only waiting to be revealed.

Conclusion

What can be said of Christian personality and freedom? The believer is a free person beyond the control of law and sin and death when and to the extent that the believer is a spirit-filled person, to the extent that the believer has given himself to the mystery that is God. The task is growing in understanding of self and in this awareness of self a growing in self-disposal as we freely choose the destiny that is given to us. The new law of freedom is exercised concretely, and this implies the particular manifestations that include the concrete love of neighbor. We are most free when we give ourselves actively in love to God through the active gift of love to others and to this world; we are most free when we allow ourselves to be what we are: individual persons who are called to share the mystery that is God, which is the fulfillment of the mystery that is man. In all that he does, the free person gives himself to the good and then he achieves freedom and becomes a person.

Notes

[1]Cf. Walstan Mork, *The Biblical Meaning of Man* (Milwaukee: Bruce, 1967), pp. 14-16.

[2]*Summa Theologica*, III, q. 16, art. 12, ad. 2.

[3]Cf. John Walgrave, *Person and Society* (Pittsburgh:

Duquesne Univ. Press, 1965), pp. 101-103.

[4]Cf. Joseph Donceel, *Philosophical Anthropology* (New York: Sheed and Ward, 1967), pp. 462-463.

[5]Albert Camus, *The Plague* (London: Hamish Hamilton, 1948), p. 203.

[6]Albert Camus, *The Rebel* (London: Hamish Hamilton, 1953), p. 19.

[7]C. D. Broad, *Religion, Philosophy and Physical Research* (London, 1953), p. 161.

[8]The main outline of this section is taken from the thoughts of John Cowburn, *The Person and Love* (New York: Alba House, 1967), pp. 33-49.

[9]Cf. John Walgrave, *Person and Society* (Pittsburgh: Duquesne Univ. Press, 1965), p. 105.

[10]*Ibid.*, pp. 103-105.

[11]Cf. Karl Rahner, "Theology of freedom," *Freedom and Man*, ed. John C. Murray (New York: Kenedy, 1965), pp. 201-217.

[12]Cf. John F. O'Grady, *Jesus, Lord and Christ* (Paramus: Paulist Press, 1973), ch. 1.

[13]Cf. Stanislaus Lyonnet, "St Paul: Liberty and Law," *The Bridge*, vol. IV (1962), pp. 229-251.

[14]Cf. Karl Rahner, *Grace in Freedom* (New York: Herder and Herder, 1969), pp. 203-264; Piet Fransen, "Grace and Freedom," *Freedom and Man*, pp. 31-69.

7

Man: Body, Soul, Spirit

The dualism that has plagued Western civilization is coming to an end. The various heresies that have emphasized the spiritual to the detriment of the bodily have been laid to rest in the quest of modern man to enjoy the bodily almost to the exclusion of the spiritual. The modern penchant for hedonism has counteracted the dualism of the past. Perhaps society has already gone too far in this freedom and glorification of the bodily; perhaps it is no more than the previous extreme of suppressing the bodily.

Man is described as body/subject today; or body spirit.[1] There is an effort to relate the many aspects of a person's life in a unified fashion. With the end of a dualism on the theoretical plane, it is predicted that soon there will be the end of dualism on the practical plane. There is an advantage of avoiding divisions and separation; there is also the advantage of dividing in an effort to understand what is united. Here we will divine man to come to a unified resolution. Man is spirit, he is psyche, and he is body.

In the history of theology there has been the constant question of whether the Bible considers man as dichotomous or trichotomous. As already seen, the Bible teaches neither. In Scripture, man has bodily aspects *(basar, sarkx)*, psychological aspects *(nephesch, psyche)*, and spiritual aspects *(ruah, pneuma)*. Man is one center with many spokes. There is no immortal soul, but only a personality destined for God for all eternity. Man lives and dies and rises as one.[2]

The words "soul" and "spirit" are fraught with misunderstanding. For the purpose of clarification, we will distinguish the two ideas. Personal being is rooted in the spirit. It is on that level, on depth of personality, that man is aware of self and is free. It is on the level of spirit that man is transcendence and related to a God who is transcendent. The soul is the psychic element of man. Here we are concerned with intellect and will and emotions. This distinction is not found in Scripture. The Bible does not distinguish mental life from the life of the spirit. The Bible is not merely psychological, it is more spiritual than anything else, but it always speaks of man as having spiritual, psychological, and physical aspects.

Spirit[3]

Man can be person because he has spirit. But what is spirit? This seems to be a philosophical question, which does not mean, however, that theology cannot be concerned with the meaning of spirit. We believe that man is created in the image of God and has a positive orientation toward God. As we try to understand the meaning of man in light of the Word of God, we approach the question of spirit as theologians and see how the elements of philosophy can help us to appreciate the biblical message.

The Bible states that God is spirit (John 4:2), and that we must worship God in spirit and truth (John 4:24). God is spirit and man is given spirit (Gen. 2:7). The early narrative of Genesis on the origin of human life teaches that the spirit of man is related to the spirit of God. This cannot refer to the neutral power of thinking or feeling or willing. Spirit must be more than the psychological; it must be the foundation for the psychological. Man can think and feel and decide only if he sees himself in relationship to something beyond the level of functional psychology. Man is related as person to that which is beyond the ordinary level. Spirit exists in relationship to meaning or to what modern philosophy calls value. The reference of man as man to that which is transcendent will distinguish spirit from the physical elements of man. Spirit is concerned with the selfhood, with self-awareness, with all of the possibilities of self, accomplished in the presence of, and reaction to, freedom.

It is spirit that gives man his apparently limitless possibilities. The gift of intellect can be meager, the power of the will affected by outside influences, the emotions can be confused, but on the level of spirit, man can become evermore as he commits himself to a value, to an ideal, to a purpose and meaning in life. The spiritual level is most properly the possibility of human life since it is here that man can transcend the limitations imposed on him by his psyche and his body. Spirit is free; spirit is the possibility of growth in self-awareness.

Theology claims that the final point of reference for which and from which our spirit exists as spirit, is the God who reveals himself to us in his Word. Spirit in man makes it possible to relate ourselves in thought, will, and feeling to the Word of God. That is why we say that personal being is founded in spirit. By means of the spirit, we perceive the Word of God addressed to us: we believe; we love; we respond and become the persons we are called to be. The spiritual aspect of man is the domain of personhood, of freedom and self-awareness; it is the possibility of transcendence and the possibility of relating to God who is spirit.

The Soul

On the psychological level, it is the psyche or soul that is most important for daily life; the psyche is often seen as the bridge between the spiritual and bodily.[4] If the bridge is clouded over, it is hard for people to function humanly. On this level of human life we encounter intellectual, volitional, and emotional activity.[5]

Even the most ordinary common sense is a gift of God and in this there is the appreciation of the intellect. The intellect is the power of perceiving the infinite, especially in the world of things. With the aid of this knowledge, the intellect gives man the power to live and act in this finite world in a practical way. The Bible is full of respect for such astuteness. Man needs intelligence in order to grasp the concrete purpose of life and live practically. It is particularly the Wisdom literature of the Old Testament that glories in the intellectual aspect of man. The Book of Proverbs is filled with the practical advice that comes from intellectual activity:

> The slack hand impoverishes, but the hand of the diligent enriches. A son who fills the granaries in summer is a credit; a son who slumbers during harvest, a disgrace. (10:4-5)

> Where words are many, sin is not wanting; but he who restrains his lips does well. (10:19)

> For lack of guidance a people falls; security lies in many counselors. (11:14)

> He who loves correction loves knowledge, but he who hates reproof is stupid. (12:1)

By his intellect man has been endowed with the power to learn what he needs for life. He knows what is an advantage for him and what is harmful, as well as what is useful for all mankind. He can form the concept of what is true and then come to the values that are behind that which is true; he carefully observes the actual world and collects facts and inquires into laws and events. This is the blessing of intellect.

The intellect is not isolated from the totality of the person. Ideas and concepts are based on sense perception and imagination, as well as made possible by the person who is growing in self-awareness. A false intellectualism can try to separate cognition from the senses and from the spirit of man. When this happens, the mind becomes arid and purely conceptual; thought becomes rigid since it lacks feeling and the freeing presence of spirit. When man becomes only the cerebrating animal, he can do no more than build machines.

The will is also an element of the psyche: man has the ability to decide and to move toward the decision. Impulse or instinct roots volitional activity as man moves toward the goal as perceived. The will directs man to become what he is through activity. It is related to the intellect that advises him and is rooted in the spirit that enables him to become. But like intellect, will is not separated from emotions and must consciously be referred to spirit. Left on its own, will becomes ruthless and brutal, crushing and destroying what it finds in its path; it becomes hardened since it lacks the softness and vitality of feeling and the perspective of freedom. The self-willed and hard-willed man is to be lamented. One aspect of what could be a beautiful life has taken over to the detriment of all else. The Bible encourages man to be what he is and strive toward the goal by decisive activity, but that goal is the glory of God who is ever merciful and faithful. The will and its activity is essential for the development of human life, but always must be inserted into the broader perspective of what comprises every person's life.

Emotions and their influence are the third element of man's psychic activity. Feeling is related to the pleasure/pain sensation as the will is related to instinct and the intellect to imagination and sense perception. Genuine feeling is not possible without the foundation in spirit and without the interaction of other psychical and physical aspects. A good meal may bring pleasure but does not bring joy unless man is operating on more than the physical level. The most delicious dinner tastes like so many ashes if it is eaten alone and without the engaging of the spirit with others.

Feeling accompanies the spiritual activity of man because feeling is concerned with values that are known. What we know and how we react in volitional activity always includes some feeling and is always based on the spirit of man. There is no possibility of separating feeling from the life of man and remaining human. Love, hatred, joy, sorrow, boldness, fear, hope, and despair and anger are present in life and influence our waking and sleeping moments. They can enhance the nobility of man if they are integrated into personality. To deny their presence can only cause problems for personality development.

These three elements of the psyche—intellect, will, and emotions—are all interrelated and are further grounded in spirit and manifested on the level of the bodily. Man is a complex unity with the integrated person holding in a creative tension all of the dimensions of his life. It is on this level of the psyche that modern psychology has offered so much.

To speak of the role of the psyche and modern psychology introduces the role of psychology in the development of personality and in the development of man's relationship to God. Many contemporary psychologists are learning that there is more to human life than the psyche. Sometimes the efforts to restore mental health only discloses the depth of a person and, in particular, his spiritual nature. This is beyond the realm of psychology and is often only hinted at in the writings of contemporary psychologists. For a

Christian approach to life the spiritual is most significant, but it is possible to develop the spiritual only if there is a degree of health on the level of the psyche. People who are suffering from psychological illness find it very hard to develop self-awareness and freedom and find it even more difficult to experience and accept a relationship to God. Just as psychological illness can cause grave problems for the bodily aspect of man, so the same illness can cause grave problems for man's spiritual activity. Psychology and theology must work hand in hand as they seek to make level the hills and make straight the paths of the human personality so that a person can come to know and respond to the offer of God. The present interest in pastoral counseling is a practical application of this need to unite the spheres of spiritual and psychological activity. The counselor who is pastor and concerned with the religious dimension of the person develops the ability to aid the person in siphoning off the emotional problems that cloud human activity. Once the problems are cleared away, the religious aspect can be handled more effectively. This is another example of how the complex nature of man is unified. Theology and psychology are concerned with healing and cooperate as they try to offer healing to the diversified client.

We have already mentioned problems when one aspect of the psyche is emphasized to the detriment of the others. When the intellect reigns supreme or the will pontificates in its harshness and determination, there is always a justified protest. In human history romantic movements have been the human response to the tyranny of intellect and will. Romantics defend the Dionysian god of feeling and life and spontaneity and freedom against the Apollonian god of reason, the sun god whose rays can singe all living things unless they are refracted. The inhabitant of the city of iron and concrete is not without reason the man who is easily beguiled with the love of the East and the longing for Nirvana. The human person and his life must be filled with a vital force or else he will become a phantom. The Creator has not made man with a reason for everything he does. The sober remark of Pascal, "The heart has reasons of which the mind is unaware," should not be lost on the Christian understanding of man. But we need not become the romantic who is hostile to intellect or will to recognize the falsity of intellectualism or hard-nosed volitionalism. Christ tells us to consider the lilies of the field and the birds of the air, and tells us also to be wise and prudent. A theology that is without heart or real sentiment makes human beings heartless and hard. On the other hand, feeling without thought tends to evaporate.

The Body[6]

If we cannot find a special Christian teaching on the soul, the same is also true for the body. The Bible is concerned with the integration of the whole man in his personal life. The account of Genesis tells us that God took earth and breathed spirit into the earth. This account expresses a fourfold truth: body and spirit belong equally to the nature of man; neither is to be reduced to the other; they are destined for each other and for God; they are adapted to each other.

The body is the means by which man communicates. He is adapted and connected and conditioned by the world through his body. The body is also the most solid and impressive manifestation of the creaturely condition of man. The person is finite, localized in this world of time and space and determined by his location. The body accomplished all of this. Through bodily functions the spirit of man reaches down to the rich soil of the earth and takes up and makes personal man's relatedness to the earth. Through the senses man learns and then develops his thought. He communicates with other people and offers himself in that communication as he accepts the offer of others. Without the physical aspects of man in his body, we would not learn, we would not communicate, we would not be able to express ourselves for what we are. Take away the bodily and man loses his contact with the world and with others.

As is evident the body also limits man. The spirit of man seeks to express itself as does the psyche. In both cases the body is not capable of the task. The spirit and psyche of man must limit their expression to the material, and the material is never the adequate expression of the nonmaterial. There is a residue that remains when the spirit of man seeks expression. Words do not completely convey thoughts; thoughts do not convey adequately the profound insights or experiences of the person. Man is always more than what he expresses, which is a constant source of pain for the truly creative person. No wonder man has always been tempted to rid himself of his body so that he can be without limitation in the expression of the spirit. But if he tries to accomplish this, he discovers that the only way a man can express himself is through the bodily. To be human is to accept the limitations of bodily expression.

In the Christian tradition there has often been the sin of contempt of the bodily. There has been the tendency to refuse to accept limitations and concentrate on the more spiritual activities of man. But what is man if he is not bodily? How can there be a creature if there is not limitation? The body is man as is his psyche and his spirit. To try to deny the bodily dimension of human life is to lose the ability to communicate and to suffer the greater loss of an awareness of dependence. A man without the body is not a human being.

Since we are most conscious of our bodily aspect there have been various theories of the relationship between body and the spiritual aspects of man.[7] A strict materialism will deny any spiritual element of man and try to explain all through the manipulation and control of genes and chromosomes. There is no doubt that there is an influence on the more spiritual aspects of man through the genes and chromosomes, but that is not a sufficient explanation of human life. An idealism will effectively remove the bodily from the domain of the truly human. This theory falls apart in the face of the irrevocable bond between the material and the psycho-spiritual existence. As we have already seen, there is an interpenetration of each dimension. A contemporary theory that sees the bodily as the symbol of the spiritual makes the most sense.[8]

In an understanding of symbolism the symbol is distinguished from the sign. The symbol is said to contain the reality it symbolizes, although not completely: the sign refers to the reality it signifies.[9] When this is applied to man, the spiritual and psychological aspect of man is the reality that is expressed in the bodily activity. The reality that is man, the person, is always more than any expression whether that be verbal or through activity and gestures or mode of life. But it is only in the bodily dimension that we can ever come to understand something of the reality that is a human person. The body is the symbol of man through which the nonmaterial reality, the person, is manifested. We can even say that a man has some control over the expression of himself; he can reveal what he wants to reveal. This is true, but only partially true. What a man is, is manifested in what he says and does. Some control is possible but not a complete control. Man cannot be only words or empty gestures; he cannot be someone and not manifest that someone. The expression that is body can never equal the reality that is person, but as symbol it contains that reality. We learn about the true person through the bodily expression. This theory of the relationship between the bodily and the nonmaterial aspect of man makes sense. It ties together the various dimensions of man and enhances the place of bodily expression.

The advantage of using a trichotomy in the explanation of the many aspects of human nature is the disclosure of the richness that is always present in human life. The disadvantage is that it tends to dissect and make man piecemeal. In every word that has been written concerning the multidimensional nature of man there is always the call to a more primordial unity. There is no such thing as body apart from psyche and spirit and vice versa. Man is one and so much one that all of his functions and possibilities are interrelated. Touch one and the others react. This is the basic insight from biblical anthropology that presents the many sides of man. The findings of contemporary psychology and philosophy add support to the earlier biblical images. The implications for a fuller Christian anthropology are varied. Two areas will be treated briefly: faith and Christian morality.

Christian Faith

Faith is the acceptance and commitment of the person to God as he has revealed himself in Jesus Christ. It is a free offer and a free response made from the very depths of a man's being.[10] It has become commonplace in contemporary theology to talk about the commitment of the total person in faith to God through Jesus Christ. We are no longer involved with an intellectual assent to the truths of faith accepted and believed as revealed; we are more concerned with the acceptance of a person and then the acceptance of what that person said. What is primary is the belief in the person.

All of this is to be found in theology books and articles, as well as in works on catechetics. In the light of this chapter, how can faith be said to be the commitment of the total person?

First, it can be said that if faith involves the whole person, then it necessarily is multidimensional, for such is the total person. Faith is fundamentally on the level of spirit. If it is through the spirit that man is related to God, then it is on that level that he is able to hear the Word of God and respond. The value to which the man seeks to commit himself in freedom is none other than the God who has revealed himself in Jesus of Nazareth. Faith demands self-awareness, as it demands freedom. It is impossible to believe and commit oneself unless one is first aware of oneself and aware of the possibility of commitment.

Faith also involves the level of the psychological. There is a noetic content to faith; it is not just a blind leap with no effort to seek understanding. There must be some content, some explanation of faith, however inadequate. Man seeks to know and to understand. In faith he hears the Word of God, seeks understanding and then, having made the Word personal, man speaks it to others. This involves the will. Man must respond and so there is a decision to accept the Word as it comes and a decision to speak the Word of God to others. Without the volitional activity in faith, there is no possibility of making the Word of God personal and no possibility to express the Word to others. There is also the emotional dimension of faith. Faith needs to grow and seeks expression on a human level. The possibility of feeling accompanies faith. Faith is a passion of love and desire and hope and joy and cannot be robbed of its emotional expression. In mystical religions, feeling plays an important role. In Christianity it should play an equally important role. The experience of union with God, which faith offers, is more than an intellectual, volitional, or even spiritual union. Union is an experience of the closeness of God, which is a state of the whole man. Every Christian is called to experience God in a tangible way. This is the goal of the Christian life and so involves the emotional aspect of man. Feeling should not be identified with faith, but should not be lacking in the experience of faith.

Faith is also bodily in its expression. We kneel, we bow, we cross ourselves, we are baptized, we receive communion, we pray together in words and gestures. Faith is not ethereal and abstract. Faith is human and shares in all of the dimensions of human life. Since man is bodily, so faith has its bodily expressions.

Morality

What is true for Christian faith is true for a Christian morality. Morality is possible only because man is spiritual and capable of accepting or refusing the significant values that are offered to him in a lifetime. Morality demands understanding and will; morality is affected positively and negatively by the emotional life of man. Morality is bodily and not just cerebral or volitional. If we attempt to speak of Christian morality as influencing and affecting the whole person, then we must include all the dimensions of the person in the discussion.

A basic insight into the freedom of man is the foundation for the contemporary understanding of fundamental and final option.[11] Man's orientation to God and his essential religious nature as well as his inability to reverse himself, easily account for the reinterpretation of mortal and serious sin.

On a more psychological level, the influence of emotions on decision and the lack of total freedom has helped moralists to evaluate the sinful condition of man and the meaning of Original Sin, as we have already seen. The man who is not multisided does not exist; a Christian morality that is not multisided is equally a phantom of the imagination. Even the tension that exists in the efforts to understand and develop as a person has encouraged thinking on tension morality.[12] Man is much too complex to discover a set of rules that will apply in every instance for every individual.

The final dimension that is present in relating faith and morality to the meaning of man as body, soul, and spirit, is that man is never complete in his life or activity. As man develops, so does faith and so does his moral stance in life. The final point of perfection is to come. This offers hope for all who are struggling to allow faith to permeate all of the human personality and respond to this presence of God through the moral activity of a good life. Man as someone to be realized in many dimensions is a blessing. Only gradually does he become the integrated person he is called to be.

Conclusion

Man as the image of God, destined for glory, is a unified and complex individual. The integration of all aspects of the human personality with the development of person in freedom is a task that is offered and a task that is hindered by his own failure and his sin. The reality of evil and the destruction of the person that takes place on a daily basis is discouraging to the person who is seeking to overcome the forces of destruction. The only way the person can develop is to believe in the possibility of future integration—a firm promise in the biblical understanding of man. It is not easy to allow the presence of God to permeate the human personality; it is not easy to respond in a perduring fashion in faith to the offer of God; it is not easy to respond to the values that are presented. When the believer sees the possibilities and gives firm assent to their feasibility, then the road to integration has begun. Body, soul, and spirit are each interrelated aspects of a single human life, each with its good qualities and each with its weakness and propensity to sin. Separation helps to understand the unity that is man's future, when he will be God's image in his total personality.

Notes

[1]Cf. M. Merleau-Ponty, *Phenomenology of Perception* (London: Routledge and Kegan Paul, 1962); Mary Rose Barral, *Merleau-Ponty: The Role of the Body-Subject in Interpersonal Relations* (Pittsburgh: Duquesne Univ. Press, 1965). Also: M. Savelsky, *Reflections on the Person from the Ethical Perception of M. Merleau-Ponty's Phenomenology of the Body-Subject* (Unpublished dissertation from Kathelieke Universiteit te Leuven), 1973.

[2]Cf. Mork, *op. cit.*, pp. 19-52.

[3]Cf. Karl Rahner, *Spirit in the World* (New York: Herder and Herder, 1968), pp. 290-297; *Hearers of the Word* (New York: Herder and Herder, 1969), pp. 53-70.

[4]Cf. Gregory Zilboorg, *Psychoanalysis and Religion* (New York: Farrar, Straus and Cudahy, 1962), p. 41. (In these pages the word "spirit" is used where Zilboorg uses "soul"; "soul" is used where Zilboorg uses "psyche.")

[5]Cf. Donceel, Ch. 5, 6, 10, 11.

[6]Cf. Jacques Sarano, *The Meaning of the Body* (Philadelphia: Westminster, 1966); Richard Zaner, *The Problem of Embodiment* (The Hague: Nijhoff, 1964); C. A. Van Peursen, *Body, Soul, Spirit: A Survey of the Body-Mind Problem* (New York: Oxford Univ. Press, 1966).

[7]Cf. Donceel, pp. 424-436.

[8]Cf. Karl Rahner, "The Theology of the Symbol," *Theological Investigations*, vol. IV (Baltimore: Helicon, 1966), pp. 245-252.

[9]*Ibid.*, pp. 228-229.

[10] The influence of faith on the total person is expressed well in Carlos Cirne-Lima, *Personal Faith* (New York: Herder and Herder, 1965), pp. 20-60.

[11]Cf. L. Londen, *Sin, Liberty and Law* (New York: Sheed and Ward, 1965), pp. 30-43.

[12]Cf. John Milhaven and David Casey, "Introduction to the Theological Background of the New Morality," *Theological Studies*, 28 (1967), pp. 213-244.

8

Male and Female

The difference between male and female reaches down to the roots of personal existence and destiny. To speak of the "self" or "person" always implies the sexual dimension. Sexuality is more fundamental than individual characteristics. No wonder that sexuality figures prominently in the thought of philosophers, psychologists, historians, and poets. It should also figure in any appreciation of man's relationship to his God. If Christianity offers an appreciation of human life then it must offer some understanding of this baffling aspect of the person.

The amount of material written these days on sexuality is beyond the capacity of any one person to read and understand. The interest in sex, the call for liberty in expression, in word and action, in all matters of sexuality, as well as the campaign for women's liberation, has generated a host of authorities on human sexuality propagating with equal authority every possible position. Here we are concerned with the biblical understanding of male and female in the hope that the Word of God may help the Christian believer as he is confronted with this particular quality and perfection of human life.

Human Sexuality

Usually sexuality is limited to the physical differences of male and female. In reality, human sexuality determines the spiritual and psychical life of man, as well as the physical. If we remained only on the level of the physical in the effort to understand male and female, much of the precise differentiation between man and the animal kingdom would be lost.[1] Man readily sees that the need for the experience of human love in sexuality, and love is more than just physical attraction. Moreover, it is through sexuality, and physical sexuality, that love is concretized and expressed, even if this is not the only way to express love.[2] Male and female is a difference that permeates all of human existence.

This embracing characteristic of human sexuality is especially evident in the development of self-consciousness. The more a man or woman grows in self-awareness, the more sexuality becomes part of the experience of the totality of human life. With the awakening of self in adolescence the sexual characteristic begins its intermingling of pleasure and pain, light and darkness, freedom and slavery. It is the source of "the human being's most intense pleasure and most pervasive anxiety."[3] Every aspect of life feels the power of sexuality and knows its ambiguity; all of which has led man into philosophical, anthropological, psychological, and sociological studies of human sexuality. This has also brought profound changes in the teaching of Christianity on sexuality as the concrete results of these studies became known and accepted and practiced within the context of Christian faith. Certainly no one can deny or fail to appreciate human sexuality as studied by secular sciences. In the Christian life, however, all of this must be viewed in light of the Word of God. For Christians, human sexuality fits within the framework of the biblical understanding of sexuality.

"Male and Female He Created Them"

The Book of Genesis simply states: "God created man in his own image; in the image of God he created him; male and female he created them" (Gen. 1:27). The statement is to the point: male and female are together the image of God. With this brief sentence a world of myth, of gnostic speculation, of cynicism and extreme asceticism in sexuality, as well as the deification and fear of sexuality, disappear. What is unusual about the attitude of the author of Genesis is his ability to say just enough and no more. Almost in all other statements about sexuality, man has said too much or too little. At times he has even cursed his sexuality, as anyone can attest. In the Bible the Word of God has linked sexuality with the image of God in man, and this merits thought. A review of some ideas already treated will enable us to appreciate more the male/female relationship.

The text in Genesis presents man as one with special dignity. This is particularly evident in light of the following verse:

> Let us make man in our own image, after our likeness, and let them have dominion over the fish of the sea and over the birds of the air and over the cattle and over all the earth, and over every creeping thing that creeps upon the earth. So God created man in his own image; and in the image of God he created him, male and female he created them. (1:26-27)

Male and female as created in the image of God share in his dominion over the earth. Together they are his vicegerents, taking his place in creation.[4] Further help in understanding this dignity of man comes in Psalm 8:

> Thou has made him little less than God and has crowned him with glory and honor; thou has given him dominion over the works of thy hand; thou has put all things under his feet. (5-6)

Man shares in the glory and majesty of God because he alone is created in his image; he shares in the glory of God because he manifests this glory in his dominion over the earth; he manifests this glory when he brings to his exercise of dominion the characteristic virtues of God himself: mercy and fidelity.[5] In the Old Testament as well as the New Testament, God's glory is the manifestation of his divinity, or the recognition of his holiness by men (1 Cor. 16:28; Ps. 96:7; Eph. 1:12; Phil. 1:11), or man's share and vision of his saving deeds (Isa. 35:2; 40:5; 59:19; Ps. 63:3). God is glorified when he is God to his people, when he expresses his covenantal attitude of mercy and fidelity. The New Testament presents Jesus as the glory of God (Phil. 2:11; Heb. 1:3). In him we have seen this glory:

> And the Word became flesh and dwelt among us, full of grace and truth; we have beheld his glory, glory as of the only Son of the Father. (John 1:14)

When we couple the full understanding of the glory of God as seen in Jesus of Nazareth[6] with the teaching of Genesis on male and female, it becomes clear that the complementarity of the sexes is fundamental to man's role of sharing in the glory of God through the manifestation of mercy and fidelity. Together male and female are sacred, together they have a responsibility in creation.

The first conclusion in the study of sexuality in the Bible situates male and female in supporting and complementing roles in creation.

"It Is Not Good for Man To Be Alone."

The complementarity of male and female is not restricted to their role in creation; they are also complementary to each other in their development. Man could have been created without this possibility of procreation and development through sexuality, but he was not. Man and woman are dependent on each other and unable to exist by themselves, unable to be totally autonomous and self-sufficient. "It is not good for man to be alone" (Gen. 2:18). In the presence of the constant danger of confusing himself with his Creator, it is good for man to have a part in an arrangement that most fundamentally binds two beings to each other and makes them dependent on each other and supplemented by each other. The arrogant idea of self-sufficient man is effectively eliminated in the need of man for woman and the need of woman for man. In no place is this so evident than in the act of procreation in which the creature shares most fully in the creativity of God and experiences the need for another. Once again with a simple word the Bible demolishes the deification and fear of sex and places it in the perspective of the mutual dependence of male and female.[7]

"They Saw They Were Naked."

The beginning of this Chapter mentioned the ambiguity of sexuality: the mixture of pain and pleasure, light and darkness, acceptance and rejection. What is recognized in human life, and attested to by psychologists, finds expression in the Bible with the words: "They saw that they were naked" (Gen. 3:7); "And I was afraid, because I was naked and I hid myself" (Gen. 3:10). The experience of sexuality points to a rent in the harmony of the sexes that the Bible relates to a primitive Fall: "And the man and his wife were both naked and were not ashamed" (Gen. 2:25). In all genuine love there is a longing that cannot be satisfied and a lack of harmony that cannot be explained only through faulty sex education.[8] Somehow man has experienced a tear in his human sexuality that defies a total mending. This does not mean that the Bible considers sexuality or the polarity of male and female as sin. Rather, sin has entered into the sexual relationship in such a way that the spirituality of male and female, as expressed in their sexuality, has become separated and is in need of harmony. The actual experience of male and female today, as in the time of the author of Genesis, causes anxiety in trying to relate the spiritual element of the person with the sexuality as personally experienced. This does not lessen the need and desire for sexual fulfillment but points to the disharmony of the original balance of the male/female relationship. Man has fallen away from genuine love and from the realm of the personal and, in this falling away from the acceptance and the need of each other, man and woman experience greed and selfishness in their sexual relations. The Bible accepts the lack of harmony and offers the possibility of repairing the damage by a return to complete love, made possible when man and woman see themselves in need of each other and in need of their God, and seek union with their God through a union of love with each other. It is a goal that is offered and it is in need of acceptance.

In Genesis the marriage union is not presented as destroyed by the power of evil and sin but it is greatly weakened. In the now shattered world, human love no longer will lead directly to the love of God. Marriage as the sacrament of the first creation has lost its power to unite all things in God. For this there was needed a new creation. The author of Genesis knew that the ideal for marriage willed by God had never been realized. Even among God's chosen people divorce was accepted as a harsh but inescapable reality. Woman was a second-class citizen in almost all of the books of the Bible, outside of Genesis. She became just another possession of man. It might even be wondered why the author of Genesis presented such an exalted picture of the relationship between man and woman if it has never been realized and apparently could never be realized. Here it is essential to recall that the narratives of Genesis are not simply nostalgic tales but hopes of what might be. The paradise of Genesis with man and woman in peace and harmony is a picture of what God intended and still intends for his creation. Man's sinfulness could frustrate the plan, but only for a time. A second Adam would gather together the broken fragments of human life and restore the harmony between man and woman. Through Jesus Christ the unity could be restored:

> There does not exist among you Jew or Greek, slave or freeman, male or female. All are one in Christ Jesus. (Gal. 3:28)

New Testament Teaching

Christ rejects the practice of divorce by appealing to the ideal of marriage in Genesis:

> Some Pharisees came up to him and said, to test him, "May a man divorce his wife for any reason whatever?" He replied, "Have you not read that at the beginning the Creator made them male and female and declared, For this reason a man shall leave his father and mother and cling to his wife, and the two shall become as one? Thus, they are no longer two but one flesh. Therefore, let no man separate what God has joined." They said to him, "Then why did Moses command divorce and the promulgation of a divorce decree?" "Because of your stubbornness Moses let you divorce your wives," he replied; "but at the beginning it was not that way. I now say to you, whoever divorces his wife (lewd conduct is a separate case) and marries another commits adultery, and the man who marries a divorced woman commits adultery." (Matt. 19:3-9)

The Pharisees objected that this ideal had never been the practice. Moses himself made explicit provision for the practice in the law. Christ does not dispute with their opinion. During the long history of God's people, certain provisions had to be made for selfishness and hardness of heart, but now the time had come for a new creation and a restoration of the relationship between man and woman. Christ returned to the ideal that was presented in Genesis, an ideal that was completely beyond a humanity infected with evil and sin, but now a new age was inaugurated. Jesus would make it possible for a man to cling to his woman and together they would become one flesh and mirror the glory of God. The lost harmony would be restored. All of creation would feel the effects of the presence of Jesus; man and woman would be restored.[9]

Jesus the risen and exalted Lord healed and reconciled broken lives. He restored to man and woman the possibility of genuine and perduring love so that the ideal of marriage was no longer hopeless. What was even more wonderful, the union between man and woman could be the sign of the union between Jesus and his Church. Just as the Old Testament had used the marriage image to portray the union between God and his people, the union of two in one flesh now can spring into a love that gradually transforms the spouses into the image of Christ and can thus transform the whole world:

> Defer to one another out of reverence for Christ. Wives should be submissive to their husbands as if to the Lord, because the husband is head of his wife just as Christ is head of his body the church, as well as its savior. As the church submits to Christ, so wives should submit to their husbands in everything.
>
> Husbands, love your wives, as Christ loved the church. He gave himself up for her to make her holy, purifying her in the bath of water by the power of the word, to present to himself a glorious church, holy and immaculate, without stain or wrinkle or anything of that sort. Husbands should love their wives as they do their own bodies. He who loves his wife loves himself. Observe that no one ever hates his own flesh; no, he nourishes it and takes care of it as Christ cares for the church —for we are members of his body. "For this reason a man shall leave his father and mother, and shall cling to his wife, and the two shall be made into one."
>
> This is a great foreshadowing; I mean that it refers to Christ and the church. In any case, each one should love his wife as he loves himself, the wife for her part showing respect for her husband. (Eph. 5:21-33)

Husbands love their wives and give themselves up for them; wives are subject to their husbands not in a subservient role, but dependent on their husbands as the Church is dependent on Jesus Christ. When this is realized, the ideal of Genesis becomes a fact of human life.

What does this mean? Male and female he created them and together they are the image of God. Human sexuality reaches down to the very roots of existence and must be actualized and realized. Man is made to be complemented by woman, as woman is complemented by man, and in this acceptance and fulfillment of his complementarity he mirrors what he is: one who is in need of another and who finds fulfillment and peace in another. Unfortunately the harmony of the sexes is an ideal to be achieved and it is not something given. The male/female relationship suffers from the presence of evil and sin and can be overcome only through much effort in much time. When achieved, the harmony of the sexes is the sign of the total harmony that man should experience with the universe and his God. The development is arduous and a process in which sexuality is humanized and personalized. This ideal is what Jesus of Nazareth offers to his followers, and when it is achieved, man becomes what he should be.

Sexual Morality

Morality is concerned with how a person lives his or her life: the choice of the good and the noble and the true, or the acceptance of their opposites. Christian morality is based on the Gospel of Jesus Christ and presupposes an effort to live a life with others that is consonant with the lived teaching of Jesus himself. Sexual morality in the Gospels and other writings of the New Testament is not spelled out in great detail. Only the broad strokes of living according to the Spirit of God through a following of Christ are offered to the believer. Sexuality is accepted as part of human life, a dimension in need of harmony and integration. When the Spirit of God fills a person, then sexuality is personalized and there are no problems of morality. The key to understanding Christian sexuality as lived experience is to personalize and integrate sexuality through the power of the Spirit of God.

Many of the problems of sexuality are involved in the failure to personalize. Any reduction of sexuality to genital sexuality is a failure to personalize and allow the other dimensions of human life to influence genital sexuality. In every case, man's great sinfulness in matters of sexuality can be traced to his propensity to make impersonal this most personal aspect of his life. Using people, even using himself in an impersonal way, causes the problems. Without personal love, sexuality is not human.

In the past, Christian morality was limited almost exclusively to sexual morality with a corresponding failure to recognize the problems that face any person in the arduous task of integrating and personalizing sexuality. Too often the sexual dimension in man was considered as nonexistent or merely tolerated instead of being seen as a great gift that offers opportunities for enrichment of the human spirit in relationship with others. The belief that man and woman were together the image of God was overlooked in an effort to root out every speck of evil and sin in the male/female relationship to the detriment of the relationship itself.

Sexual morality today has taken a different turn. It is readily admitted that sexuality colors all of human existence, not in the sense of genital sexuality but in the sense of man's need for woman and woman's need for man. Arguments on what is permitted and what is possible appear endless as Christian moralists try to respond to the ambiguity of sexuality in everyone's life. The solution is not to multiply distinctions, but rather to return to a simpler biblical approach of complimentarity and the need to personalize sexuality. It remains one, though very important, dimension of the human personality. It is to be integrated by the firm acceptance of its existence, coupled with the desire to personalize sexuality. The return to the Bible and its approach to sexuality may help powerfully in the solution of some of contemporary society's questions on sexuality.

Sexual differentiation permeates the whole of human existence. Masculinity is not limited to a genital function, nor is femininity. The biological differences are not just one compartment of human life without influence on any other area. The chemical, glandular, and functional aspects of human sexuality affect the psychological and spiritual nature of the person as well. While there is surely great discussion these days on the role of social conditioning and differentiation of the sexes, all the conditioning possible cannot prescind from biological differences. If we strive to see the person in a totality, then there must be an influence in every aspect of human life coming from such a fundamental dimension as sex.

The woman's role in life is different from a man's. The possibility and actuality of motherhood brings about a relationship to life that cannot be the same for the male. Even on a strictly chemical and physical level, the monthly changes in a woman's body affect her personality and cannot be overlooked.

The closeness to life that a woman experiences can cause a false sense of bondage. Many times woman can be content to live a life limited and circumscribed by the home and a family. In many instances this limitation is imposed by the male, but too often it is easily and quickly accepted by the female.

Male characteristics often give birth to arrogance, with a sense of being completely free. The man can tend to seek objectification and in so doing, become harsh. If it is a feminine characteristic to be falsely bound, it is a masculine characteristic to be arrogantly free.

Certainly no one should claim that any individual is lacking some of the qualities and characteristics of the opposite sex. Every man has some of what we term feminine characteristics and every woman has some of the "so-called" masculine characteristics. The human person runs the spectrum of qualities with personalities of extreme femininism and extreme masculinity, something more to be lamented than blessed. If mention is here made of such characteristics, it is because the majority of people have tendencies in a definite direction. General characteristics are good generally, and not exclusively.

If there is true complementarity, then the tendencies of masculine and feminine personalities are part of that mutual interaction just as they bring problems and false positions in the relationship. Complementarity between male and female does not imply superiority, but difference. Male needs female and vice versa. One perfects the other in outlook and nuances and tendencies. Imperfections become accepted and modified as there is a mutual exchange in life. Male and female are always in need of each other as they strive to live out a life in which there is a continual return to a genuine love that alone will overcome the lack of harmony and the pain that persists in their relationship. To celebrate and enjoy the differences is one of the beauties of human life.

The modern movement for feminism has done much to emancipate woman and overcome some of the hindrances to the development of the meaning of woman. Often, however, it has gone to the opposite extreme, claiming that the only difference between man and woman is biological and social conditioning. This is the failure to see how much the difference of sex colors human existence. There is no need for claiming sameness in the struggle for equality. It must be admitted that man has dominated history, culture, and the conditions of law and education for the most selfish of reasons and short-sighted motives. Woman has been riveted to her natural destiny and limited to that position, which has prevented her from the development of her spirit as one who is called to reflect in her specific difference the image of God. Woman is still a slave of man in many respects and has a long struggle before she attains her freedom. We know much more of the meaning of man than the meaning of woman since man has been given many more opportunities and freedom to develop and express his masculine qualities. This is yet to be actualized for the woman. In spite of this crying need, it would prove ultimately disastrous for both men and women if all of the drive for freedom and expression in the feminist movement is directed to attaining equality without difference. Once again it is the Christian Scriptures that offer assistance.

If we start with the biblical concept of spirit expressing itself in matter and concentrate on the interrelationship of humanity, the meaning of existence is not an impersonal culture but a being in love and being in community as male and female. The relationship of the sexes becomes consequential for human destiny. Instead of a difference in degree between male and female, there is a difference in kind; instead of thinking in terms of stages of development, we think of parallel terms. To be a woman is to be human and at times inhuman in a different way than man. A woman is not less human or less inhuman. There is a right and wrong on both sides of the relationship with an eternal struggle between man and woman waged with passion and resolved only in time and with much sacrifice. The primal truth is always the same: male and female are together the image of God. This cuts away the inferiority and elevates both to a complimentarity. The Creator has made man and woman not with different values but different kinds of values that are in need of each other. Each is called to develop as person to live in love in the same degree, but in different ways. The man will often shape life but he will depend on his woman to unite life.

Some may complain that there is too often a subordinate role in the sexual relationship. There is a different function but not a difference in value. The special possibility to serve life as a woman is a privilege and not a humiliation. We have already seen that the attitude of the Bible sees woman as a helpmate, but not in the sense of subservience. Mutual service is the supreme proof of the helpmate as well as the proof of a mature and developed human life. From the center of mutual service there should issue forth a transformation of all values derived from him who came to minister to and not be ministered to and who by that mode of service revealed the meaning of life.

In a world that often tends to deify sex and in a Church that often approaches sex with caution and alarm, the sober remarks of Genesis remain a firm mooring for the one who is trying to live a Christian life and integrate his sexuality into that belief:

> God created man in his image; in the divine image he created him; male and female he created them. (Gen. 1:27)

Notes

[1]Cf. D. Morris, *The Naked Ape* (New York: McGraw-Hill, 1967), pp. 43-84. The author considers man only as an animal, which is the chief weakness of the book.

[2]Cf. E. Brunner, *Man In Revolt* (Philadelphia: Westminster, 1947), p. 347.

[3]Rollo May, *Love and Will* (New York: Norton, 1969), p. 38.

[4]Cf. G. Von Rad, *Old Testament Theology*, vol. I (London: Oliver and Boyd, 1962), p. 146.

[5]Cf. J. L. McKenzie, "Glory," *Dictionary of the Bible* (Milwaukee: Bruce, 1965), pp. 313-315.

[6]Cf. John F. O'Grady, *Jesus, Lord and Christ*, ch. IX.

[7]The New Testament continues the doctrine of mutual dependence and service, especially in Ephesians 5 where Paul compares the male-female relationship of Christ and his Church. A similar relationship between Yahweh and Israel is seen in the Song of Songs.

[8]Cf. Rollo May, *Love and Will* (New York: Norton, 1969), p. 39.

[9]The meaning of "except for unchastity" has long been discussed in Scripture and theology. Cf. A. Mahoney. "A New Look at the Divorce Clauses in Matthew 5:32; 19:9," *Catholic Biblical Quarterly*, 30 (1968), pp. 29-38; T. Fleming, "Christ and Divorce," *Theological Studies*, 24 (1963), pp. 106-120.

9

Man as History: Individual and Corporate Existence

The present age seems to have finally discovered history. Man is time and lives in a world of time; he is history as an evolving world continues to envelope him.[1] The great surprise is that man has always been history and time, and so will he remain.

Earlier visions of human existence admitted historical development; that is too obvious to deny. Nevertheless, man continued to think that he was impervious to history; his nature was static; it was the same for the cavemen, for the Greeks and Romans, the man of the high Renaissance and the man of mortar and steel and nuclear fission. Man drifted through a sea of movement and change, but was relatively untouched; he was born, lived, and died. So the process continued without ever affecting the fundamental structure of human "nature."

The Bible tells us that God is the Lord of history and has entered history in Jesus, his Son. God's ways with men created a true history of salvation. The event of Christ was prepared for many centuries in Israel's growing religious awareness. History was made when Christ was preceded and anticipated in the hopes of the Jewish people for the Messiah. With the advent of Jesus a new dimension was added to man's religious hopes: a final revelation of the Kingdom of God would come. Christianity became a historical religion, based on the influx of movement and change and becoming. Man was moving out and onward into a destiny that he was pulling into the present.[2]

In intervening years the biblical outlook seems to have been lost in favor of a more static and unchanging consideration of human nature. Time and its influence on human life became a peripheral issue with concentration placed on the essential and unchanging elements of human nature. If we could discover what is properly man's and his alone, then this could be applied to all men of all times and places without being affected by the presence of time and space.

The twentieth century has rejected this unchanging aspect of man and has returned to an appreciation of time. Man is not static in his nature; he is dynamic and developing, becoming more than what he ever was with a newness of being. Individuals change and become; so also the human race changes and becomes. This is the new insight into life proffered today, which is in truth a very old insight. It offers great value since it challenges and prods and evokes a response. It is the basis for a future hope and the sure cure for pessimism and discouragement. As long as man can be other than what he is, hope springs eternal.

There are dangers as well. If this chapter emphasizes the advantages, it does not minimize the problems. When an age has discovered history, the danger is to espouse historical relativism. This must be avoided. Man is history but is not an indefinite, drifting whimsical stream of life. Real growth can never be completely unpredictable. In every development, which is a true becoming and not merely change,[3] there is a fundamental identity that evolves itself in continuity with what has been. To understand the meaning of man as time, as well as avoid historical relativism, we must talk about the meaning of history as well as the individual and corporate existence of man.

Man in History

When we consider man in history, the immediate foundation for such a consideration is the desire to see man in his situation. The term "situation" is somewhat recent in philosophy, but like many other ideas, has a long tradition. It connotes the concrete conditions surrounding man, the phenomena to be studied. There are different periods of a man's life, different social conditions, backgrounds, and education. The more traditional meaning of *situs* usually connotes the place where man is located, a physical dimension of human life. Modern philosophy includes the psychological location of man as well. Situation involves man caught in time and caught in place, affected and affecting both. Time and space make man historical.[4]

In the early Middle Ages, theologians considered man as being immersed in history and engaged in a series of events that influenced the road he travelled from an initial deed to a final destination. Somehow what man would eventually become depended on all of the intervening events and decisions rendered meaningful in the last and definitive act. Time was not an indifferent succession of events, but an organized sequence. The basis for this thinking was the Bible.

The Bible was a record of the sacred history of humanity. It described man as a traveler completely oriented toward God as his final and historic destiny. God had entered history in a final and definitive way with Jesus Christ and now all of human history was influenced by his presence. Christianity rejected the cyclic notion of Greek history in favor of history as the expression of man's responsibility to implement God's plan, with life or death as the final heritage. The Bible saw time as the progression and continuous maturation of man in light of the Word of God. The believer in the Bible saw himself beginning as a creation of God, progressing through life, and reaching a final goal. Time and history were as much a part of life as was the air that a man breathes.[5]

The biblical orientation to man in history was not, however, the chief basis for later medieval reflection on time. That basis was provided by Augustine. What was read in the Middle Ages were his treatises, with less attention to his *City of God* and *The Confessions*. These latter works portrayed the great bishop's thought on time much more accurately than his other works. The result was that the medieval thinkers accepted a modified Augustianism that was little more than Neoplatonism. Change is considered in the Platonic system as an imperfection; man in his more spiritual nature must strive to maintain relative immobility. The concrete conclusion was the failure on the part of medieval thinkers to accord time and history its full measure. They often discounted becoming and regarded change and mutability as a misfortune from which man must free himself. Man was seen to exist more properly in an immutable eternity with history as only a temporary scaffolding.[6]

The reading of the Bible encouraged Thomas Aquinas and the Victorines to reject this idealism of Augustine. These men afforded to created beings their existential density and in so doing created the necessary condition for the understanding of man as historical. Time enters into the very definition of man as the essential coordinate of his existence in the world. Creation continues in time and man is in time as a cooperator with the Creator. It is unfortunate that Thomas Aquinas did not develop his understanding of man in history in a more complete fashion. Even he was influenced by an essentialistic philosophy that saw man as participating in an immutable essence even while caught in history. For Thomas the paradox was never resolved. For his commentators, it was resolved more in favor of the essential and unchanging nature of man, with man in history falling once again into shadows.[7]

The Christian Meaning of History

There is no particular Christian philosophy of history; there is only a Christian understanding of history.[8] The Bible sees man not as an isolated individual but rather as part of the history of mankind as a whole; he is an individual called by God to share in his glory, but called as a member of a community, caught in time and becoming in space. The same Scriptures see man as not just historical in the sense of inevitable process but see history as made up of decisive moments on the part of God and man. The Christian idea of person and the Christian idea of history are complementary; each requires the other. In the Christian understanding of history the contradiction between the temporal and sinful world and the eternal will of God is overcome by concrete events. Redemption is a real, historical event involving the entrance of the Word of God into space and time. The content of Christian faith is a historical person, Jesus of Nazareth. Even the acceptance of faith, the hearing and the response, is historical, caught in particular space and time, without which there is no possibility for being a Christian. There is a Christian understanding of human history that starts with the event of the incarnation. Everything depends on this historical intervention of God and all of human history must be related to this event. Jesus of Nazareth determines the historical character of personal existence as well as the personal character of history, for with him a decision has been made that has changed the present and the future of mankind.[9]

The Person as Historical

The Romans referred to history as *Res Gestae*, things that have been done. Action is the element of history. The characteristic element of history is not that things happened, but that something was done; history is made where personal decisions are made. This gives the character of uniqueness and unrepeatableness to the historical situation; this distinguishes history from what happens in nature. Decision alone separates what took place afterward from what was previous. Julius Caesar knew the meaning of history when he crossed the Rubicon: *"Alea jacta est"* ("The die is cast!") The historical quality of existence is the quality of decision.[10]

For the Christian, person is not a being in eternal repose nor does person grow naturally as the flowers grow. Person is being in decision; human life is a decisive answer to a destiny full of responsibility. What a person has been influences what he is and what he will be. There is no decision that does not imply consequences for the individual as well as for others. Its gravity is seen in the understanding of the past.

For the Greeks the past meant nothing. In a cyclic understanding of history the past does not exist as past but only as part of an eternal return. For the Christian the past is the honor and the guilt that he bears. The believer is determined by his past since he has been made through decisions that are never completely lost. One who does not take the past seriously always thinks that he can start fresh without the influence of what has been. To take the past seriously shows the seriousness of history and decision.

The Christian who must take the past seriously could very well despair if he has only his personal decisions in his consciousness. For the believer the past is fraught with sin and failure that still influence the present. If this were all, then the future could not look promising. But the past is also influenced by the decision of God and the decision of Jesus Christ:

> Even when you were dead in sin and your flesh was uncircumcised, God gave you new life in company with Christ. He pardoned all our sins. He canceled the bond that stood against us with all its claims, snatching it up and nailing it to the cross. (Col. 2:13-14)

God has forgiven us all our sins in the death of his Son. The Christian can always start again without any fear of having the decision on the part of God and his Christ overcome by man's personal decision. The future of mankind is good because it has been decided irrevocably by the decisive entrance of God into human history in the incarnation of his Son. Even here, however, there is a need for an understanding and making personal the decision for or against God through the acceptance or rejection of Jesus Christ. This personal decision will determine all that the Christian ever does. What will follow for him as well as for the human race will be influenced by the final Word of God in Jesus Christ. Compared with this decision on the part of God, and the decision to accept Jesus Christ, all other decisions are relativized. The once-and-for-all event has already taken place; the power of evil is overcome:

> His death was death to sin, once for all; his life is life for God. (Rom. 6:10)

Jesus is the decisive answer of God to human history offering himself and making perfect the human response to God:

> Unlike the other high priests, he has no need to offer sacrifice day after day, first for his own sins and then for those of the people; he did that once for all when he offered himself. For the law sets up as high priests men who are weak, but the word of the oath which came after the law appoints as priest the Son, made perfect forever. (Heb. 7:27-28)

Through our relationship to this historical event, our past is stamped and our present is marked in favor of a good future. As decision is the fundamental element of human history, the decision on the part of God and Jesus Christ has been made in favor of man and now must be made personal by individuals.

The second element of human history is community.[11] Existence with others makes history. History is a destiny for community as it is a community of personal decisions. There is always a continuity between generations, a historical heritage. Man is in need of historical consciousness that arises from a strong sense of tradition. One who disowns his own past will take still less into account the past of others; he will think of himself as an isolated individual, which will destroy the historical sense of personal life. The meaning of being historical is solidarity with others as well as decision-making.

Christian thought is most conscious of the community dimension of human life and history. Men are called to share in the life of God as members of a community whose fate has already been determined by the Word of God; individuals must commit themselves to live a community life of prayer and good works and contribute to the holiness of God's people. We are now one in Christ:

> There does not exist among you Jew or Greek, slave or freeman, male or female. All are one in Christ Jesus. (Gal. 3:28)

Our solidarity shows itself in the Christian willingness to live in favor of community, to stand for every human being. We are united with all people through our love that we have already received from the life, death, and resurrection of Jesus Christ. Men are united and walls are broken down when they turn from their selfishness and decide in favor of the other. This is history: decisions made in and for community.

The Personal Meaning of History

Christianity professes that the meaning of life and the course of human history is found in the experience of persons. Nature is only the stage on which the relationship of person to person, and in particular, the relationship of man as person and God is played out. There is a consciousness of solidarity of the human race, a conviction of human sinfulness and a greater belief in a common redemption. Instead of an everlasting process of nature, the drama of world history is a temporal course of freely willed activities of persons in community. There is a vital connection between the personal and the historical.

Ancient peoples often regarded the circle as the essential symbol: there was a firm belief that nothing new really happens. The ancient Jews refused to accept this nonhistorical appreciation of human life. The Lord God of Israel was the God of the covenant and this covenant with God was the content of history. History is what takes place between God and his people. No other nation understood history or religion in this sense.[12] In accordance with this belief, Israel saw its own life in terms of the personal. The main concern of the national life of Israel was not to be centered on culture or civilization or conquest, but the obedience of a nation to God and the unity of the members of that nation with one another based on their relationship to God. From the beginning the ethos of Israel was personal and social, manifested in the twofold commandment of love of God and neighbor:

> Therefore, you shall love the Lord, your God, with all your heart, and with all your soul, and with all your strength. (Deut. 6:5)

> Take no revenge and cherish no grudge against your fellow countrymen. You shall love your neighbor as yourself. I am the LORD. (Lev. 19:18)

Whenever Israel failed in her responsibility to the personal covenant and trusted more in her alliances with the nations, she suffered the wrath of God. History was personal and involved the personal response to a God who had intervened on her behalf. It was his plan—and it was a good plan—and not blind fate that ruled human life and destiny.

The personal understanding of history was completed in Jesus Christ. History does not mean the history of one group of people with God, but indeed is a history of humanity derived from God and going to God. Every individual and every human community is a fully qualified member of the whole. The new people of God are not bound by any natural presuppositions; all are called to share in the glory of God, since all are made for Jesus Christ (Col. 1:15-

20). Every appearance or possibility of a collective blind destiny has been destroyed; there is a new way of existence offered to every man, and this is inaugurated, not by a cosmic catastrophy, but by the advent of Jesus of Nazareth. In him the will and love of God is revealed; in him history and eternity have become united just as in him the human and the divine are joined. In him there is the meaning of the origin and the end of the world:

> In him everything in heaven and on earth was created, things visible and invisible, whether thrones or dominations, principalities or powers; all were created through him, and for him. (Col. 1:16)

He is the meaning of history, and he is not an abstract principle; Jesus of Nazareth is personal. In the love that he gives to men the union and communion between God and man and the union of all persons among themselves have been realized. The goal of human destiny was revealed as a common destiny of peace and harmony (Eph. 1:1-14). He disclosed the plan of God and realized it in himself. In him there is present what human history is called to be: God and man are united and men are united with one another, all through personal decision. A human life, which included a human death, is the disclosure and the foundation of the actual realization and end of human history. The cycle of the external return has been broken; the line of history is extended; it has a beginning and an end that is Jesus Christ.

Person Is Historical, Human History Is Personal, Is the Message of Christianity

This chapter began with the assertion that man is caught in history, progressing and developing as he moves through his decisions in community. We have also seen that man is becoming and developing in his personality and his freedom. The ideas are closely related, because man is historical, bound in space and time; his decisions are time-conditioned, equally caught in space and time. There is no final or irrevocable decision until man has exercised his final and irrevocable option. Decisions may perdure, they may be intended to last, but there is never a total commitment by man to anyone or anything as long as he lives. There is only the time-conditioned commitment. Even the life of Jesus can be seen as fulfilled and finalized only in his death. Until that event, his decisions were time-conditioned as are ours.[13] Some may react that this is man's tragedy; it is equally his glory. As long as man is in history, he has the possibility of development and change; this prevents him from making a total once-and-for-all decision in favor of the good, in favor of God; it equally prevents him from making the same decision in favor of evil.[14] It is not without import that the Gospel messages call us continually to repentance, to change our way of living, to look at life differently and begin anew. Conversion is not a once-and-for-all thing; it is a life-long process. How easy it would be if the decision made in Christianity were once and for all; but that would not be human. Man never does anything in a total or complete way; he is too immersed in history and too dependent on history as he works out his own life. The possibility of sin and virtue presupposes the possibility of becoming. That involves history.

Individual and Corporate Existence

We usually do not think of individual and corporate existence in terms of history. If decision is the basis for history and community is the presupposition of history, then the person who makes the decision has an individual as well as corporate existence. Human existence is personal and corporate at the same time and with the same intensity. Man was created by God as a responsible person and as a member of the human family with a corporate responsibility. Man is "I" and "We" because both constitute a fundamental aspect of human existence.

Individual Existence

The decisions that make up history are made by individuals. In a Christian context, man's call to respond to the Word of God makes man the individual set apart from the masses and independent. At first sight individual existence may seem to have nothing to do with responsibility. In reality it has much to do with responsibility. Man alone among all the entities of nature is aware of his exclusive identity with himself; he is self-conscious, which involves responsibility for self-existence. Man is responsible to God, to himself, and to others, for his self-existence as well as the self-existence of others.

What separates man from the animals and the individual from the group is the call of God. God calls each person by name and never confuses his creatures; he has not created a person as just an example of the species, but as one particular person whom he loves and destines for glory and communion with himself. God values the individual person and will not exchange one person for another; he is the Good Shepherd who leaves the flock to look for the lost sheep (Luke 15:3-7). God never depreciates one person for the sake of another; he gives his rain and sun to all in like measure and has created man to share in his own personal world:

> When I behold your heavens, the work of your fingers, the moon and the stars which you set in place—What is man that you should be mindful of him; or the son of man that you should care for him? (Ps. 8:4-5)

God has called man as an individual to responsibility, and that call to respond is unconditional and demanding. There is a task given to the individual that can never be fulfilled by anyone else. This is why every man is indispensible; none can be replaced. God gives the call and the task that is directed personally and uniquely. Man is not just one of the group. This responsibility, which is personal, brings man to the fullest appreciation of his isolation. At the core of man's being is a metaphysical aloneness; the individual belongs to God and is called by God and cannot be replaced. The life given is personal life as a gift and can be completed only when the gift is returned. It was Augustine who prayed: "You have made us for yourself, O God, and our hearts can never rest until they rest in you." The profound appreciation of man's isolation prompted Kierkegaard to remark:

> When I stand before God I am unconditionally an individual. Here is absolute eternal solitude in which no Christian fellowship can be of help; I am alone face to face with my God. I must believe, must decide, must hear the electing Word of

God, and no church, no priest, no Bible, can take this responsibility from me.[15]

Often men may try to escape this responsibility. It is impossible. When a man tries to have others decide for him, he is deceiving himself and will destroy himself. Even to refuse to decide is a decision. The individual is responsible for every detail of his life and can take no refuge in others. Man is free to decide. He can say "yes" or "no" but in every case he has decided and is responsible. He is called accountable to God who has first called him; he is accountable to himself and must accept the consequences of his decision; he is accountable to others who are affected by his decision. More often it is easier to avoid responsibility than to accept it. This is only the short view of life. Kierkegaard offered the final blow to the avoidance of decisions. Man will one day stand before his God and answer for his life.

Corporate Existence

It is the paradox of Christianity and of life that what gives man an absolute value as a self also places him just as absolutely in community and demands that he live with others. The individual shares a corporate existence. All that exists is connected existence. The world is united in biological and anthropological strains; there are national connections and interdependence; there is blood relationship, but community is present only in and through free decision. Man is called to community and is forced to live in dependence on others, but it is only through his personal choice that true community arises. The paradox is that the more a man chooses to love and live in community, the more he realizes his own individuality.[16]

Greek philosophy regarded friendship as the basis of community. Christianity regards love as the basis. Friendship depends on shared value, or sympathy, and involves exclusiveness. The New Testament basis of community can never be friendship; it is based rather on acceptance of the other, and wishing the other well, promoting the other and acknowledging the beauty and the goodness of the other. It is this love that God has revealed in the sending of his Son.

God created man primarily for a union with himself and so man is never totally alone, but man is also created for communion with his fellow-men. A covenant has been established that calls men together to share a life in union with God. It is God's people who exist as well as God's chosen members of that people. The calling of man has also accomplished the calling together of men; the *klasis* (calling) issues in the *ekklesia* (community called). Man can fulfill himself when he lives in love, and this is possible because of the gift of God. All that is human is disposed for this community by the Creator. Man is so created that he can become the individual only through the other. The "I" becomes the "I" through the "Thou." Human life is the mutual exchange of giving and receiving. It involves the Gospel axiom that states: "Whoever will save his life will lose it and whoever will lose his life will save it" (Matt. 16:25). Personal existence, corporate existence, sacrifice, and self-sacrifice belong to one another. Love combines the challenge of sacrifice for the sake of the other, with the call to find oneself. The two ideas are one.

The Individual and Humanity

Person is created for community and this is why we have the individual who needs others. How then can we consider our common humanity? Does Christianity have anything to offer for an appreciation of humanity?

An enthusiasm for humanity is common to many people and many societies. There is nothing specifically Christian about interest in all that is human. In fact, Christianity is often accused of disinterest in humanity and in humanism. If concern for humanity is based on man's achievements, or creative powers, or control over nature, then that concern must be short-lived. The death and destruction of the wars of this century, the use of creative powers and talents to further the control of evil and destruction, the misuse and abuse of nature, does not augur well for any future of humanity. We are on the brink of despair if we have no future other than ourselves. Religion alone offers an antidote to this despair.

Christianity believes that the common heritage we have as members of the human race is based on the unity of mankind in origin and in goal. Man is created in the image of God and is destined to share in his glory. Moreover we believe that the revelation of God in Jesus of Nazareth is also the revelation of humanity. In him we have learned the destiny of man and have learned the meaning of living a human life for the sake of others. This unity in origin and destiny is completely independent of all biological, paleontological, and scientific findings. Humanity may never be a unity from the point of view of the zoologist, but humanity is one in the sense of *humanitas*, the shared origin by a creating God and the shared destiny of communion with one another and with this God.

There is a Christian humanism based not on the achievements of mankind but on the incarnation of Jesus Christ which points back to man as created in the image of God. Man is singled out by his Creator in an unparalleled way as one in whom creation reaches its peak and whose redemption is the meaning and goal of human history. Man, not the male or female, not the talented or untalented, the black or the white or the yellow or brown or red, is the bearer of spiritual value. All who bear the human face are of God. The only thing that matters is whether man returns in his freedom and through his decision to his origin, or chooses to remain in his alienation and in opposition to the Word of God. The meaning of man's being is not secured in something that cannot be altered, but is secured in a perduring decision in favor of his God. Man is the individual person, called in time with others to respond to his God and become what he is always destined to become: one with others and one with his God.

Conclusion

To be human is to be time-conditioned as an individual who is also part of a community. No escape is possible. Rather than flee from what is pervading human life, the developing and becoming person revels in his own historicity, believing that at no age or at no level has the final goal been reached. As long as man is alive, the possibility is offered to move into a different future. Nor can man settle for a totally isolated existence. The pull to others and community based on a loving and free decision is too strong to overcome. Man needs others to understand and love what he is himself. The possibility of history and time offers the continuous unfolding of what might be. Somehow as the individual moves through life he maintains the divinely fashioned uniqueness that is his, and he discovers himself as never-again-to-be-repeated through a relationship with others. History and time make this possible, for without it, man would be condemned to settle down and learn to live without richness. That would never be human, nor could it ever be divine.

Notes

[1]Cf. Jean Mouroux, *The Meaning of Man* (New York: Sheed and Ward, 1952), pp. 1-18; Wolfhard Pannenberg, *What is Man?* (Philadelphia: Fortress Press, 1970), pp. 68-71; Jean Guitton, *Man in Time* (Notre Dame: Notre Dame Univ. Press, 1966), J. T. Fraser, ed., *The Voices of Time* (New York: Braziller), 1966.

[2]Cf. Karl Rahner, "History of the World and Salvation History," *Theological Investigations*, vol. 5 (Baltimore: Helicon, 1966), pp. 97-114.

[3]In contemporary philosophy there is a marked difference between becoming and change. Becoming signifies development on a personal level; change usually designates the more superficial alteration.

[4]Cf. J. M. Robinson, *Theology as History* (New York: Harper, 1967), p. 210; G. G. O'Collins, "Is the Resurrection an Historical Event?" *The Heythrop Journal*, 8 (1967), pp. 383-384. William Luijpen, *Existential Phenomenology* (Pittsburgh: Duquesne Univ. Press, 1969), pp. 237-243.

[5]Cf. Emil Brunner, *Man in Revolt* (Philadelphia: Westminster, 1947), pp. 448-449.

[6]Cf. R. G. Collingwood, *The Idea of History* (New York: Oxford Univ. Press, 1956), pp. 46-56.

[7]Cf. N. D. Chenu, *Toward Understanding St. Thomas* (Chicago: Regnery, 1964).

[8]Cf. Emil Brunner, *Man in Revolt* (Philadelphia: Westminster, 1947), p. 435.

[9]Cf. Karl Rahner, "Christianity and the New Man," *Theological Investigations*, vol. 5 (Baltimore: Helicon, 1966), pp. 135-153.

[10]Cf. Emil Brunner, *Man in Revolt* (Philadelphia: Westminster, 1947), p. 440.

[11]*Ibid.*, p. 443; Soren Kierkegaard, *The Concept of Dread* (Princeton: Princeton Univ. Press, 1957), pp. 22ff.

[12]Cf. C. R. North, "History," *The Interpreter's Dictionary of the Bible*, (Milwaukee: Bruce, 1965).

[13]Cf. Karl Rahner, *On the Theology of Death* (New York: Herder and Herder, 1961), pp. 65-75.

[14]Cf. Karl Rahner, "The Theological Concept of Concupiscence," *Theological Investigations*, vol. 1 (Baltimore: Helicon, 1961), pp. 364-369.

[15]Quoted in Brunner, *op. cit.*, p. 285.

[16]Cf. Teilhard de Chardin, *The Future of Man* (New York: Harper, 1964), pp. 134-135.

10

Man: Worker and Artist

Most people like to avoid work. It is a drudgery, it is monotonous, and it often does not involve a sense of accomplishment. Too few people exercise the artistic talents they have. Leisure to express oneself creatively seems never to be found. The Bible sees man as a worker and as creative. Christian tradition offers the same picture. The question arises: what does it mean to be Christian and to work and to be creative?

Man: The Worker

Greek culture looked down on physical labor.[1] Only a slave worked. The perfect gentleman of Aristotle would never soil his hands. Toil should be avoided and relegated to the less cultured. The educated man used his mind and not his body for work. A similar tradition is present today. Socially it is better to be a white-collar worker than a blue-collar worker. Working with the mind connotes a better level of culture, education, and breeding. This notion is common today and flows from a long classical tradition. It is foreign, however, to Judaism and Christianity.

In Judaism, work was a divine command levied upon all men: "Six days you shall labor and do all your work" (Ex. 20:9). Even before the Fall, Genesis sees a need to work:

> The Lord then took the man and settled him in the garden of Eden, to cultivate and care for it. (2:15)

Work is as natural as the rising of the sun and its setting:

> You made the moon to mark the seasons; the sun knows the

> hour of its setting. You bring darkness, and it is night; then all the beasts of the forest roam about; young lions roar for the prey and seek their food from God. When the sun rises, they withdraw and couch in their dens. Man goes forth to his work and to his tillage till the evening. (Ps. 104:19-23)

This theology is brilliant in its imagery but still does not explain the drudgery and tediousness of work. Only when the power of evil and sin is joined to the command to work does the Bible explain this dimension of human life. Genesis joins sin and work and projects a penitential character to all work. The struggle between the farmer and the herdsman, not unlike the struggle between the cattlemen and sheepsters in this country, is a bitter rivalry ending in the death of the herdsman (Gen. 4:2-9). The earth is full of thorns and thistles causing pain for the man who seeks to survive:

> To the man he said: "Because you listened to your wife and ate from the tree of which I had forbidden you to eat, Cursed be the ground because of you! In toil shall you eat its yield all the days of your life. Thorns and thistles shall it bring forth to you, as you eat of the plants of the field. By the sweat of your face shall you get bread to eat, until you return to the ground, from which you were taken; for you are dirt, and to dirt you shall return." (Gen. 3:17-19)

What should have been an enjoyable task has become a discipline that robs man of energy and interest. The work day has become a sorrow to man; the need for work has ushered in rivalry and bitterness and brought destruction in its wake. In Genesis man must learn to live with the thorns and conquer their power; he must strive to overcome the bitterness and live in peace. Unfortunately, the history of mankind has known too much of the competition and pain of work and too little of the resolution of work into a peaceful time of cooperation among men.

The New Testament presents Jesus as a worker or an artisan:

> Is this not the carpenter, the son of Mary, a brother of James

> and Joses and Judas and Simon? Are not his sisters our neighbors here? (Mark 6:3)

As God worked in creation (Ex. 20:11), so his Son would work on earth. There is no sense of shame in Jesus as the carpenter. It was a respected position in life. Nor must we assume that he was an unskilled carpenter. He lived the greater part of his adult life not as an itinerant preacher, but as a man who worked with his hands and fashioned objects of wood to be used and enjoyed by others.

In the later writings of the New Testament, Paul supported himself as a tentmaker (2 Thess. 3:7-8), and commanded that if people refused to work then they should not be given any food (2 Thess. 3:10). Work was part of human life and would be part of the Christian life. If man was to exercise dominion over creation (Gen. 1:28) and overcome the thorns of the earth, he would have to learn to work with the strength of his arms and the sweat of his brow. What he would make would be good and would be blessed and would contribute to the coming of the new creation. The fruit of the earth would be joined to the work of human hands and together there would be offered to the Creator a gift that fulfilled the command of God that man should work.

Interpretations of the Meaning of Work[2]

A theology of work has often suffered from a narrow viewpoint. The preceding paragraph points out three possible interpretations to the meaning of work: a penitential view that concentrates on the curse associated with work as a result of the Fall (Gen. 3:17-19); the creationist view that is based on the role of man to dominate creation (Gen. 2:28); and the eschatological view that sees man as contributing to the new creation (Isa. 65:17-25) which God himself will initiate.

The penitential view seems to be the most common among believers. The idea that man is cursed and must work as a result of the Fall has figured prominently in the folklore of the past and is still present in the minds of most Christians. Work is to be accepted because it cannot be avoided; it is seen as pain and suffering to be endured since it is inevitable.

The creationist viewpoint has a more positive approach. As

man was created with power and authority to dominate and control, he is to strive to exercise that power over creation. What has been given is the need of someone "to till" and "to water." The creation cannot be understood apart from the need of man to dominate and control, prescinding from any aspect of the influence of evil and sin. Such a viewpoint of work stresses the ability of man to continue the perfection that is already present in creation.

The third viewpoint, the eschatological, concentrates not on the first creation, but on the second. With the creationist viewpoint it shares the belief in man's power to dominate and control, but differs in perspective since it points much more to the new creation, which will replace the present order. Man is destined to work to dominate and control, as he works to transform the present order into the new creation—the new heaven and the new earth that will see the fulfillment of all of man's dreams.

Each approach has its advantages and its element of truth. A true theology of work must include some elements of each. There is a pain and drudgery associated with work; work can tend to divide people and cause rivalry and suffering. The earth is full of thorns and succumbs to man's influence only with much toil. There is a goodness that is already present in creation that man must dominate and control; there is a final perfection of this universe that is yet to come and to which man is called to make his contribution. A true Christian approach to work involves the penitential character and creationist approach and the eschatological hope. The penitential view without the other two robs man of hope; the creationist view alone fails to explain the problems encountered with work; the eschatological view makes no sense without the understanding of the present and the past. For the believer today a combination of all three is necessary to understand the place of work in a Christian perspective.

The Meaning of Work

A more pressing question is the precise meaning of work for the individual as well as for the group. There has to be a collective meaning and purpose for work, as well as a sense of meaning and purpose for the individual worker.

With regard to the collective purpose, all men should contribute to the unity and integration of all things. Over and beyond the life of the individual, there is a moving purpose for work that sees a future in which the contributions of individuals will contribute to the overall perfection and integration of the universe. This alone gives a sense to collective work. The accomplishments of space travel can never be attributed to any single individual. It is only through the cooperation and contribution of thousands of people throughout the world that we could ever have reached the space age. The unity and harmonious working of a great many talented people accomplished the first step on the moon.

The meaning of individual work, however, has to be more than some future integration. There has to be a sense of meaning that is present as the individual worker makes his contribution. Certainly work offers the individual the possibility of expanding himself. There is a renunciation of the purely natural state of creation with the sense of challenge that is offered to the individual. Another possibility is realized as the worker shapes something new from raw material, whether this be a building or a garden. A sense of dignity and accomplishment accompanies man's efforts to work as he installs himself in part of his world. There is also present the love of the world in work as well as a love of others. Something good comes from work that can be offered to others. The farmer has his crops that feed and delight his family; the laborer makes his contribution to a building that will aid people in living. This is the sense and meaning that work can offer.

The picture presented here of man the worker seems quite positive, in spite of the penitential aspect of work. The ideas presented are part of the Judaic-Christian tradition, but do not present the full picture. Man the worker has his problems, intensified by the pace of life in the twentieth century and the demands made upon man to respond to needs. A work ethic seems to have overtaken the imagination of man and is in need of correction.

The Christian and the Work Ethic[3]

The one image that is central to contemporary man is the image of man the worker. Space travel is becoming commonplace; people no longer become excited about moonwalks unless there is a possible loss of human life. Machines transform the face of the earth. Niagara Falls is turned off and on; superhighways slice through the most powerful of mountains; bridges span deep gulfs; skyscrapers fight one another to be the tallest in the world. Man is a worker who does things and does them quickly. Such power makes man feel omnipotent. There is nothing that he cannot do, given time and talent and money. It is all possible and delayed only because of accidents or unavailable resources. In time all problems will be erased and whatever man sets out to accomplish will be realized. In such a scheme there is little need for God; man has become a god to himself. The only problem is that man the all-powerful worker is not the all-perfectly happy man.

Karl Marx sees man as an economic commodity. In spite of his humanism he would use man as a good to be consumed in favor of society; so many workers could accomplish so much for the economy and should learn to rest content. The prospect does not offer much possibility for happiness and contentment. In the presence of his buildings and bridges and roads and aircraft and space travel, man the worker suffers anxiety and anguish and even abandonment. He may well have the power to create but does not have the power to create meaning for himself. Has he made the machines or are the machines making him? Is man the toolmaker becoming himself a tool?

Ordinary amenities of society point out the tragic image of man the worker. First acquaintances usually ask: "What do you do?" A man's identity is centered on what he has or can accomplish. Take away the function and modern man has little to offer himself or others. When function and efficiency and frenzied activity become the identifying qualities of a human life, then man suffers alienation. He is out of harmony with himself, with others, and with all of creation. If human life is relegated to the useful and the successful interests of capital gain, the respect for human life will plummet at ever-increasing speed. Work is necessary for man but must be joined to man who is also the artist and man who is also the one who plays. No one should try to avoid work, but if anyone settles for a work-oriented life, his or her life will be poor and far from human. The Christian perspective lays claim to a firm belief in man the artist and celebrator that modifies man the worker.

Man the Artist

In human history there has always been an interest in the true, the good, and the beautiful. By these three qualities man has striven to install himself as part of this world and master of the universe. Truth gives birth to scientific and intellectual activity; good encourages man to seek moral activity based on the response to others' needs, and the beautiful entices man to create and produce craftsmanship and artistic creations. By the presence of the three activities, man controls his world. What is evident is that all three are necessary. Theory and moral activity are in need of the refinement of artistic and productive work. To concentrate on one without a corresponding interest in the other causes man to fail in his efforts to master and subdue the earth. Theory offers man new hope and directs his activity; moral action based on the good overcomes the rivalry in work; artistic and productive works modify the theory and accomplish what is possible. Together they form a unified interaction of human qualities and possibilities.[4]

Christian faith sees man as free and distinct from the world but part of the world, called to perfect what is given to him. The world is not perfect but is to be perfected by the activity of man in moral action and in artistic as well as intellectual activity. If man is to shape the earth, then he is affected by what he has done and has affected others. He remains apart from his world but immersed in its development. His own existence is intensified by his artistic activity making the world a dramatic festival in which people become what they are called to be.

Conceived broadly, art is that by which man helps to install himself as part of this world; in the Christian context, it is the means by which man fulfills and perfects and molds the earth that is given to him, participating in the creativity of God. Man is destined to share in the power of God to create, destined to make his contribution to this world, making it a more perfect and more beautiful world by what he has done. Some may add that this participation in creation is very limited compared to the creative power of God. In some sense it is as absolute as God's power. If man creates, then what is created exists only because of the individual and without him the creation would never be. Man is not needed to sustain his creative act but is necessary for the creation to exist.

There is a contribution that the individual alone can make. The world is now better because of what one person has accomplished. Everyone has this ability. No one is restricted. Some may have more talents than others but no one is bereft.

The various forms of art demonstrate the possibilities of artistic activity for everyone. If man is caught in time and space, so are his art forms. They depend on time and space and can be divided according to their position into the temporal, the spatial, and the temporal/spatial art forms.

The temporal art forms are addressed to hearing and sound. Poetry is the art of beautiful word and music is the art of beautiful sound. Poetry is meant to be read aloud; it lies dead on the printed page and comes alive only when spoken, to return to repose once the words have passed. Music is also caught in time. It exists as fleeing moments of sound remembered and bound together by the listener. Once the time has passed, the music lies equally dead in little black dots on a piece of paper. Without time poetry and music would not be.

Space too has its art forms. The sense of sight and lines and form and color creates architecture and sculpture and painting. Each depends on space and occupies space and remains rooted in location. The architect has his building as a permanent monument, the sculptor has his statue, and the painter his picture. Each has its place and can be enjoyed at anytime. The works are permanent and will remain as long as man does not choose to destroy, or does not permit their destruction. The Parthenon has withstood the ravages of time and would remain forever if man would allow it to remain. The *Pietà* has captured the compassion of a mother for her dead son, marred only by the destructive force of man himself. Rembrandt and Rubens and El Greco and Monet died long ago but still offer to modern man the beauty of their creation. The spatial arts are more lasting than the temporal arts and more easily appreciated. They depend on space and can overcome the transitoriness of time. Some arts are a combination of space and time. Dance is both involved in space and caught in movement in time. It is there, but then is lost as the time passes. The same is true for drama. Space is required to enact this aspect of life; but once enacted, it is gone.

Everyone has the ability and the drive to share in these art forms. Every man is an artist, no matter how primitive that art may be. To use beautiful words, to choose carefully the right expressions, is part of human life. Even the most uncultured and uneducated man seeks to express himself with all the beauty that he can muster. Love is the natural prod for beautiful words. Someone in love needs no prompting to be careful in what words he speaks to his beloved. It is an art form and part of life. The same is true for the temporal art form of music. Long ago Congreve wrote, "Music has charms to soothe the savage breast." What was true in the time of Congreve has always been true. Music has healing affects; it calms and brings peace; it can equally excite and bring man to a pitch of ecstasy. Children and old people know and appreciate music. It brings a richness to life that is so often missed by those who are caught up in the affairs of the world. Even the mentally retarded appreciate music and sometimes far better than the successful man of the world. The art of beautiful sound belongs to man to listen to and share.

Singing is also an ever-present reality. The creative instinct of beautiful sound is given in the human voice. Not everyone can be an opera star but everyone can enjoy singing. Parties liven up when there is someone at the piano; religious activities become celebrations with the addition of singing. Give man the opportunity to sing, remove his inhibitions, and he will join with the larks and the nightingales. Music is part of being alive and life is dead without it.

The spatial arts also have their presence in human lives. The art of line and form and color is displayed in the arrangement of a room, in the building of a motor, the planting of a garden, the making of a hat, or the sewing of clothes. Color and its use is present in the choice of clothes to wear, painting of a house, coloring of Easter eggs, as well as in the painting of masterpieces and the sculpturing in marble. Every person uses the art of lines and form and color.

Drama and dance are also part of the human scene. The grace of an athlete in basketball or baseball is the same quality that is displayed in ballroom dancing. Movement in rhythm has more manifestations than in the ballet. Acting in drama forms part of everyday life. We all wear masks and act out a drama that may very well be far from personal reality. They are art forms and they are part of human life. Man is artist in all that he seeks to do in the light of his personal contribution of doing and making something of this world, and making something that is beautiful as his personal contribution.

Art and Society

A discussion of art and man's talents must include the relationship of society to the artist. In spite of the personal and social effort that art entails, it remains in the end a happy accident that is still a creation. The work that is accomplished is a testimony of the individual who desires some communication with those who see or hear the artistic work. This is the problem. Art demands intelligibility if it is to be a true communication, but often this is precisely what is lacking. The artist is a man who has his insight into reality that he strives to concretize and express in a material way through sound or matter. If the horizon of the artist is broader than the horizon of society, there is bound to be opposition and violence. Society can view and judge only within the purview it has reached. If the artist has already gone beyond this limit, there will be a problem of communication and intelligibility. At any given time the art expression could be more advanced than the era of the artist and thus cause a lack of intelligibility. The only hope is that in the future its own truth and beauty will become accepted when society has expanded its horizons. This does not mean, however, that art is to be private or limited to a few. Where art becomes esoteric, then art ceases to be itself. Only in face of the community and the world can art be what it is meant to be. Eventually if the art is good, then society will come to appreciate what it was offered in the distant past. True art wills out and passes the test of time.

The Individual Artist

Thus far we have concentrated on everyman the artist. Some men are more the artist than others. The great artist is a person endowed with unusual talents. His whole being cries out when they are in use as well as when they are dormant. The artist passes through trials and experiences that can never be entirely appreciated by the masses of people. An artist is different.

The millions of works of art that delight audiences are not merely the results of programming. The art form is the result of the creative imagination of the artist. The talents of the artist and the external stimulation make works of art. Even this is not sufficient to describe the different quality of artists.

Cézanne tried to formulate the particular artistic quality and referred to the "motive" within the artist that excites him to action. Something moves the artist to create a tangible expression of his insight into reality. Others refer to inspiration, the crucial moment when the art form reveals itself in the mind of the artist. The everyday world vanishes and is replaced with the world of imagination, of phantoms, and deep insights into life.

External forces also help. The artist often uses historical events to help give rise to ideas for art. But the artist does not find his source of inspiration in the external world; he makes his inspiration; he is looking for a springboard for his creative imagination that is the real source of his works. This explains why some people can see the same thing, read the same book, study the same object and come away with nothing more than some information. The artist will see more and end up with an idea in germinal form that he must express in some art form. The difference is in the man himself. To some, God has given greater capacity for creativity.

We have been talking about something that exists in the mind of the artist and that he eventually will express concretely in his work. We really do not know much about this "something" in his mind. For a lack of a better word we can borrow the word "form" from philosophy and think of the relation between the idea in the mind of the artist and the matter he will use. The form is what he wants to express; the matter is the vehicle he uses for the expression.

The art form in the mind of the artist can never be defined. It can never be adequately known. All we know are the effects, and even the artist himself cannot fully know what he is doing until it is finished. The artist must wait until the work is completed and then he knows what previously existed only in his creative self. This lack of knowledge explains one of the saddest moments of the artist's life. When the art work is finished, often he feels as if he is a failure. What he sees before him, or hears, is not the masterpiece that existed in the mind. He feels frustration because the germinal form has not been expressed in the matter. The reality he wished to capture has escaped his control. The material is never equal to the spiritual.

There remains one final interest in the study of the workings of an artist. It takes time for the form in the mind of the artist to find its body, its expression. Sometimes an artist can look back over a number of years between the initial contact with the inspiration and the final execution. In that period, the form may have changed considerably in the mind of the artist while in reality it has not changed but has only been seeking its bodily expression. Once it has arrived, the artist knows it and moves to completion. While it is still in embryonic form, no one can force it into existence. Time must pass until the artist suddenly knows that the conditions have been fulfilled and he completes his work. As long as the form is alive, the artist works. Once it dies, the work of art, whether completed or not, is finished. The artist can never force the inspired form; it is there or it is absent.

Theology of Art

Thus far we have concentrated on the human dimensions and meaning of art and man the artist without giving consideration to any particular Christian or theological appreciation of man the artist. It is difficult to talk about a Christian theology of art since the Bible, the main source of Christian theology, is relatively silent on this subject. For the Jewish Scriptures the lure of beauty could be a snare, and in fact this was a temptation that had to be faced in the Old Testament times. Exodus warns against images:

> You shall not carve idols for yourselves in the shape of anything in the sky above or on the earth below or in the waters beneath the earth; you shall not bow down before them or worship them. For I, the Lord, your God, am a jealous God, inflicting punishment for their fathers' wickedness on the children of those who hate me, down to the third and fourth generation. (20:4-5)

The tradition of opposition to artistic works continued in Christianity in the early centuries, but not without its opponents. The catacombs are richly decorated with art forms that certainly contributed to the understanding of the new religion. Later the development of ritual and song and special buildings caused a change in the attitude of the Christian Church that eventually developed into the Church as patron of the arts in the Middle Ages. The history of the relationship of art and the Christian Church is left to other writers. Here some comments will be made on a theology of art.

As there has been a threefold accent in the theology of work, a similar trifocal theology of art is present in the writings of Christian theologians. Paul Tillich concentrates on the message of the cross and its influence on art; Nicolas Berdyaev looks to consummation; and Etienne Gilson, Jacques Maritain, and other Roman Catholic philosophers and theologians focus attention on art as the response to God as Creator.

Paul Tillich[5]

Tillich offers a theology of art that is based on the theological principle of transcendence and God as ground of being. Man's experience of his world points beyond itself toward a ground of being and meaning. Art, like all else, indirectly conveys the self-transcendent character of the world so that the religious quality of art does not depend on its content. All art is sacred. The one fly in the ointment is the experience of man as fallen. For Tillich the cross of Jesus is in the center of his interpretation of human existence and thus of culture and of art. To exist is to be fallen and Christians are to bear witness to that from which they have fallen. This is particularly evident in art that points beyond what is the experience of man and at times offers some glimpses of the existence that man finds as his destiny. It is the cross and death of Jesus that has shattered man's temptation to erect the symbol into some absolute. As Jesus, the symbol of God, sacrificed himself to forestall any attempt at idolatry, so art must always point beyond itself and recognize the possibility that it has to become the media for the manifestation of what is truly ultimate. The cross becomes the center of the theology of culture and of art.

When religion is defined as ultimate concern, no matter how

secular the fashion in which the concern is expressed, and religious symbolism is described in terms of transparency to the ground of being, the question of content in art is irrelevant. The standard by which aesthetic images are judged is their ability to point beyond their own form and content toward the inexhaustible power of being that animates all things.

The contribution of Tillich to a theology of art is his ability to see the fallenness of man and judge this experience through the cross of Jesus. He sees art as manifesting this quality of human existence and, at the same time, a human existence which needs to learn that what is here is not ultimate. What is lacking in these views is the play element of art and the Christian picture of God as creating and creating good. To exist means to be fallen, but also to be called to a fulfillment of existence in the midst of a world that is participating in this goodness. The Christian community and a theology of art must unite creation as good with the cross as well as a consummation of creation yet to come.

Nicolas Berdyaev[6]

The freedom of man and his vocation to creativity characterizes all of the writing of Berdyaev. For him, "Artistic creativeness best reveals the meaning of the creative act."[7] Art is not content with just seeing; it rejects all that is visible and tangible in favor of what no eye has seen nor ear heard. In the mind of the artist and in his creation, a transfigured world is born that conforms to the demands of man's liberty. Art is a repudiation of this world, an avowal of human freedom, and a protest against present bondage. Art, moreover, is a token of man's proper destiny. What the artist does is a response to the divine appeal for assistance to actualize the good and transfigure the tragic possibilities of man's primordial freedom. In all, it is a quest for the eschatological beauty that will constitute the Kingdom of God.

Berdyaev concentrates exclusively on the consummation of man. His image of the artist is one of the rebel who rejects what is offered as inferior and is moved constantly beyond the fragility of present life and existence into a transformed world. But when eschatology is divorced from the goodness of creation already present, it becomes little more than "a revelation of a kingdom which is not of this world and which signifies that there is no making out anything in this world."[8] When Berdyaev rejects Genesis along with Tillich and defines art as a passion for eternity, then he must condemn the artist's venture to discover and express more of the world around him. Berdyaev's perspective is one that must be present in a Christian theology of art, but consummation and eschatology cannot be the overriding concern.

Etienne Gilson

The third individual who takes a different approach to a theology of art is a philosopher, Etienne Gilson:[9]

> In a created universe whatever exists is religious because it imitates God in its operations as well as in its being. If what precedes is true, art, too, is religious in its very essence, because to be creative is to imitate, in a finite and analogical way, the divine prerogative, exclusively reserved for HE WHO IS, of making things to be. . . . Each artist, then, while exerting his often anguished effort to add new types of beings to those which make up the world of nature, should be conscious of the resemblance between his finite art and the infinitely perfect efficacy of the divine power. All truly creative art is religious in its own right.[10]

The Creator has given to man the ability to create. Whether he knows it or not the artist responds to a great invitation "to join in the praise of God by cooperating with his creative power and by increasing, to the extent that man can do so, the sum total of being and beauty in the world."[11]

This third perspective, art as a response to the Creator, is more fundamental than the previous attempts at a Christian theology of art. The world is good and beautiful and man must recognize the present beauty and goodness and express this reality. Even in the midst of a fallen world man is called to perfect and fulfill what is already present. The cross of Jesus is real and assures the Christian that he will not succumb to a false idolatry, but the cross of Jesus does not exhaust the meaning of Jesus. Jesus is "the new creator and the actuality behind a new imagination and a new creation."[12] The artist participates in this new creation by celebrating the beauty that is present now and has always been present in creation; he recognizes the fallenness of man and rebels against the pains of existence and works toward the final consummation of all things. This is the true theology of art. Cross, creation, and eschaton each has its place and its contribution.

Tillich and Berdyaev both appraise the artist's venture in the light of estrangement from ultimate reality, from God. This interpretation is appropriate but not sufficient. Faith in God the Creator is also necessary. For the believer called to be an artist, there must be the firm belief in the goodness and beauty of this world. Only with this foundation can there be any hope for true artistic accomplishments. All of art, whether great or something less than great, is always a happy accident. We all struggle against the chaos and formlessness that seems to surround our lives:

> My anguish, my anguish, I writhe in pain. . . .
> I looked on the earth and lo it was wasted and void;
> and to the heavens and they had no light . . .
>
> I looked and lo there was no man,
> and all the birds of the air had fled. (Jer. 4:19a, 23, 25)

As God triumphed over the chaos and the formlessness of Genesis, so man struggles in his artistic endeavors today. The biblical image of creation provides the foundation for an interpretation of the artist's venture with the theme of consummation emphasizing the ambiguity and dialectical character of all art. The story of the cross stresses the principle of discrimination by which we appraise our efforts to install ourselves as part of this world and bring this world to completion. The fallenness of man is involved in his creativity and cannot be overlooked. When individual believers strive to unite these aspects of human life into a unity, they fulfill their destiny as artists.

Conclusion

The ability of a man to go beyond the narrow limits of space and time, even as he is captured in their clutches, gives birth to the artist. Human transcendence gives foundation to what a man can create as he tries to rival the creative power of God. It is a human characteristic to create because every man has the possibility of transcendence.

If transcendence is the foundation for artistic work, man as spirit in the world is the possibility. The spiritual aspects of the person always seek expression and strive to concretize the insight into life in forms of line and color and sound and movement. In each case the nonmaterial reality surpasses its expression. Man is spirit in the world and the world can never capture sufficiently the expansiveness of the human spirit.

For the Christian viewpoint, man is artist when he fulfills the biblical injunction to build the earth and manifest in his dominion some of the qualities of the divine. The glory of God is made visible in the human effort to display this glory in terms that are seen and heard. The goodness of the world in creation, the cross as the axis for all human life, and the final consummation of creation are all involved in artistic activity. Finally, man is artist and creative because man is of God.

Notes

[1]Cf. Edward Kaiser, *Theology of Work* (Westminster: Newman, 1966), p. 33.

[2]Cf. J. L. Illanes, *On the Theology of Work* (Chicago: Scepter, 1967); Dennis Clark, *Work and the Human Spirit* (New York: Sheed and Ward, 1967); Louis Savary, *Man, His World and His Work* (Paramus: Paulist Press, 1967).

[3]Cf. Sam Keen, *Apology for Wonder* (New York: Harper and Row, 1969), pp. 117-150. The author presents the problems associated with the work ethic as well as some attempts at solutions.

[4]Cf. Alois Halder, "Art," *Sacramentum Mundi*, vol. 1 (New York: Herder and Herder, 1968).

[5]Cf. Paul Tillich, *Theology of Culture* (London: Oxford Univ. Press, 1959); *The Protestant Era* (Chicago: Univ. of Chicago Press, 1948); *Dynamics of Faith* (New York: Harper, 1957).

[6]Cf. Nicolas Berdyaev, *The Meaning of the Creative Act* (London: Gollancz, 1955); *The Divine and the Human* (London: Geoffrey Bles, 1949); *Freedom and the Spirit* (London: Geoffrey Bles, 1935).

[7]Cf. Nicolas Berdyaev, *The Meaning of the Creative Act*, p. 225.

[8]Cf. Nicolas Berdyaev, *Dream and Reality* (New York: Macmillan, 1951), p. 225.

[9]Maritain takes the same general approach as Gilson and it is upon Maritain that Gilson depends. He is cited here rather than Maritain because of the greater ease with which he presents his ideas. Cf. J. Maritain, *Creative Intuition in Art and Poetry* (London: Harvill, 1953).

[10]Etienne Gilson, *Painting and Reality* (New York: Pantheon, 1957), p. 294.

[11]*Ibid.*, p. 295.

[12]William Lynch, *Christ and Apollo* (New York: Sheed and Ward, 1960), p. xiv.

11

Man the Celebrator

Everyone has experiences that defy description. For a moment what was dark becomes bright and the world shines as it never shone before. A walk after a fall rain refreshes; sailing off Cape Cod, the fury of an unexpected storm enveloping the person in wind and rain; the first experience of a jet aircraft as it lifts off the ground and begins to climb majestically into the ever-receding blueness of sky; the magic of a wedding day; the warmth of a Christmas at home. Each is an experience of the whole person that gives insights into life and makes people full and alive. In each moment of rapture, some new knowledge is gained on an intellectual level, but the more fundamental and more important change is in the person involving the emotional, the physical, the spiritual and the bodily. Man as a multidimensional participant is a celebrator of life.

Frequently in the business of life we tend to emphasize the intellectual and the notional aspect of living and are too conscious of the work ethic that has predominated in our culture. We live in a world of ideas and images and notions that bounce in and out of the mind at a staggering rate. Life is analyzed by the sociologist, probed by the psychologists, computerized by the efficiency experts, and regulated by the economist. No wonder that some people are beginning to revolt against the control of the machine, the organization, and the sterile idea. Life has to be more than the rise and the fall of the stock market, corporate profits, increases in salary, visits to an analyst, and sociological and demographical studies. Life is personal and full of surprises; it is a mystery that calls for living. If man is an artist as well as a worker, he is also a celebrator, one who sees wonder and is festive and has dreams that exist only in the world of imagination.

Today there are many devotees of celebration who dwell on the experience of life by the total person and who bless the efforts to make the days and weeks of the year come alive and vibrant. Everyone is called to celebrate the life they have, but is this just a word, another idea that will fade from sterility? How is man a celebrator? What does it mean and how can a Christian approach to life respond to this aspect of life?

The meaning of celebration needs refinement if we are to understand how it is part of life. Before this is done, some examination of approaches to God are necessary if we are to understand the role of celebration in the Christian life.

We usually think of God in terms of mental images; he is Creator, Judge, Lawgiver, Father, Provider, Supporter. But God is also present in the lives of people and manifests himself to them at times and places that defy description. There are conceptual approaches to God that emphasize the intellectual and the notional; there are equally present experiences of God that are far more encompassing in their effect on the human person.[1]

Both approaches are part of the religious experience. We come to believe in God and feel his presence and try to translate this experience into words that are never equal to the task. The effort to translate, however, clarifies the experience and we grow in our appreciation of the presence of God in our lives. The conceptual flows from the nonconceptual and clarifies the nonconceptual.[2]

Until very recently the Christian religion emphasized the conceptual approach to God. People were nurtured on this idea and frequently were suspicious of any experience of God as strange and unreal; today there is a change. If Christian anthropology expresses belief in the total person and if faith is something that is emotional and psychological, then an awareness of God that is more than intellectual should be part of the human experience and should help a person appreciate the closeness of God. Man is a celebrator and is necessarily so, for in this celebration of life there is not only present an aspect of the mystery that is man, but there is often revealed an aspect of the mystery that is God revealing himself to man. Goodness and mercy and salvation and fidelity are not abstract religious ideas; they are real, present in the lives of people who are real. To celebrate life and revel in its wonder and festivity and fantasy involve the possibility of moving beyond what is offered to an awareness of the foundation of the goodness in life, God.

We begin with some thoughts on the meaning of celebration and will conclude with the meaning of celebration for the Christian life. Once again, man created in the image of God with a destiny that is God himself is the ultimate foundation for the hope and enjoyment that is always present with man the celebrator.

Wonder[3]

July 20th, 1968, marked a new achievement for all of us: "One small step for man, a giant step for the human race." With unbridled enthusiasm the President of the United States remarked that it was the greatest day since creation. On that day millions of people saw the first human foot leave its mark on the moon. Think back to that evening. The room had an eerie silence; there was enthusiasm but it was a quiet enthusiasm mixed with fear and apprehension. Slowly the tension began to increase as Neil Armstrong emerged from the Lem. Hair stood on end; goose pimples ran up and down the spine. Then Armstrong stood firmly on the surface of the moon and momentarily millions relaxed and sank into joyful relief. It was a wonderful evening, a moment full of wonder and a joy for life, but with it all there was an element of anxiety and fear. No one knew for sure what would happen as Armstrong emerged and that alone caused fear. What could not be overcome was the sense of joy and accomplishment.

Wonder is the human reaction to some insight into life and brings with it a mixture of joy and fear. The insight of July 20th was the accomplishment of man: what man can do and has done that leaves future possibilities at his feet. Fear was also present in the midst of the unknown. We all learned something that made us joyful, but the experience also induced caution with the fear that what we had learned might also cause pain.

A flock of scarlet tanagers also brings wonder. A red-winged blackbird is a delight that tells us something about the beauty of creation and the beauty that is given to all of us. It also can bring fear and anxiety as expressed by the author of the eighth Psalm:

> When I look at the heavens, the work of thy fingers the moon and the stars which thou has established, What is man that thou art mindful of him and the son of man that thou dost care for him? (3-4)

The beauty of the world can always bring awareness of questions: the meaning of human life, or the fear that it has no meaning. It brings joy and enthusiasm and anxiety about what might be behind this beauty, if anything; in both cases, anxiety arises.

The sensational can easily generate wonder; the commonplace can do likewise. A sparrow can cause as much of a reaction as walking on the moon. In every case there is an insight into life that is far more than an intellectual appreciation; it is an experience of the total person—a mixture of joy and fear, pleasure and pain. Wonder is the most basic ingredient for celebration.

Festivity: The Affirmation of the Insight Into Life[4]

Festivity is something all enjoy, but it is hard to describe. It is either well known or can never be known by words. A seventy-year-old mother starts to do some of the modern dances at her daughter's wedding and all react quickly that such activity is too strenuous. But she is in a festive mood; her last child was settled for life and so in such times people do strange things.

Harvey Cox in *Feast of Fools* speaks of three elements of festivity:[5] excess, affirmation of life, and juxtaposition. People go too far in festive moods, stay up too late, eat too much or drink too much or dance too much and feel it the next morning. Festivity always allows a short vacation from the tried and true and the conventional and stuffy. Without some infraction of the more structured formulas of daily life, festivity would not be festivity. Excess, going beyond the limits of daily life, always characterizes festivity.

The second element in festivity is the affirmation of life. No one can be festive in a negative way. Excess without the affirmation of life is just plain excess and brings no new insight into life. Joy in the presence of sorrow, life in the midst of death, is festivity. It is not so strange that the Vienna Orchestra continued to play as the Germans marched into the city; they would be festive and affirm life in the midst of what would soon be death for so many. *Finnegans Wake* is another good example of the affirmation of life, and perhaps there are still some around who have had the good fortune to have attended an old-fashioned Irish wake. The affirmation of life is evident. Even the custom of Mardi Gras is the affirmation of life and the good times of life on the eve of what was once austerity and fasting. In every case the goodness of life is emphasized for a true festive mood.

The final element in the Cox scheme of festivity is juxtaposition. It would be nice to have people in a Christmas mood all year round but it would not be realistic. What makes Christmas, Christmas, is partially that it is a once-a-year occurrence. There has to be contrast; no one can be festive all the time. Without the winter, who could appreciate the spring? Without the cold bleakness of January and February, the signs of green life in April would not be noticed. Without 364 nonbirthdays, the one birthday would lose all its glitter; without the anticipation of the festive mood, impatiently awaited, the richness would seep out of life and contribute to dullness. No one can be festive all the time, and this fact only enhances the moments of festivity.

The affirmation of insight into life, accompanied by retreat from the daily aspects of life, often to excess, coming at intervals, is the second ingredient for celebration.

Fantasy: How Things Might Be[6]

Thus far celebration through wonder and festivity has been involved with time. Wonder drives us back into time even as it happens now; wonder makes us aware of how things are and how things have been if we merely open our eyes. Festivity also happens now with an emphasis on the present and without worry or even consideration of yesterday and tomorrow. Without some future orientation, however, wonder brings no lasting effect; without a future, festivity is running away. What ushers in the future is fantasy: how things might be.

The rain may never fall till after sundown,
By eight the morning fog must disappear . . .

There's a place for us, somewhere a place for us,
Peace and quiet and open air . . .

It is not so strange that the *Oxford History of the American People*[7] should end with some lyrics from *Camelot*:

Don't let it be forgot, that once there was a spot,
For one brief shining moment that was known as
Camelot.

Perhaps both Camelot and the oblique reference to the Kennedy years are both past orientated, but in reality they are future orientated: how things might be, even if they never were in the past. Take away fantasy and there will be little enthusiasm for life. Why is it that Walt Disney often appeals as much to adults as to children? Children live in the fantasy world as real; adults would like the fantasy world to be real. Cinderella does not exist but what a joy if it happened. Things might be so different. If all people had was their past and the present, how sad life would be. Birthdays, wedding days, graduation days are all glorious because they mark the adventure into the future. After five or ten or fifteen years when things have just not worked out as hoped and planned, if all people had was the past and the present without any future possibilities, then life would be bleak. With a future, life can be exciting and creative; take it away and dullness and boredom rush in.

Celebration involves wonder as insight into life, festivity as the affirmation of this insight, and fantasy about how life might be because of this insight.

Celebrations

Birthdays, anniversaries, marriages, holidays, graduations, promotions, reunions, holy days are all part of our yearly efforts to celebrate. In each case, there is insight into life, there is festivity, and there is fantasy.

Two people commit themselves to each other in marriage to love each other, to grow old gracefully together, to raise a family, and to share life. The wonder is there: life involves other people who will love each other, but how will this marriage work out?

What will it be like five years from now or ten or twenty? Joy and the fear are part of the insight. Festivity is also present. We affirm life and marriage even when marriage does not seem to be on the best of grounds these days; we often go to excess in celebrating: eat too much and drink too much; and there is contrast: people don't get married every day. Fantasy is also present: perhaps this marriage will be the ideal marriage, perhaps in spite of all the pain and suffering this couple will grow in gentleness and love. Perhaps for these two things will be different. Take away any of the three elements and there is no true celebration.

Anniversaries are also celebrated. Again, there is insight into life, the affirmation in festivity, and the fantasy. Whether we celebrate the beginning of life, the beginning of a marriage, the birth of a country, there is always insight and festivity; but in such celebrations the more important element is fantasy: how things might be. Many people today find it hard to celebrate the Fourth of July. Perhaps it is because they have lost hope in the future of the U.S.A. We can recall the past event, the birth of the country, but if there is no future, there can be no celebration. A couple on the verge of divorce cannot celebrate their anniversary; for them there is no future together. Nor can birthdays be celebrated if there is no enthusiasm for the future. Take away the future from anyone and that person is already dead and waiting only to be buried.

Celebration is based on wonder, festivity, and leads us into the future as we come to see just what can be in the midst of what is. Celebration is glorious and makes us more human.

Celebrations: Experiences for the Total Person

Celebrations are human because they involve the total person: the complexity of intellect, will, emotions, bodily activity, sensory perception, and the enjoyment of others and their presence.[8] As a total human experience, people are necessary for celebrations if only to share insight into life; life is not celebrated in lonely splendor.

One could wander through Europe enjoying the beauty, feeling a sense of awe at seeing the Alps for the first time, Notre Dame at night, and the charm of winter in Luzerne; but if there is no one to share these with, no one with whom to celebrate, one would be poorer in spite of the experience. People make celebrations and affect other people.

Light and color and good food and good wine and atmosphere and flowers and music and dress are all part of celebration and contribute to a fuller experience. They are surely not as essential as a basic insight into life, but such externals do help.

A husband wishes to take his wife out to dinner to celebrate their anniversary. He goes to much pains to pick the right restaurant with the right atmosphere, lights, food, and music. She, in turn, goes to great pains to feel and to look pretty. Flowers are given, candles glow, and so do the people. Anything that can contribute to the experience of the celebration finds a place and enhances the evening.

There are times, no doubt, when the wine is great, the music fine, the atmosphere superb, but the celebration never gets off the ground. It would have been just as good to have stayed at home. The heart of celebration is insight into life with the affirmation of life and fantasy. If this is lacking, all the trimmings are hollow and are as ashes in the mouth. The heart can be enhanced by the externals but cannot find a substitute. Perhaps an episode from *West Side Story* can make this clear. Maria feels pretty. The atmosphere is a small dress shop in New York, the lighting poor, the costume is a bolt of cloth—and yet there is a celebration. Maria is in love; she has found someone who wants her and needs her and loves her and she has her insight into life. The experience is not without the fear: she is Puerto Rican and he is not. She has her festivity: the affirmation of life in the midst of what does not seem too good; she goes to excess as she waltzes around the room with a bolt of cloth. She has her fantasy: how things might be ("There's a place for us, somewhere a place for us"). The externals are not the greatest, but there is a celebration, which shows that externals may be present or not; always, however, there must be wonder, festivity, and fantasy.

Celebration and Faith

Some may argue that this chapter has avoided the more spiritual or Christian dimension of life. The role of faith and the Gospel of Jesus Christ may not seem so evident. In reality this is not true.

The present chapter is written in the perspective of man's orientation to God, or the relationship of nature to grace.[9] There is no reality that is strictly secular, no experience of man that is totally devoid of grace. If God has entered into a relationship with man, that relationship is on the level of a total experience and not just on the level of the conceptual. There are approaches to God that are not so evidently religious, but for that reason are not irreligious. Christianity has often been accused of living in a distant past that has no meaning, or in a distant future that does not yet exist, with a disdain for the earthly and the present. That some believers have encouraged this viewpoint is granted; that such is the heritage of Jesus Christ is denied. Salvation, the peace and harmony and love that is promised and given to us in Jesus, is not reserved exclusively for eternity. Salvation is NOW and part of our everyday life, just as damnation is a part of NOW and part of daily life.[10] For the believer there must always be a celebration of life in the sense of wonder and festivity, even as the believer in fantasy looks forward to a future that is richer, when what is begun will be fulfilled.

To believe in God and in Jesus Christ is to see the goodness that is present in life and creation and man and woman and friendship and parties and anniversaries and birthdays and every day. If salvation means anything, it means that God and his Christ are present in our world and make our world worth living and loving. To one who believes, there is always something new in life; there is always a reason to be festive; there is always a possible better future breaking into the present. If believers would wake up and come alive, Christianity would offer so much more to people who are starving for life. Faith tells us that nothing is outside the influence of God; nothing happens that cannot in some way bring some good. Faith assures us that even in the midst of evil and sin and destruction and loss of life, there is always the rebirth that gives an eternal hope. Life has a meaning that is not just drab. Anyone can become so involved with the details and troubles of life that he misses the balloon. For the believer in Jesus Christ, it is a crime to miss the balloon. Man is a celebrator because man is alive and called ever more into life. He needs his wonder, his insight into life; he needs moments of festivity and, above all, he needs his fantasy: how things might be! This is all very nonconceptual but can be equally valid in an approach to God. Nietzsche could not believe in a God who could not dance. The Christian God is one who dances to the delight of his followers.

Celebration and Christian Liturgy[11]

We have spoken of life as a gift. The celebration of life can help us to appreciate the gift we have received and encourage us to offer gratitude. The traditional way in which one is grateful for life is to worship.[12] Some thoughts on Christian worship and celebration are very much in order in any Christian appreciation of man.

The conceptual and nonconceptual approach to God are both part of the human experience. In an amazing way liturgy participates in both. Liturgy is the celebration of God's presence among his people; it is the experience of the total person that makes one aware of the presence of God in a human fashion, bringing a change in attitude and leading the participant into a deeper appreciation of his relationship to God; liturgy is thanksgiving for the gift of life and for the life of Jesus Christ. Certainly liturgy is conceptual since it involves ideas and images and concepts and is based almost entirely on reading and listening to the Word of God. But liturgy is also nonconceptual; it appeals to more than the intellect; it creates an atmosphere and envelops the person in its appeal. A recall of the liturgy of the past and a consideration of present-day liturgy will help clarify the place of the nonconceptual and the place of celebration in worship.

Traditional Liturgy

Christian liturgy of the past created an atmosphere. For Roman Catholics the offering of Mass in Latin created a sense of wonder; an aura of the mysterious pervaded Sunday morning. In the Protestant tradition, liturgy was almost limited to a listening to scriptural readings accompanied by the minister's sermon. Occasionally there was the dignified reception of the Eucharist with people paying very close attention to the ritual enactment of the Last Supper. Both traditions offered different insights into the meaning of life as the year developed. If anything, the transcendence of God and the awe that must accompany any effort to approach God were predominant. People were "moved" by the sound of Gregorian chant intoning the *Hodie Christus natus est* of Christmas, or the passion of Good Friday. It was more than just an intellectual experience; it involved the whole person.

There was festivity with the affirmation of faith and the God-man relationship as well as juxtaposition and the excess that is always present when faith is expressed. There was also the fantasy as we all were offered thoughts on the future, and in particular, the future life with God. The former liturgy contained the elements of celebration that appealed to the total person and not just to one aspect of what it means to be human. It had its results as well, with countless numbers of people dedicating their lives to the practice of the Christian faith.

What is interesting to recall is that this same period had in its catechetics a very narrow approach to God. What was offered to children was not the experience of God, but a carefully delineated set of questions and responses. The catechism was far from a non-conceptual approach to the Christian faith. Children were asked to memorize responses that were supposed to stay with them as they grew up. It was an intellectual approach to God and the Christian faith with little effort to appeal to more than the intellectual. Even the liturgy began to suffer too much from this intellectual approach, with a loss of participation and a loss of cultural adaptation. There was a need for change to restore celebration of the total person to liturgy.

The Liturgy of Today[13]

The liturgy of today continues a tradition from the past in an effort to appeal to the total person, but it has been adapted and changed. There is still the emphasis on the insight into the full meaning of life, but now more opportunities are offered to experience this insight. To begin with, the Roman Catholic liturgy is in the vernacular, which should help people enter more deeply into the meaning of the experience of God. The priest faces the people so that the sense of sight is more involved; there is greater communication by words and song between priest and people; there is an effort to simplify the appointments of a church so as not to distract from the celebration of the liturgy. All are directed to helping people experience wonder and insight into life all the more.

The Protestant tradition has had its own liturgical revival with an increase in the celebration of the Eucharist and the use of contemporary culture in its celebration. The restoration of movement and ritual and sense perception to the more traditional Protestant liturgy is part of the same experience in the Roman Catholic tradition. Everyone seems to experience the need for liturgies that celebrate the awareness of God and the goodness of life and is seeking ways to express this awareness in ways that make sense and have meaning today.

The new liturgy also has its festivity with more emphasis on this element of celebration than in the past. Sunday should be more festive than other days of the week; there is the affirmation that life is good and people are good, and that God is alive and good. This affirmation is made even as we are conscious that we are not always the people we profess to be. There is the juxtaposition and the excess of faith as was present in the past; there is the fantasy as well. We celebrate together that God is present among us; people from all walks of life can gather and listen to the same Word, eat from the same table, and even wish one another well in the gesture of peace. Surely this is fantasy: how things might be when all men can live as one.

Liturgy and Celebration

When liturgy is celebrated, it involves the total person. No aspect of the human personality is left out. People come together as a faith-community to experience some new insight into their lives and their relationship with God. The total person is affected: the emotional, the bodily, the mind, the heart, the spirit; each finds expression in what happens and hopefully each becomes holier and manifests more the qualities of God: each person strives again for the mercy and fidelity that characterizes God, and in so doing gives glory to God. An atmosphere is created in which the participants express and become affected by what is expressed. The fundamental intuition into life is impressed on the individual worshiper not only in an intellectual sense, but in a way that brings involvement of the total person. The celebration of liturgy has long recognized the humanness of involvement of the total person. Our experience with a good liturgical celebration is fundamentally not conceptual; at the same time, it is not without its conceptual elements. The liturgy of the Word is conceptual, but fits into the larger picture of the religious experience of people expressing faith together in ritual and experiencing the presence of God. Christians in liturgy move from the nonconceptual to the conceptual, and in that movement become different people as they experience the nearness of God in Christ. Liturgy is more than emotional; it is more than intellectual; it is human and involves all that is human. For this reason, it is evident that liturgy should form an integral part of Christian life.[14]

People must participate in and feel a part of the celebration; the priest or minister as leader must help to develop the prayerful atmosphere. The Word of God must be proclaimed; the use of light and color and sound and music and vestments and movement and dance all have a part and all together have their effect. When we speak of the presence of the Church as the presence of the worshiping community and the epiphany of the Church,[15] we are close to the New Testament. When people of faith come together as members of the household of saints to express their faith together and celebrate their life and their relationship to God and to their fellow-men, they are changed. Liturgy fulfills its purpose and makes them more human and more Christian and brings an enthusiasm for life and God and people.

Life can be so wonderful if we open our eyes. Even in the midst of tragedy and failure, there is a goodness about man that can never be erased. He is created in God's image and has a destiny that is God himself. Life is never without its insights and is always in need of festivity and fantasy. When we combine the celebration of life with gratitude to God, then we worship God and become better people. Liturgy becomes human and draws us nearer to God and to one another. David could dance with joy in front of the ark; Christians for 2,000 years have sung out the praises to God with faith and with vigor; believers have prayed together and have been changed through their prayer.

Man always has a need for celebration and has a need for God. The two are not totally disparate. When we appreciate life we can never be far from God. Dag Hammarskjold once remarked: "God does not die on the day when we cease to believe in a personal deity, but we die on the day when our lives cease to be illuminated by the steady radiance, renewed daily, of a wonder, the source of which is beyond all reason."[16] If we believe in God and in his Christ we have to believe in life and wonder. For those who at least believe in wonder, God can never be far off. To be human is to celebrate. For the Christian, God is always the basis for celebration.

Notes

[1]Cf. John F. O'Grady, "Traditional Images of God," *American Ecclesiastical Review*, 163 (1970), pp. 73-80.

[2]For a brief presentation on religious experience see Alistair Kee, *The Way of Transcendence* (Baltimore: Penguin, 1971), pp. 3-31.

[3]Cf. Sam Keen, *Apology for Wonder* (New York: Harper and Row, 1969), pp. 21-60.

[4]Cf. Harvey Cox, *The Feast of Fools* (Cambridge: Harvard Univ. Press, 1969), pp. 21-47. I have modified some of Cox's positions on the meaning of festivity, but in general the thoughts are derived from his pages.

[5]*Ibid.*, pp. 22-23.

[6]*Ibid.*, pp. 59-67. Cox speaks of fantasy as "advanced imagining" (p. 62). I prefer to speak of fantasy as "how things might be, even if they never will be."

[7]*The Oxford History of the American People* (New York: Oxford University Press, 1965), p. 1122.

[8]Cf. Sam Keen, *To a Dancing God* (New York: Harper and Row, 1970), pp. 38-81. This book does not offer the clear reflections on celebration as his previous work, but does present how celebration affects the total person.

[9]This has been treated at length in chapter 3.

[10]Cf. John F. O'Grady, *Jesus Lord and Christ* (Paramus: Paulist Press, 1973), ch. VI.

[11]This has been treated previously in my article: "Liturgy: Catechesis for the Total Person," *The Priest*, 28 (1972), pp. 18-26.

[12]Cf. Keen, *Apology for Wonder* (New York: Harper and Row, 1969), pp. 206-212.

[13]Cf. Henry Horn, *Worship in Crisis* (Philadelphia: Fortress 1972). The author presents some important thoughts on the contemporary liturgical movement and some problems present in the approach.

[14]Cf. *The People Worship*, ed. Lancelot Sheppard (New York: Hawthorn, 1967), pp. 69-80.

[15]Cf. J. J. Von Allmen, *Worship: Its Theology and Practice* (New York: Oxford Univ. Press, 1965), pp. 42-56.

[16]D. Hammarskjold, *Markings* (New York: Knopf, 1964), p. 56.

12

Man and Nature

Christian theology in the recent past has not been noted for great interest in cosmology. Theologians were satisfied with dealing with the God-to-man relationship and vice versa, and often overlooked man's environment. This has not always been the case. Religions have consistently been concerned with the universe and they need this concern. "Religion is concerned with our reactions of purpose and emotion due to our personal measure of intuition into the ultimate mystery of the universe."[1] If we are to talk about a Christian anthropology, we must talk about man's relationship to nature.

The Bible: Basis for a Christian Understanding of Nature

Any foundation for the role of man and nature in the Judaic-Christian tradition rests on an understanding of Genesis. God created all things, is responsible for all that lives, and all that God created is good (Gen. 1:2). At the height of creation is man himself to whom God gave dominion. We have already seen the meaning of "created in the image of God": man is to exercise dominion by manifesting the qualities of God; he is to be the vicegerent: "God set man in the world as the sign of his own sovereign authority, in order that man should uphold and enforce his God's claims as Lord."[2] This is the basis of man's role in the universe.

Throughout history man will fulfill his role of sharing in the glory and majesty of God when man is responsible in his decisions. The authority of man in creation has to be a God-like authority. This does not mean that God is responsible to another for his creation, as is man, but that God cares for his creation; He is faithful, trustworthy, and consistent in his concern. As God is, so man must strive to become. This is true even if man cannot always see the constancy in God's activity. It is faith that assures us that God is bringing a good thing to its conclusion:

> Accordingly, let those who suffer as God's will requires continue in good deeds, and entrust their lives to a faithful Creator. (1 Peter 4:19)

Man is responsible for creation in another sense: he must render an account before God:

> But you, how can you sit in judgment on your brother? Or you, how can you look down on your brother? We shall all have to appear before the judgment seat of God. (Rom. 14:10)

As man is to rule creation, so his rule is to be wise, reflecting the qualities of God. Dominion is given to man but not without a call to account based on stewardship. This viewpoint is quite different from a purely biological view that sees man, as the most resourceful of all animals, capable of controlling his environment. When Christian theology speaks of control and stewardship and man as the vicegerent of God, the purpose and theology of creation enter the scene. Man cannot do with his environment whatever he wishes.

The Bible presents clear indications of the repercussions in nature that result when man fails to exercise responsible dominion. The classic example is in Genesis with reference to the Fall and the cursing of the soil because of man's sin (3:17). To the authors of Genesis, man's sinfulness has not only affected himself but has also affected his environment. In the prophets—in Isaiah, Hosea, and Job[3]—there are other examples of the relationship between the fulfillment of man's responsibility to God and the blessing of nature and the failure of man and the cursing of nature.

The New Testament offers a similar belief. St. Paul relates man to creation now and in the future:

> I consider the sufferings of the present to be as nothing com-

> pared with the glory to be revealed in us. Indeed, the whole created world eagerly awaits the revelation of the sons of God. Creation was made subject to futility, not of its own accord but by him who once subjected it; yet not without hope, because the world itself will be freed from its slavery to corruption and share in the glorious freedom of the children of God. Yes, we know that all creation groans and is in agony even until now. Not only that, but we ourselves, although we have the Spirit as first fruits, groan inwardly while we await the redemption of our bodies. (Rom. 8:18-23)

Man is responsible before God; as long as he refuses to play the role of God's vicegerent in creation and fails to exercise his dominion as one created in the image of God, the entire world is frustrated and dislocated. It is only when man fulfills his role as son in relationship to Jesus that the groaning of nature will be silenced. As long as man abuses his own life, he will abuse all of creation and will suffer the consequences.[4]

The Bible speaks of a complementarity of cosmology and theology, and this is necessary for any religious appreciation of man. We cannot speak of man and his nature and destiny prescinding from his environment. The question remains: why have we not learned to protect our environment, why have we continued to abuse what is given? A study of the medieval synthesis between cosmology and theology and its subsequent separation may help us to understand why we have lost our sense of relationship to the universe and how this loss has caused problems of great magnitude.

The Medieval Synthesis Between Cosmology and Theology

The theology of the Middle Ages concentrated on the unity and harmony of the universe and interpreted this unity in the light of an appreciation of God and man. The basis of this unity, however, was more often the Greek philosophy of Plato and Aristotle than the Word of God in Scripture. Plato offered his vision of the world of ideas that was reflected in the created order, bringing a perfection to the universe that mirrored the perfection in the world of ideas. Aristotle saw the universe dependent on a first mover with each element maintaining its natural tendencies.

Within such a synthesis of the world, the Christian theologians inserted their understanding of God and man. God was viewed as the Almighty, all-knowing Creator of a perfect world; man became the entrapped spirit yearning for the heavens and the world of the spirit. With some simplification it can be said that the medieval theologians and people saw the universe as a perfect order in which there was no change and a perfect order in which there was established a close hierarchy of beings.

Within this context, the task of man was to realize in his own life, in his own thinking, in his morals, in his art and social life the reflection of the same perfect and hierarchical order he observes in the universe. Man is called to contemplate and admire the work of God.

There were many advantages to this world-view. Everything was submissive to faith because all was submissive to the all-powerful and all-knowing God. Man should learn to overcome his attachment to this world in favor of the future world.

Equally evident were the disadvantages. Man lost his sense of perfecting and changing the universe; his sense of dominion was lost in the control of faith and the religious institution. Science, which needed freedom, fell under control of faith and the Church. Such a system could not long survive.

The Loss of the Medieval Synthesis

Within medieval theology this world outlook was closely related to faith; so it is understandable that the theologians and the Church would suspect any effort to change this outlook. Tinkering with the world-view amounted to tinkering with faith. But even the threat of the all-embracing ecclesiastical institution could not sure-up forever the old cosmology.

The destruction of the old cosmology that had predominated since Aristotle was not accomplished in a day. Step by step the old view was eroded, with the first step taken by Copernicus.[5] He offered his theory of the centrality of the sun more for philosophical reasons than scientific, but in spite of his failure in science, the publication in 1543 of *De revolutionibus orbium caelestium* marked the beginning of a scientific critique of the old cosmology.

The man who contributed most to the destruction of the old order was Galileo (1564-1642). His theory of method in science based on observation and experimentation destroyed the argument from authority. Galileo's story is sufficiently known today and perhaps more intelligible, if not defensible, in the light of the unity of thought between faith and the world perspective that characterized the medieval synthesis. The invention of the telescope aided his theory of heliocentrism; through it, he discovered spots on the sun, which was in opposition to the former doctrine of the perfection of the heavenly bodies.

The discovery of a new star by the Danish astronomer Tycho Brahe in 1572 brought into question the static notion of the universe. With this discovery the possibility of a changing universe was no longer dismissed as fanciful.

The final blow to the medieval synthesis was delivered by Isaac Newton with the law of gravity. The medievalists summoned the power of God and angels to move stars and planets. With the discovery of gravity, there was no longer any need for such intervention. The solar system functioned by its own dynamics and its own laws.

The concrete results of this loss of unity between faith and the world was a liberation for man. The universe was no longer under some religious control; man is the ruler of the universe if he can unlock the secrets of his world. This new possibility gave entrance to the dominance of science. Man was no longer a contemplative in the world; he must find his own place, and in this search he must control the place of everything else.

The one dissonant note in the process was man's loss of responsibility before God. We have seen that the medieval theology had God intervening in the universe even to the extent of moving the planets. The development of science made this activity superfluous. To the question of the role of God in such a synthesis some philosophers responded with deism (Locke, Rousseau, Voltaire, Hume). For them, God was the great architect or watchmaker; once he created the world, he was no longer interested in its activities since it could manage very well on its own. Others (Baruch Spinoza) offered a doctrine of pantheism. Still others drew the logical conclusion of atheism (Diderot, D'Holbach). The old cosmology was bankrupt. If God was said to be necessary only for the start of the process, what prevents man from seeing matter as eternal and having in itself the power for organization and complexity? Change your world-view and if your concept of God does not agree with the new world-view, it cannot long survive. The very important result of this process was the complete independence from God that blossomed in the favor of this new world-view. It was man's world; he could do as he wished.

The Third Cosmology of the Twentieth Century

Many scientists consider that in this century we are on the verge of a third cosmology. The first Aristotelian cosmology persisted for more than 2,000 years until the sixteenth century. The second cosmology from Copernicus and Galileo lasted up to this century; it was not a real and coherent view of the universe, but only the first attempt to discover the universe in its spatial dimensions. With the discoveries and theories of Einstein, the giant telescope of Mount Palomar, the quantum theory, and the more recent space exploits, some scientists believe that we are on the threshold of a new age of science.[6] In this new age, science is no longer separated from other disciplines. Rather, man is more aware that all human knowledge is interconnected. "The modern conception of nature is of a continuous evolutionary process linking the purely physical with the biological, the biological with the psychological, and the psychological with the social, moral, artistic, and religious experience of man."[7] Evolution, development, process have become the slogans of the new age, bringing with it a more basic innovation of the third cosmology: the role of man in the new universe.

Once man views the universe as a self-sufficient system of energy, he must see his responsibility to develop this system. Today man is conscious that he is immersed in space and time, that he is an individual capable of decision and responsibility. He is responsible to his past, but equally so for his present in which he lives as he strives to build his future. He will become himself only when he is willing to pay the cost of developing.

Man has changed his vision of the world. No longer does he see the heavens under the control of God; no longer does he see the earth as perfect and static; no longer does he see a need for a synthesis of theology and the cosmos; no longer does he listen to words about the wonder of God and creation and his responsibility before God. Instead he sees himself as developing and becoming, much the same as his world is developing and becoming; he is aware of the possibilities that are given to him and is striving for the integration of these possibilities in a human mode of life; he knows that he is free to make of his life whatever he wants and is determined to act in spite of approval or disapproval; he senses the urgency of the one life that is given to him and the few years that are his to make his mark; he knows that the world is his responsibility and revels in the challenge that it offers; he sees himself totally and not piecemeal, and seeks a life that will respond to his totality; he sees his responsibility to this world and to the future and believes that he has the means of controlling and changing this world. The one sour note in this picture is the question of whether man will survive to accomplish all that he hopes. Can the environment sustain much more of man's abuse?

Christian Responsibility and the Environment

With the demise of the medieval synthesis and the new developments of the twentieth century, man may well have come of age. The question is whether the divorce of religion from nature and the role of God in man's life is possible without detriment to the environment. Some have claimed that the Judaic-Christian understanding of man as created in the image of God is directly responsible for the abuse of the environment. It seems instead that a loss of the meaning of dominion in Genesis and the further separation of the religious dimension of life from the environment has added to the failure to appreciate the need for man to contribute to the betterment of the environment rather than seek to destroy it. This is not to say that religion and religion alone will save the environment. It is to say that religion can make a significant contribution to the salvation of man's earth. It is this that needs explanation.

Genesis presents man as Lord of the universe, but not one to whom God has given a blank check. Man is to be a wise and faithful steward, held accountable for the responsible use of the goods of creation. Dominion means to foster, encourage, and bless—and not to destroy. Jesus demands that his stewards have the qualities of fidelity and wisdom (Luke 12:42). Paul echoes the same belief when he says:

> The first requirement of an administrator is that he prove trustworthy. (1 Cor. 4:2)

No man has the right to abuse the goods of God's earth. Such activities violate the sacredness of life, the intelligence of man, and the integrity of the universe. To talk abstractly is not sufficient; there are practical conclusions for any Christian theology of man and his environment. For too long a time we have allowed theology to be divorced from cosmology; it is time that the Christian approach to life and creation once again offer a guide to the desire of modern man to develop, control, and master his world. It is one thing to speak about the future of man in a scientific and technological age, but this cannot ignore the possible destruction of man, not by some act of God but by man himself. Christian attitudes must characterize our role on this planet.

A theology of ecology is needed. A restatement of the facts and the needs is not necessary; this is all too evident in the ever-declining amount of clean air and water and space and the burgeoning of waste. A theology of ecology begins with the firm conviction that all being is relational.

The Bible assures us that man is relational, as is all of reality. The basic ideas of the Bible—God, man, love, hatred, sin, grace, covenant, fidelity, truth—are all relational words. The words point to the meaning behind the words: man is not alone in this world; he is part of the whole and in need of the whole for survival and for a fruitful survival. As Paul remarks in 1 Corinthians:

> If one member suffers, all the members suffer with it; if one member is honored, all the members share its joy. (12:26)

A second premise for a theology of ecology is that relation brings dependence. Each element of the whole is "beholding" to the other. The choice of the word "beholding" is carefully calculated. To behold is not just to see; to behold is to regard with a sense of honor and reverence. Man beholds creation. Jesus teaches us to behold the lilies of the field (Matt. 6:28). "To stand beholding means that one stands within creation with an intrinsically theological stance."[8]

We have already seen that man is history. Too often in the past man as history was separated from man as nature. If there is to be a theology of ecology, man as history must be joined to man as nature. Redemption is historical and has implications for all of creation. Even the enigmatic eighth chapter of Romans at least suggests that creation waits for human operations by which men of faith will truly become what they are called to be, sons of God, and not simply the most resourceful of all animals, which in nature will redound and bring about the perfection of the universe.

Finally, as we understand the meaning of salvation we realize that God loves this world, man and woman, and their neighbors and the whole earth. It is a garden of joy and labor that awaits the fullness of salvation when all will be restored.

When we accept the world as relation, when man is beholding to all of creation, when the believer manifests his faith that all of creation shares in salvation, we will have developed a theology of ecology. Lest this be considered too abstract and too separated from life, there are some attitudes that the Christian must develop.

Christian Attitudes for Man and Nature

Progress in the exercise of responsible dominion depends on an awareness of what can and should be done. There are sins against stewardship that must be overcome.

Responsibility for the future—Christians believe that the future of man is God and that this future is assured by the coming of Jesus Christ. We are basically a people who look beyond the present and prepare for the future. Since the future perspective is part of the Christian outlook, believers can never use things in the present so as to destroy them for the future. Responsibility extends into the future with its future generations. To be concerned only for the present and for the immediate is a failure in Christian stewardship. We must be concerned with the wanton waste of natural resources in order that the goods of creation will be present for future generations.

Responsibility for others—A third of the world's population often suffers greatly because of the consumer habits of one-tenth of the world's population. To use things for ourselves in such a way that others are deprived of basic needs is sinful and cries for justice. There are imbalances in the world economic order that must be redressed. Economic imperialism is more damaging than political imperialism since it is more subtle and more devastating for the future. Affluent nations must learn to adapt to a more modest standard of living in order to raise the level of living conditions of all people. Stewardship demands that we share with the brother in need (Matt. 25:31-46).

Responsibility to use goods wisely and not wastefully—We have the false opinion that there is an unlimited supply of everything. Power, energy, water, natural resources are finite and not infinite. We destroy the environment as quickly as we have destroyed species of life. Cultural practices must be re-examined as well as economic practices. It is not necessary to be subservient to fashion, to plan obsolescence in our products. There is a limited supply on this earth of all goods. Man must learn to believe this is true and act accordingly.

Pride in work—Man is a worker and must see work as fulfilling a need for himself and others. If more people took pride in their work, our products would last longer and have greater value and versatility. To contribute further to a throw-away culture will only add greater destruction to the environment.

Respect for creation—The true Christian personality sees value in the earth and in the world. He has respect for all of creation as well as for the noble achievements of man. This is not to be taken for granted. There is need for education in respect for the planet made practical by signs of that respect. People will never be convinced of the need to cooperate with programs for the enrichment of the environment unless they first respect their planet.

There are many other practices that will be necessary for man to resolve his relationship with the environment. The foregoing are offered only as a beginning. There is need for a reassessment of the relationship between Christian theology and nature made practical in the lives of believers. Nor is this just another abstract principle of theology. It involves the survival of the human race.

There has already taken place a divorce between theology and science. In many respects this has brought great benefits to mankind. It has also caused problems. When man is left on his own and has no sense of responsibility for creation, he will tend to destroy what is given. Theology offers the possible balance of man's need for control and his exercise of responsibility through the concept of Christian stewardship. We may well be on the threshold of a new cosmology that is more lasting than the previous cosmologies; we are also on the threshold of possible destruction. Science needs theology to limit its power just as theology must take science into consideration in its task to respond to the needs of contemporary man. There is a theology of nature and a Christian approach to nature that is expressed in the Bible and finds expression in the concern for the universe on the part of believers.

In an age of religious secularization, it can easily be said that the present concern for ecology is nothing more than the secularization of the Judaic-Christian tradition. No longer does man talk about man created in the image and likeness of God having dominion over the universe to be exercised responsibly, but the end result is the same. There is a value contained in this religious doctrine and if the value were always appreciated, we would not be in the position we find ourselves today. Without the cloak of religious doctrine, man today has accepted the value and is interested in making the value acceptable to all. At least it can be said that there is no contradiction between the doctrine of man in the Bible and the understanding of man's responsibility today to clean up his world that he himself has dirtied up.

There seems to be another aspect that we should also consider here before we conclude, and that is the convergence of values that seems to characterize our society. We see man as more than an economic or political or scientific entity; man is social and historical and in need of the good and the beautiful as well as the useful and the economic; man is involved with the future as well as the immediate present; man has responsibilities to the unborn generations as well as to his own life and family. Certainly we can say that this is also part of the Judaic tradition, but it has not always been evident in Western society and today it is accepted not for religious reasons, but for humanitarian reasons. This understanding of man, perhaps more than anything else, is responsible for the new attitude of man toward his environment. If this attitude spreads among men, and today it is still far from the accepted notion, then we will have a better environment; we will improve our quality of life far more effectively and more quickly than all the speeches and laws and marches can ever hope to do. For then we will be acting because of our understanding of ourselves.

In the Christian tradition, there have been few believers who have ever achieved the level of love for creation attained by Francis of Assisi. Even in a secular age he offers a romantic approach to creation that stirs the imagination. Christians must learn to pray and praise God in his creation in a way similar to the poor man of Assisi:

Canticle of Brother Sun

Be praised, my Lord, with all Your creatures,
Especially Sir Brother Sun,
By whom you give us the light of day!
And he is beautiful and radiant with great splendor,
Of You, Most High, he is a symbol!

Be praised, my Lord, for Sister Moon and the Stars!
In the sky You formed them bright and lovely and fair.

Be Praised, my Lord, for Brother Wind
And for the Air and cloudy and clear and all Weather,
By which You give sustenance to Your creatures!

Be praised, my Lord, for Sister Water,
Who is very useful and humble and lovely and chaste!

Be praised, my Lord, for Brother Fire,
By whom You give us light at night,
And he is beautiful and merry and mighty and strong!

Be praised, My Lord, for our Sister Mother Earth,
Who sustains and governs us,
and produces fruits with colorful flowers and leaves!

Notes

[1]Alfred N. Whitehead, *Adventures of Ideas* (Cambridge: Univ. Press, 1961), p. 165.

[2]Gerhard Von Rad, *Old Testament Theology* vol. I (London: Oliver and Boyd, 1962), p. 144.

[3]Cf. Isaiah 11:5-9; Hosea 2:21-23; Job 5:17-23.

[4]Cf. C. F. Moule, *Man and Nature in the New Testament* (Philadelphia: Fortress Press, 1967).

[5]Cf. Thomas Kuhn, *The Copernican Revolution* (Cambridge: Harvard Univ. Press, 1957).

[6]Cf. F. Hoyle, *The Nature of the Universe* (New York, 1960).

[7]E. Harris, *Revelation through Reason* (London, 1958), pp. 57-58.

[8]Joseph Sittler, "Ecological Commitment as Theological Responsibility," *IDOC*, 9 (1970), p. 79.

Conclusion

Everyone seems to desire to know more about the meaning of human life. A world run mad, with powerful forces for survival or destruction, is often thrown back upon the need to question and to seek some answers. Dreams are often the result of the questioning process with faint hopes that somehow, somewhere, sometime, the dreams may be realized. This is the ever-receding hope of mankind.

A study of a Christian understanding of man, man in the light of the Word of God, is one possible solution. It is not the only solution but one among many. It is not the only answer that can be given to the riddle of human life. There are more responses than opportunities to offer the response. Over 2,000 years have passed in the Christian tradition, and in relationship to its Jewish heritage, another 2,000 years. What has made sense to many people can continue to make sense to future generations.

Man is created in the image of God and is called to share a responsible dominion together with woman over all of creation. Man has a destiny to reflect the glory of God: His mercy and His fidelity, and His need of a community to accomplish this task. It is a good foundation for any approach to the meaning of life.

The future of mankind is God himself. This he has established in the sending of his Son, Jesus Christ. All men are destined to share in the glory of God and find happiness and contentment in God himself. There is no sadistic God behind the scenes condemning without reason, arbitrarily calling one to salvation and the other to endless suffering. There is only the attitude of a gracious and loving parent who is wise enough to allow freedom of choice to everyone. God is clear in his approach to human life and human meaning; it has been established through years of man's refusal to love; the final word has been spoken and that word is good.

Among the many nations of the world, God has chosen two groups to be his special place of revelation: Jews and Christians. This election calls for an acceptance of responsibility to strive to help others to see the value in life and in belief in the God of Abraham, Isaac, Jacob, who is Father of Our Lord and Savior, Jesus Christ. Christians and Jews have a position in the world unlike others. They are to be the sign of salvation to others, offering concrete signs of God's goodness through the love that they manifest in their lives.

As a result of what man is, we can believe that everyone has a religious dimension in his life; there is a positive orientation toward God that is reflected in the desire of man for transcendence and for peace. There is no such thing as a universe unaffected by grace, but only one universe in which the powerful presence of God is discovered in every aspect of life. With such a positive orientation it is hard for man to go wrong. Yet he has done just that.

Man lives in an evil world and contributes to that evil by his own sin. Pride, selfishness, greed, envy have plagued human society for as long as man remembers. It has always been this way in recorded history and the present does not seem to be an improvement. Evil is real and as contemporary as war and violence and suffering and death. The beautiful image of a tranquil life has been ruined.

On these foundations the Christian bases his approach to life. If anything, the scales are tipped in favor of goodness. In an age in which evil and destructive forces are so evident, it is essential to recall this goodness. Whatever else can be said of man—his nature as person in dialogue, his total personality, his historical dimension, his sexual life, his work, his art, his celebrations—all is influenced by the foundations. What man is now depends on what he has been becoming. He is a mixture of good and evil and multidimensional. With this basic outlook the Christian can approach any appreciation of human life and have a perspective that will stand him in good stead. Man is good from his origin even as he is vitiated by sin.

There is no need to try to summarize the preceding pages. There is no need to try for an integration of so many ideas. That is left to the individual reader. There is one dimension, however, that should be recalled. If we are ever to become what we are called to be, we need fantasy in every aspect of our lives: How things might be!

Too often discouragement and frustration and despair plague even the most faithful of believers. There is lost a sense of the future and there is forgotten all that has been already promised and fulfilled in the past. Christians have to learn to have vision; Christians must strive to see what is offered even in the midst of what is actual. Fantasy can liven up the dullest of human lives; it can change the face of the human community and the Christian Church.

Elsewhere we wrote that salvation is now and is made evident in the lives of believers. Mankind's future is not in the hands of some dark force. The power that controls human life is good and interested in us. Jesus assures us that:

> We know that God makes all things work together for the good of those who have been called according to his decree. Those whom he foreknew he predestined to share the image of his Son, that the Son might be the first-born of many brothers. Those he predestined he likewise called; those he called he also justified; and those he justified he in turn glorified. What shall we say after that? If God is for us, who can be against us? Is it possible that he who did not spare his own Son but handed him over for the sake of us all will not grant us all things besides? (Rom. 8:28-32)

Life has meaning because we have the witness of the life of Jesus Christ who lived for others:

> All this I tell you that my joy may be yours and your joy may be complete. This is my commandment: love one another as I have loved you. There is no greater love than this: to lay down one's life for one's friends. (John 15:11-13)

There are values present in human life, even if they are not accepted. As long as there is life there is a fundamental value that is the foundation for that life:

> Praised be the God and Father of our Lord Jesus Christ, who has bestowed on us in Christ every spiritual blessing in the heavens! God chose us in him before the world began, to be holy and blameless in his sight, to be full of love; he likewise predestined us through Christ Jesus to be his adopted sons—such was his will and pleasure—that all might praise the glorious favor he has bestowed on us in his beloved. (Eph. 1:3-6)

Jesus Christ is the friend of all: "You are my friends if you do what I command you" (John 15:14).

This is the fantasy that is needed by all. We must all try to believe that things can be different, even if we never live to see the change; we must try to have the enthusiasm for life that alone gives meaning and sense and finds value in the presence of so much pain and suffering.

Fantasy: How things might be, even if they never will be, is needed by all today and is offered in a Christian perspective.

Beginnings are always ominous since we never know where they will end. This approach to Christian anthropology is a beginning. There is much more that must be said: the meaning and place of grace, the development of the Christian life, death and the fulfillment of the Christian life. At least it is a beginning and is offered as such.

BIBLIOGRAPHY

CHAPTER 1

BOOKS

Barthelemy, Dominique, O.P., *God and His Image: An Outline of Biblical Theology*. London: Geoffrey Chapman, 1966.

Berkouwer, G. C., *Man: The Image of God*. Grand Rapids, Michigan: William B. Eerdmans Publishing Company, 1962.

Eichrodt, Walter, *Man In the Old Testament*. London: SCM Press Ltd., 1951.

Ferris, Theodore, *The Image of God*. New York: Oxford Univ. Press, 1965.

Kummel, Werner Georg, *Man in the New Testament*. Trans. John J. Vincent. Philadelphia: The Westminster Press, 1963.

LeTroquer, René, *What Is Man?* vol. 31 of the *Twentieth Century Encyclopedia of Catholicism*. New York: Hawthorn Books, 1961.

Mascall, E., "The Question of Man," *Theology of the Future*. London: Darton, Longman, 1968.

Moeller, C., "Renewal of the Doctrine of Man," *Theology of Renewal*, vol. II. New York: Herder and Herder, 1968.

Niebuhr, R., *The Nature and Destiny of Man*. New York: C. Scribner's Sons, 1941.

Prenter, R., *Creation and Redemption*. Philadelphia: Fortress Press, 1965.

Rahner, K., "Theology and Anthropology," *The Word in History*. New York: Sheed and Ward, 1966.

Rust, E. C., *Nature and Man in Biblical Thought*. London: Lutterworth Press, 1953.

Schlier, H., "Man in the Light of the Earliest Christian Preaching," *The Relevance of the New Testament*. New York: Herder and Herder, 1967.

Sullivan, John Edward, O.P., *The Image of God*. Dubuque, Iowa: The Priory Press, 1963.

ARTICLES

Bluhm, H., "Luther's View of Man in His Early German Writings," (Lecture), *Concordia Theological Monthly*, 34 (October 1963), 583-593.

Feinberg, C. L., "The Image of God," *Bibl. Sacra*, 129 (1972), 235-246.

Feuillet, André, "The Christ-Image of God," *The Bible Today*, 21 (1965), 1409-1414.

Gleason, Robert W., S.J., "The Concept of Man in the Old Testament," *Dominicana*, 50 (1965), 13-30.

Glock, C. Y., "Images of God, Images of Man and the Organization of the Sacred Life," *J.S.S.R.*, 11 (1972), 1-15.

Kenny, J. P., "The Perfect Image: Jesus Christ," *The Way*, 5 (1965), 192-203.

Luyten, J., "Anthropology of the O.T.," *Louvain Studies*, 5 (1974), 3-17.

Navone, J., "In Our Image and Likeness," *The Bible Today*, 8 (1963), 492-499.

Pelikan, J., "Doctrine of Man in Lutheran Confessions," *Lutheran Quarterly*, 2 (February 1950), 34-44.

Ricoeur, P., "The Image of God and the Epic of Man," *Cross Currents*, 11 (1961), 37-50.

Rousseau, R., "Secular and Christian Images of Man," *Thought*, 47 (1972), 165-200.

Scanlon, M., "Convergence in Theological Anthropology," *CTSAP*, 29 (1974), 283-299.

Stuermann, W. E., and Geocoris, K., "Image of Man (Perspective of Calvin and Freud)," *Interpretation*, 14 (January 1960), 28-42.

CHAPTER 2

BOOKS

Barth, Karl, *Church Dogmatics*. G. W. Bromiley and T. F. Torrance, ed. Edinburgh: T. and T. Clark, 1957. (Vol. 11, 2nd part, ch. VII.)

Calvin, John, *Institutes of Christian Religion*, 2 vols. *The Library of Christian Classics*, vol. XXI, John T. McNeill, ed.; trans., Ford Lewis Battles. Philadelphia: The Westminster Press, 1960. (Bk. III, Ch. 21, Sec 5 and 7.)

Farrelly, John, O.S.B., *Predestination, Grace and Free Will*. Westminster, Md.: The Newman Press, 1964.

Guardini, Romano, *Freedom, Grace and Destiny*. New York: Pantheon Books, 1961.

Kerr, Hugh T., ed., *A Compendium of Luther's Theology*. Philadelphia: The Westminster Press, 1966. (p. 36ff.)

Luther, Martin, *Lectures on Romans*. Trans. and ed. by Wilhelm Pauck. *The Library of Christian Classics*, vol. XV. Philadelphia: The Westminster Press, 1961.

ARTICLES

Blythin, I., "Patriarchs and the Promise," *Scottish Journal of Theology*, 21 (1965), 56-73.

Cunliffe-Jones, H., "Predestination," *Scottish Journal of Theology*, 3 (1950), 409-415.

Dion, H., "Predestination in St. Paul," *Theology Digest*, 15 (1967), 144-149.

Fahey, T., "Romans 8:29," *Irish Theological Quarterly*, 23, (1956), 410-412.

Fitzmeyer, J. A., "Aramaic 'Elect of God' Text from Qumran Cave IV," *Catholic Biblical Quarterly*, 27 (1965), 348-372.

James, E. C., "Is Foreknowledge Equivalent to Foreordination?" *Bibliotheca Sacra*, 122 (1965), 215-219.

Lambrecht, J., "Man Before and Without Christ: Rom. 7 and Pauline Anthropology," *Louvain Studies*, 5 (1974), 18-53.

McDonnell, A., "Those Whom He Has Chosen," *Dominicana*, 48 (1963), 109-119.

Reynolds, S. M., "Surpreme Importance of The Doctrine of Election and The Eternal Security of he Elect as Taught in the Gospel of St. John (10:29)," *Westminster Journal of Theology*, 28, (1965), 35-41.

Robinson, D. W. B., "Salvation of Israel in Romans 9-11," *Reformed Theological Review*, 26 (1967), 81-96.

Simonin, T., "Predestination, prescience et liberté," *Nouvelle Revue Théologique*, 85 (1963), 711-730.

Solomon, A., "The New Testament Doctrine of Election," *Scottish Journal of Theology*, 11 (1958), 406-422.

Sutcliffe, Edmund, "Many are Called but Few are Chosen," *Irish Theological Quarterly*, 28 (1961), 126-131.

Vigouroux, F., "Predestination," *Dictionnaire de la Bible* (Paris: 1912), tm 5, 594-595.

CHAPTER 3

BOOKS

Lubac, Henri de, *The Mystery of the Supernatural*. New York: Herder and Herder, 1967.

Rahner, Karl, *Nature and Grace*. New York: Sheed and Ward, 1964.

Shepherd, W., *Man's Condition*. New York: Herder and Herder, 1968.

Segundo, J. L., *Grace: The Human Condition*. New York: Orbis, 1973.

ARTICLES

Alfaro, J., "Person and Grace," *Man Before God*. New York: Kenedy, 1966.

Allen, Paul, "Nature and Grace," *Review for Religious*, 24 (March, 1965).

Bechtle, R., "Karl Rahner's Supernatural Existential: A Personalist Approach," *Thought* 48 (1973), 61-77.

Dietz, Donald, "Nature and Grace," *Homiletic and Pastoral Review*, 54 (July, 1964), 894.

Franch, P., "Grace, Theologizing and the Humanizing of Man," *CTSAD*, 27 (1972), 55-77.

Gallagher, Joseph, "Nature and Grace," *Catholic World*, 199 (July, 1964), p. 255.

Hazelton, R., "Homo Capax Dei: Thoughts on Man and Transcendence," *Theological Studies*, 33 (1972), 735-747.

Kottukapally, J., "Nature and Grace: A New Dimension," *Thought*, 49 (1974), 117-133.

Lonergan, B., "Natural Desire to See God," *Collection* (New York: Herder and Herder, 1967), 84-95.

Lubac, Henri de, "Nature and Grace," *The Word in History* (New York: Sheed and Ward, 1966), 24-40.

McCool, G., "The Philosophy of the Human Person in Rahner's Theology," *Theological Studies*, 22 (1961), 539-552.

Motherway, T., "Supernatural Existential," *Chicago Studies*, 4 (1965), 70-103.

Potter, Gerald, "Nature and Grace," *Worship*, 39 (January, 1965), 56.

Rahner, K., "Concerning the Relationship Between Nature and Grace," *Theological Investigations*, vol. I (Baltimore: Helicon, 1961), 297-317.

Schlitzer, Albert, "Nature and Grace," *Thought*, 40 (Summer, 1965), 298.

TeSelle, E., "Nature and Grace in the Form of Ecumenical Discussion," *Journal of Ecumenical Studies*, 8 (1971), 539-559.

Trethowan, Illtyd, "The Mystery of the Supernatural," *The Downside Review*, 84 (October, 1966), 397-407.

Wright, John H., "The Mystery of the Supernatural," *Theological Studies*, 27 (June, 1966), 278.

CHAPTER 4

BOOKS

Bertrands, A., *The Bible on Suffering*. DePere, Wisconsin: St. Norbert Abbey Press, 1966.
Boros, Ladislaus, *Pain and Providence*. Baltimore: Helicon Press, 1966, pp. 52-89.
Hick, John E., *Evil and the God of Love*. New York: Harper and Row, 1966, p. 403.
Lavelle, Louis, *Evil and Suffering*. New York: Macmillan Company, 1963, pp. 30-34, 59-90.
Lewis, C. S., *The Problem of Pain*. New York: Macmillan Company, 1955.
Maly, Eugene, *Sin: Biblical Perspectives*. Chicago: Pflaum, 1973.
Régamey, Pius-Raymond, O.P., *The Cross and The Christian*. St. Louis: B. Herder Book Co., 1954.
Ricoeur, Paul, *The Symbolism of Evil*. New York: Harper & Row, 1967, part II.
Segundo, J. L., *Evolution and Guilt*. New York: Orbis, 1974.

ARTICLES

Ahearn, B. M., "Fellowship of His Sufferings" (Pauline), *Catholic Biblical Quarterly* (January, 1960), 1-32.
Blenkincopp, Joseph, "We Rejoice in Our Sufferings," *Way* (Winter, 1967), 3-56.
Boros, L., "Suffering and Death," *New Testament Themes for Contemporary Man* (Englewood Cliffs: Prentice-Hall, 1969), 126-139.
Clarke, Thomas, "The Problem of Evil," *Theological Studies*, 28 (1967), 119-128.
Janssens, L., "Ontic Evil and Moral Evil," *Louvain Studies*, 4 (1972), 115-156.
O'Grady, John F., "Evil and the Power of God," *Homiletic and Pastoral Review*, 71 (1971), 437-442.
Teilhard de Chardin, Pierre, "The Meaning and Constructive Value of Suffering," *Jubilee* (June, 1962), 21-23.

BOOKS (ORIGINAL SIN)

DeRosa, Peter C., *Christ and Original Sin*. Milwaukee: Bruce Publishing Co., 1967.
Haag, C., *Is Original Sin in Scripture?* New York: Sheed and Ward, 1969.

Schoonenberg, H. Piet., *Man and Sin*. Notre Dame, Indiana: Univ. of Notre Dame Press, 1965.

ARTICLES (ORIGINAL SIN)

Alszeghy and Flick, "An Evolutionary View of Original Sin," *Theology Digest*, 5 (1967), 197ff.

———, "A Personalistic View of Original Sin," *Theology Digest*, 15 (1967), 190ff.

———, "What did Trent Define about Original Sin?" *Gregorianum*, 52 (1971), TD 21 (1973), 57-65.

Condon, Kevin, "The Biblical Doctrine of Sin," *Irish Theological Quarterly*, 34 (1967), 20-36.

Connor, James, "Original Sin: Contemporary Approaches," *Theological Studies*, 29 (1968), 215-240.

Daly, G., "Theological Models in the Doctrine of Original Sin," *Heythrop Journal*, 13 (1972), 121-142.

Fuchs, Joseph, "Sin and Conversion," *Theology Digest*, 14 (1966), 292ff.

McCord, J. I., " 'Know Thyself'; The Biblical Doctrine of Human Depravity," *Interpretation*, 3 (1949), 142-153.

Nossal, A., "Protestants on Original Sin," *TD*, 21 (1973), 57-65.

Padavano, Anthony, "Original Sin and Christian Anthropology," *Catholic Theological Society of America Proceedings*, 22, (1967), 93-133.

Rahner, Karl, "Original Sin," *Theological Investigations*, vol. 1, (Baltimore: Helicon, 1961), 28-44.

Reese, James, "Current Thinking on Original Sin," *American Ecclesiastical Review*, 157 (1967), 92-100.

Smulders, Pierre, "Evolution and Original Sin," *Theology Digest* (1965), 175ff.

Venneste, C., "Le Décret du Concile de Trente Sur le Péché Originel," *Nouvelle Revue Theologie*, 87 (1965), 688-726, and 88 (1966), 581-602.

Wren-Lewis, J., "What was Original Sin?" *Expository Times*, 72 (March 1961), 177-180.

CHAPTER 5

BOOKS

Francoeur, Robert T., *Perspectives in Evolution*. Baltimore: Helicon Press, 1965.

Huxley, Julian, *Evolution in Action*. New York: Harper, 1953.

North, Robert, S.J., *Teilhard and the Creation of the Soul*. Milwaukee: The Bruce Publishing Company, 1967.
Ong, Walter J., *Darwin's Vision and Christian Perspectives*. New York: The Macmillan Company, 1960.
Rahner, Karl, *Hominisation*. New York: Herder and Herder, 1968.
Rust, Eric C., *Evolutionary Philosophies and Contemporary Theology*. Philadelphia: Westminster Press, 1969.
Schoonenburg, Piet, S.J., *God's World in the Making*. Pittsburgh: Duquesne Univ. Press, 1964.
Schoonenburg, Piet, S.J., *Man and Sin*. Trans. Joseph Donceel, S.J. Notre Dame, Indiana: Univ. of Notre Dame Press, 1965.
Trooster, Dr. S., S.J., *Evolution and the Doctrine of Original Sin*. Trans. John A. TerHaar, New York: Newman Press, 1968.
von Koenigswald, G. H. R., *The Evolution of Man*. Michigan: Univ. of Michigan Press, 1963.
Wolterek, Henry, *What Science Knows About Life*. Massachusetts: M.I.T. Press, 1965.

ARTICLES

Alexander, A., "Human Origins and Genetics," *Clergy Review*, 49, (1964), 344-353.
Alzeghy, Zohan, S.J., "Development in the Doctrinal Foundation of the Church Concerning the Theory of Evolution," *Concilium*, vol. 26 (New York: Paulist Press, 1967).
Birch, C., "Participatory Evolution," *American Academy of Religion*, 40 (1972).
DeLetter, P., "If Adam Had Not Sinned," *Irish Theological Quarterly*, The Thomist, 17, (1954), 469-509.
__________, "The Reparation of Our Fallen Nature," *The Thomist*, 23 (1960), 564-583.
Dolch, Heimo, "Sin in an Evolutive World," *Concilium*, vol. 26 (New York: Paulist Press, 1967), 75-73.
Donceel, Joseph, S.J., "Causality and Evolution: A Survey of Some Neo-scholastic Theories," *The New Scholasticism* 39 (1965), 295-315.
Ebeck, H., "The Hour of Transcendence: Origin of Man's Soul," *Philosophy Today*, 8 (1964), 71-83.
Grispino, J., "Polygenesis and Original Sin," *Homiletic and Pastoral Review*, 63 (1967), 17-22.
Henry, M., "Does the Concept Soul Mean Anything?" *Philosophy Today*, 13 (1969), 94-114.
Mackey, J., "Original Sin and Polygenism: the State of the Question," *Irish Theological Quarterly*, 34 (1967), 99-114.

Melsen, Andreas V., "Natural Law and Evolution," *Concilium*, vol. 21 (New York: Paulist Press, 1967), 49-59.
Metz, Johannes, Ed., "The Evolving World and Theology," *Concilium*, vol. 26 (New York: Paulist Press, 1967), 184.
O'Donovan, L., "Evolution Under the Sign of the Cross," *Theological Studies*, 32 (1971), 602-626.
O'Rourke, J., "Some Considerations About Polygenism," *Theological Studies*, 26 (1965), 407-416.
Rahner, Karl, S.J., "Evolution and Original Sin," *Concilium*, vol. 26 (New York: Paulist Press, 1967), 61ff.
Seidel, G., "The Problem of the Soul in Contemporary Thought," *American Benedictine Review*, 19 (1968), 24-31.

CHAPTER 6

BOOKS

Ayer, A. J., *The Concept of a Person*. New York: St. Martin's Press, 1963.
Barrett, William, *Irrational Man*. Garden City, New York: Doubleday and Company, 1958.
Brunner, Emil, *Man in Revolt*. Philadelphia: Westminster Press, 1947.
Cassirer, Ernst, *An Essay on Man*. New Haven, Conn.: Yale Univ. Press, 1965.
DeClity, C. W., S.J., *The World of Persons*. New York: Sheed and Ward, 1967.
Heschel, Abraham J., *Man is Not Alone*. New York: Harper and Row, 1966.
__________, *Who Is Man?* California: Stanford Univ. Press, 1965.
Johann, Robert B., *Building the Human*. New York: Herder and Herder, 1968.
Küng, Hans, *Freedom Today*. Trans. Cecily Hastings. New York: Sheed and Ward, 1966.
Luijpen, William, *Existential Phenomenology*. Pittsburgh, Pennsylvania. Duquesne Univ. Press, 1965.
Marcel, Gabriel, *Problematic Man*. New York: Herder and Herder, 1967.
Monden, Louis, *Sin, Liberty and Law*. New York: Sheed and Ward, 1965.
Mouroux, Jean, *The Meaning of Man*. New York: Sheed and Ward, 1948.
Murray, John Courtney, S.J., ed., *Freedom and Man*. (New York: P. J. Kennedy and Sons, 1965).

Tillich, Paul, *The Courage to Be*. New Haven, Conn.: Yale Univ. Press, 1952.

Von Balthasar, Hans Urs, *The God Question and Modern Man*. New York: Seabury Press, 1967.

ARTICLES

Adler, M., "Intentionality and Immateriality: Excerpts from The Difference in Man and the Difference It Makes," *New Scholasticism*, 41 (1967), 312-344.

Berlinger, Rudolf, "What is Freedom," *Philosophy Today*, 3 (1959), 281-287.

Bonner, H., "Spiritual Man in a Technological Age," *Humanitas*, 6 (1971), 277-293.

Gini, A., "B. F. Skinner: The Nature of Man and The Concept of Freedom," *A. Ben. R.*, 24 (1973), 74-88.

Kaspar, W., "Christian Humanism," *CTSAP*, 27 (1972), 1-17.

Knoebel, T., "Divine Grace and Human Freedom," *Thought*, 49 (1974), 43-55.

Metz, Johannes B., "Freedom as a Threshold Problem Between Philosophy and Theology," *Philosophy Today*, 10 (1966), 266.

Murray, John C., "Freedom, Authority, Community," *The Catholic Lawyer*, 15:2 (Spring 1969), 158-168.

Rahner, K., "Christian Humanism," *Journal of Ecumenical Studies*, 4 (1967), 369-384.

________, "Experiment: Man," *Theology Digest* (1968), 57-69.

________, "Freedom in the Church," *Theological Investigations*, II (1963), 89-109.

________, "Self-Redemption and Taking Up One's Cross," *Theological Investigations*, 9 (New York: Herder, 1972), 253-257.

Sablone, G., "Man Before God in the Philosophy of Karl Jaspers," *Philosophy Today*, 11 (1967), 155-165.

Walgrave, J., "Man's Self-Understanding in Christian Theology," *Louvain Studies*, 5 (1974), 48-58.

CHAPTER 7

BOOKS

Buber, Martin, *The Knowledge of Man*. Maurice Friedman, ed. New York: Harper and Row, 1965.

Donceel, J. F., *Philosophical Anthropology*. New York: Sheed and Ward, 1967.

Lonergan, Bernard J., *Insight, A Study of Human Understanding*. New York: Philosophical Library, 1956.
Maritain, Jacques, *The Degrees of Knowledge*. New York: Charles Scribner's Sons, 1959.
Sarano, Jacques, *The Meaning of the Body*. Philadelphia: Westminster Press, 1966.
Scheler, Max, *Man's Place in Nature*. New York: Noonday Press, 1961.
Sertillanges, A. D., O.P., *The Intellectual Life*. Westminster, Md.: The Newman Press, 1952.
Tyrrell, F., *Man Believer and Unbeliever*. New York: Alba, 1974.
Van Croonenburg, Englebert J., *Gateway to Reality: An Introduction to Philosophy*, Pittsburgh: Duquesne Univ. Press, 1963.
Zaehner, R. C., *Matter and Spirit*. New York: Harper and Row, 1963.

ARTICLES

Burnell, D., "Kant and Philosophical Knowledge," *New Scholasticism* 38 (1964), 189-213.
Burns, J., "Spiritual Dynamism in Maréchal," *Thomist*, 32 (1968).
Farrelly, J., "Religious Reflection and Man's Transcendence," *Thomist*, 37 (1973), 1-68.
Heelan, Patrick, "Matter in a Contemporary Setting," *Studies*, 55, (1966), 299-311.
MacKinnon, E., "Understanding According to Bernard J. Lonergan, S.J.," *Thomist*, 28 (April 1964), 97-132; (July 1964), 338-372; (October 1964), 475-522.

CHAPTER 8

BOOKS

Arnold, F. X., *Woman and Man: Their Nature and Mission*. New York: Herder and Herder, 1963.
Bird, Joseph and Lois, *The Freedom of Sexual Love*. New York: Doubleday and Co., 1966.
DeKruiff, T. C., *The Bible on Sexuality*. Trans. by F. VanderHeyden. Wisconsin: St. Norbert Abbey Press, 1966.
Duvall, Evelyn, *Why Wait Till Marriage?* New York: Association Press, 1965.
Grelot, Pierre, *Man and Wife in Scripture*. New York: Herder and Herder, 1964.

Hettlinger, Richard F., *Living With Sex: The Student's Dilemma*. New York: The Seabury Press, 1967.

Jeanniere, Abel, *The Anthropology of Sex*. New York: Harper and Row, 1967.

Kennedy, E., *The New Sexuality, Myths, Fable and Hang-Ups*. New York: Doubleday, 1972.

O'Neill, Robert and Donovan, Michael, *Sexuality and Moral Responsibility*. Washington: Corpus Books, 1968.

Oraison, Marc, *The Human Mystery of Sexuality*. New York: Sheed and Ward, 1965.

Ryan, Mary Perkins, *Love and Sexuality*. New York: Doubleday and Co., 1967.

Wood, Frederick, C., *Sex and the New Morality*. New York: Association Press, 1968.

ARTICLES

Callahan, Sidney, "Human Sexuality in a Time of Change," *Christian Century*, 85 (1968), 1077-1080.

_________, "The Future of the Sexually Liberated Woman," *Critic*, 30 (1972), 78-80.

Greeley, A., "Friendship and Marriage," *Ecumenist*, 10 (1972), 65-71.

O'Sullivan, E., "Humanizing Sexuality," *Furrow*, 25 (1974), 355-362.

Rosales, V., "Human Sexuality, A Question of Knowledge and Attitudes," *Linacre*, 38 (1971), 107-112.

Springer, Robert, "Christian Love and Sexuality," *Theological Studies*, 28 (1967), 322-330.

Wood, Frederick, "Sex Within the Created Order," *Theology Today*, 22 (1965), 394-401.

CHAPTER 9

BOOKS

Balthasar, Hans Urs von, *A Theological Anthropology*. New York: Sheed and Ward, 1967.

Berdyaev, Nicholas, *The Meaning of History*. Cleveland: Meridian Books, 1968.

Bultmann, Rudolf, *History and Eschatology*. New York: Harper, 1957.

Chifflot, Thomas G., *Approaches to a Theology of History*. New York: Desclée, 1955.
Connolly, J. M., *Human History and the Word of God: The Christian Meaning of History in Contemporary Thought*. New York: Macmillan 1965.
Guitton, Jean, *Man in Time*. Notre Dame: Univ. of Notre Dame Press, 1966.
Haselden, Kyle, and Hefner, Philip, eds., *Changing Man: The Threat and the Promise*. New York: Doubleday and Co., 1967.
Pannenberg, Wolfhard, *The Meaning Of Man*. Philadelphia: Fortress Press, 1970.
Rahner, Karl, *On the Theology of Death*. New York: Herder and Herder, 1961.
Robinson, James M. and Cobb, John B., *Theology as History*. New York: Harper and Row, 1965.
Shinn, Roger, *Man the New Humanism*. Philadelphia: Westminister, 1968.

ARTICLES

Boyd, A., "Rahner, Metz, Schillebeeckx: A Futuristic Encounter," *Homiletic and Pastoral Review*, 66 (1966), 942-949.
Crowe, F., "Pull of the Future and Link with the Past: On the Need for Theological Method," *Continuum*. 7 (1969), 30-49.
Lynch, W., "Toward a Theology of the Secular," *Thought*, 41 (1966), 349-365.
Rahner, Karl, "Christianity and the New Man," *Theological Investigations*, vol. 5 (Baltimore: Helicon, 1966), 135-153.
———, "Theological Observations on the Concept of Time," *Theological Investigations*, vol. 11 (New York: Seabury, 1974), 288-308.
Walgrave, J., "History of Theology," *Louvain Studies*, 4 (1973), 362-373.
Windsor, A., "Natural History and Human History," *Downside Review*, 83 (1966), 131-144.

CHAPTER 10

BOOKS (Worker)

Chenu, M. D., *The Theology of Work*. Chicago: Henry Regnery Co., 1963.

Clark, Dennis, *Work and the Human Spirit*. New York: Sheed and Ward, 1967.

Kaiser, Edwin, *Theology of Work*. Westminster, Maryland: The Newman Press, 1966.

Richardson, Alan, *The Biblical Doctrine of Work*. London: SCM Press, 1963.

Wicker, Brian, *Work and the Christian Community*. Glen Rock, N.J.: Paulist Press, 1965.

ARTICLES

Davis, P. M. C., "Work and the Making of a Christian World," *Irish Theological Quarterly*, 35 (1968), 91-116.

May, W., "Animal Laborans and Hober: Reflections on a Theology of Work," *Thomist*, 36 (1972), 626-644.

Rich, Donald W., S.J., "The Theoretical Bases of a Theology of Work," *Irish Theological Quarterly*, 31 (1964), 228-239.

BOOKS (Artist)

Berenson, Bernard, *Aesthetics and History*. London: Constable, 1950.

Dean, W. D., *Coming to a Theology of Beauty*. Philadelphia: Westminster Press, 1972.

Dixon, John W. Jr., *Nature and Grace in Art*. Chapel Hill: Univ. of North Carolina Press, 1964.

Eversole, Finley, ed., *Christian Faith and the Contemporary Arts*. New York: Abingdon Press, 1962.

Gilson, Etienne, *The Arts of the Beautiful*. New York: Pantheon Books, 1965.

Harned, David Baily, *Theology and the Arts*. Philadelphia: Westminister Press, 1966.

Maritain, Jacques, *Creative Intuition in Art and Poetry*. New York: Pantheon Books, 1953.

Tejera, Victorino, *Art and Human Intelligence*. New York: Appleton-Century-Crofts, 1965.

Van Der Leeuw, Gerardus, *Sacred and Profane Beauty*. London: Weidenfield and Nicolson, 1963.

Weiss, Paul, *Religion and Art*. Milwaukee: Marquette Univ. Press, 1963.

CHAPTER 11

BOOKS

Alves, Ruben, *Tomorrow's Child*. New York: Harper and Row, 1972.

Berger, Peter, *A Rumor of Angels*. New York: Doubleday and Co., 1969.

Cox, Harvey, *The Feast of Fools*. Cambridge: Harvard Univ. Press, 1969.

Horn, Charles, *Worship in Crisis*. Philadelphia: Fortress Press, 1972.

Huizinga, Johann, *Homo Ludens: A Study of the Play Element in Culture*. Boston: Beacon Press, 1955.

Keen, Sam, *Apology for Wonder*. New York: Harper and Row, 1969.

———, *To a Dancing God*. New York: Harper and Row, 1970.

Kent, Corita, *Footnotes and Headlines*. New York: Herder and Herder, 1967.

Lynch, William, *Christ and Apollo: The Dimensions of the Literary Imagination*. New York: Sheed and Ward, 1960.

Moltmann, J., *Theology of Play*. New York: Harper and Row, 1972.

Otto, Walter, *Dionysius: Myth and Cult*. Bloomington: Indiana Univ. Press, 1965.

Pieper, Joseph, *In Tune with The World: A Theory of Festivity*. New York: Harcourt, Brace, 1965.

Rahner, Hugo, *Man at Play*. London: Burns and Oates, 1965.

von Allmen, J. J., *Worship: Its Theology and Practice*. New York: Oxford Univ. Press, 1965.

Vos, Nelvin, *For God's Sake Laugh*. Richmond: John Knox Press, 1967.

ARTICLES

Moltmann, J., "How Can I Play When I'm In a Strange Land?" *Critic*, 29 (1971), 14-23.

Morgan, J., "Religious Myth and Symbol," *Philosophy Today*, 18 (1974), 68-84.

Reese, J., "Biblical Roots of Celebration," *American Ecclesiastical Review*, 163 (1970), 289-297.

CHAPTER 12

BOOKS

Barnette, H., *The Church and the Ecological Crisis*. Grand Rapids: Eerdmans, 1972.

Cobb, J., *Is It Too Late?: A Theology of Ecology*. Milwaukee: Bruce, 1972.

Faricy, Robert L., S.J., *Teilhard de Chardin's Theology of the Christian in the World*. New York: Sheed and Ward, 1967.

Klotz, J. W., *Ecology Crisis*. St. Louis: Concordia, 1971.

Leon, Arnold E., *Secularization: Science Without God?* London: SCM Press Ltd., 1967.

Lutz, P. E., Santmire, *Ecological Renewal*. Philadelphia: Fortress Press, 1972.

Moule, C. F., *Man and Nature in the New Testament*. Philadelphia: Fortress Press, 1967.

Sherrell, R., *Ecology Crisis and New Vision*. Richmond: John Knox Press, 1971.

Teilhard de Chardin, Pierre, *Building the Earth*. Wilkes-Barre, Pa.: Dimension Books, 1965.

________, *The Appearance of Man*. Trans. J. M. Cohen. New York: Harper & Row, 1956.

ARTICLES

Croose, Parry R., "Human Needs and the New Society," *Teilhard Review*, 9 (1974), 72-80.

DeWolf, L., "Christian Faith and our Natural Environment," *IDOC*, 9 (1970), 3-15.

________, "Theology and Ecology," *American Ecclesiastical Review*, 164 (1971), 154-170.

McCormick, Richard, "Current Theology," *Theological Studies*, 32 (1971), 66-122.

Megivern, J., "Ecology and the Bible," *Ecumenist*, 8 (1970), 69-71.

McGinn, T., "Ecology and Ethics," *IPQ*, 14 (1974), 149-160.

Obayashi, H., "Nature and Historicization: A Theological Reflection on Ecology," *Cross Currents*, 23 (1973), 140-152.

Sheets, J., "Theological Implications of Ecology," *Homiletic and Pastoral Review*, 71 (1971), 57-66.

Shepherd, J., "Theology for Ecology," *Catholic World*, 211, (1970), 172-175.

Sittler, Joseph, "Ecological Commitment as Theological Responsibility," *IDOC*, 9 (1970), 75-85.